The Feminist Dilemma

The Feminist Dilemma

When Success Is Not Enough

Diana Furchtgott-Roth
and
Christine Stolba

The AEI Press

Publisher for the American Enterprise Institute
WASHINGTON, D.C.
2001

Available in the United States from the AEI Press, c/o Publisher Resources Inc., 1224 Heil Quaker Blvd., P.O. Box 7001, La Vergne, TN 37086-7001. To order, call toll free: 1-800-937-5557. Distributed outside the United States by arrangement with Eurospan, 3 Henrietta Street, London WC2E 8LU, England.

Library of Congress Cataloging-in-Publication Data

Furchtgott-Roth, Diana
    The feminist dilemma: when success is not enough / Diana Furchtgott-Roth and Christine Stolba
        p. cm.
    Includes bibliographical references and index.
    ISBN 0-8447-4129-9 (cloth: alk. paper)
    1. Feminism—United States. 2. Women's rights—United States.
3. Women—Employment—United States. 4. Sex discrimination—United States. 5. Equality—United States. I. Stolba, Christine. II. Title.

HQ1421 .F87 2001
305.42'0973—dc21

                                                              2001033325

ISBN 0-8447-4129-9

1 3 5 7 9 10 8 6 4 2

The AEI Press
Publisher for the American Enterprise Institute
1150 17th Street, N.W.
Washington, D.C. 20036

Printed in the United States of America

To Harold
To my sisters, Catherine Remick and Cynthia Stolba

Contents

Acknowledgments

This book could not have been accomplished without the help of many individuals. Audrey Williams was a superb research assistant, keeping track of numerous drafts and statistical changes. She was supported by AEI interns Rebecca Barnett, Christina Bishop, Ann Chandler, Helen Christodoulou, Jennifer Gravelle, Elizabeth McPike, Theodora Rodman, Marissa Roy, Haley Schaffer, Stephanie Schweitzer, Susan Sheybani, and Shannon Sneed.

The book benefited from detailed comments from numerous people, including Christina and Fred Sommers, Richard Epstein, Roger Clegg, Susan Gessler, Beth Kevles, Rosalind Udwin, and Edward Cowan. Any remaining errors are, of course, the authors' own.

Thanks as well to the staff and board of the Independent Women's Forum, who provided invaluable assistance and encouragement on this project. Barbara Ledeen, cofounder of the Independent Women's Forum, was, as always, a never ending source of inspiration and ideas.

Finally, we owe a large debt of gratitude to Christopher DeMuth, president of the American Enterprise Institute, and David Gerson, executive vice president, who encouraged and supported our work from start to finish with critical comments and crucial guidance.

The Feminist Dilemma

1

Setting the Stage

In a day and age when women are piloting space shuttles, starting their own businesses, and even running for president, it is easy to forget just how far we have come. It was not so long ago that women in America lacked equal standing in society and in the eyes of the law. In the eighteenth century, for example, women spent the better part of their lives bearing and rearing children—if they survived childbirth at all—and making contributions to their family's economies through physical labor. Although many women engaged in work outside the home, as midwives, teachers, tavern owners, or shopkeepers, most lacked basic civic rights, including the right to own property, to cast a vote in an election, or to serve on a jury.

Such barriers to formal equality remained intact throughout the nineteenth century, as industrialization, geographical expansion, and immigration transformed the nation. Many middle-class women turned their attentions to voluntary associations and other reform groups, as well as to a burgeoning movement for women's suffrage, while their immigrant sisters worked as factory laborers, and recently emancipated African American women worked as agricultural laborers or domestic servants.

The economic and social changes of the era generated ferment about women's place, and by midcentury a small cohort of activists had convened to declare an organized movement for women's rights, made plain in the 1848 Declaration of Sentiments drafted at Seneca Falls, New York. A radical demand for equality in all spheres of society, the Seneca Falls declaration strongly rejected the notion

1

that a woman's place was limited to the domestic realm. At the same time, a quieter revolution was taking place as increasing numbers of women pursued higher education. The efforts of early activists bore their first formal fruit in 1920, when women won the right to vote with the passage of the Nineteenth Amendment to the U.S. Constitution.

Despite having achieved the vote and some access to higher education, by law and custom women in the postsuffrage era still lacked full equality. They were denied access to most of the professions and many jobs.

The lingering constraints of womanhood were just what the feminists of the 1960s and 1970s—the "second-wave" feminists—challenged. Led by Betty Friedan's call to arms in *The Feminine Mystique*,[1] that generation of women's rights activists launched a real revolution by demanding equality in the eyes of the law and expanded opportunities in the social realm. Like their suffragist forebears, they took their case to the country's legislators. The laws guaranteeing equal opportunity, such as the Equal Pay Act of 1963 and Title VII of the Civil Rights Act of 1964, are their most admirable legacy.

Thus, America's early feminists fought to increase women's options by providing equality of opportunity—as property owners, at the ballot box, in schools, and in the workplace. They fought for women's civil and legal equality, and it is a testament to the strength of the American democratic ideal that they succeeded. Women are now fully equal members of American society, and their success is worth celebrating.

But that success has created a dilemma for some contemporary feminists, especially those whose "second-wave" activism has now become a full-time business. For them, the accomplishments women have made as the result of equal opportunity are not good enough. They seek equal outcomes. As we shall show, contemporary feminism has lost its way by turning its back on the fundamental principles of the early feminist movement; today, feminists pursue public policies that would enshrine equality of results at the expense of equality of opportunity. Where once feminists demanded and received the right to equal pay for equal work with the Equal Pay Act, now they demand that the government set wages to favor female-dominated occupations. Once, feminists challenged discriminatory restrictions on female education; today, their campaign is for "gender equity" in education, an idea that begins with the illogical notion that, without discrimination, men and women would achieve absolute proportionality in all educational fields. Similarly, where once feminists boldly challenged the American public to end the practice of sex-segregated job advertisements and to give qualified women a chance to enter the professions, today, feminists claim that discrimination is to blame if women do not choose to enter all fields in numbers equal to men.

If, as many feminists claim, that represents an evolution in feminist thought, then it is a movement toward a type of society more socialist than democratic. Americans were granted the right to *pursue* happiness, not a guarantee that they would achieve it. Such was the opportunity that our society represented—and still represents—to those outside: the possibility of innovation, experimentation, and, most important, for individual choice. But in the name of broadening equality and freedom, feminists today are waging a campaign that would reduce both—for men and women. Feminists want to lay claim to the rhetoric of choice: in a democracy, words such as *freedom, choice,* and *equality* are powerful concepts. But feminists do not want to face the consequences of that rhetoric. That is not choice. Rather, it is authoritarian social engineering masquerading as choice.

With the push toward defining equality for women as numerical parity has come a skillful change in the language feminists use to describe women's rights. Government-mandated wage guidelines, also known as comparable worth, become "pay equity"; preferential programs for women such as government-subsidized or government-mandated day care or maternity leave are now billed as "working women's rights." Working women whose careers top out before the level of chief executive officer are described as hitting a "glass ceiling," whereas men in a similar position have just peaked. Rather than demanding equal opportunity, feminists are lobbying for preferential rights for their own interest group.

Some feminists have always boldly admitted that their aim is not a full range of choices for women but *their* choices for women. During an interview with Betty Friedan in 1975, French feminist Simone de Beauvoir said that women should not be given the choice to stay home with children, because, if they had that choice, many women might take it, and women's advancement into male-dominated areas of society would slow.[2] Contemporary discussions rarely produce such candor. But, as we shall see, that sentiment still thrives below the surface of feminist discourse. Because the results of women's choices have not always led to equal numbers of men and women in education and employment, feminists claim that women are the victims of discrimination.

Of course, women still face challenges, and discrimination and harassment are still unfortunately a part of our society. But data show that they are not systemic problems in the United States nor ones without solutions, and the laws that are in place serve to protect all individuals. Feminists are, however, winning their war to redefine equality as numerical parity. In administrative agencies such as the Equal Employment Opportunity Commission and executive branch offices such as the Department of Education's Office for Civil Rights, the feminists' message of equality of outcome now reigns. Federal agencies and all private-sector firms with more than fifteen workers are required to keep records of all workers, divided into sex and a multitude of racial categories. Many vacancies are targeted for men or women, blacks or whites, Asian Americans or Native Americans, and both federal agencies and private firms live in fear of a poor report by the EEOC. When men are underrepresented, as is the case in the U.S. Department of Health and Human Services, no efforts are made to increase their hiring, but the EEOC is known to set its sights on firms with a low representation of women, even in the absence of complaints.

It is important to note that contemporary feminist groups are not disinterested, public-spirited observers and impartial critics of government policies. During the past two decades, feminist organizations have been some of the most successful fundraisers in the nonprofit world, with grants from government, foundations, and private corporations. Thus, feminist groups have a financial stake in continuing to claim that women are second-class citizens and that the struggle for women's rights is never won. Without the banner of victimhood to rally around, feminist coffers would run dry.

The facts about women's achievements are impossible to ignore. While this book examines the central arenas where feminist efforts to redefine equality have made the deepest inroads, it also presents the facts about women's success. Chapter 2 lays out the issue that initially inspired the writing of this book, namely feminists' insistent claims of continuing discrimination in the face of women's obvious achievements in so many fields. We describe how feminists have moved from a message of equality of opportunity to one that emphasizes equality of outcomes.

The overwhelming evidence of women's success at the secondary, college, and university level belies feminists' claims of discrimination in education, as we discuss in chapter 3. More women than men attend college, and more women than men receive bachelor's and master's degrees. But many women choose to pursue fields that pay less than those dominated by men. For example, women receive a majority of degrees in public administration and English literature, and a minority of degrees in mathematics and engineering. We explore whether such choices are evidence of discrimination and assess feminists' proposals to transform education.

In chapter 4 we engage another element of the feminists' dilemma in coming to terms with women's choices. We look at the wide range of job choices available to women. Feminists frequently claim that women face discrimination in their choice of careers. They point, for example, to the paucity of women in such traditional blue-collar professions as mining and construction or to the small number of female CEOs. We suggest, however, that women have many reasons to prefer not to enter those professions and that they value job flexibility or shorter hours. In examining job choice, the great distance between what women in the real world are doing and what feminists say they should be doing is impossible to ignore.

Women's job choices have a significant effect on their lifetime earnings and workplace advancement. Those are the topics of chapter 5. We discuss contemporary feminists' main pillars of "proof" of workplace discrimination—the "wage gap" that supposedly exists between men and women and the "glass ceiling" that prevents women from advancing—and assess their validity. We note the misleading claims repeatedly made by feminists about women's wages and present evidence that demonstrates that when such vital factors as education, experience, and consecutive years in the work force are considered, pay between men and women is about the same. In addition, we refute the myth of the "glass ceiling" by noting that common sense and a cursory glance at the history of professional school degrees reveal the existence of a corporate pipeline through which women only recently began moving. Again, choice—not discrimination—explains the lack of perfect male–female proportionality in wages and advancement.

In chapter 6 we describe the costs to society of another favorite feminist weapon: sexual harassment law. Although sexual harassment law was initially intended to target egregious cases of sexual extortion, it is now being used as a means of monitoring a wide range of behavior and speech in the workplace, much of it benign. We explore the arguments of feminist legal theorists who call for the further expansion of sexual harassment law and point to the potential costs of such expansion, including the costs to women in the workplace.

It is inconsistent that at the same time that contemporary feminists claim that women can do anything done by men, they also call for more laws that would require employers to provide women with specific benefits, such as paid maternity leave or subsidized child care. The necessity for and the cost of such required benefits are the subject of chapter 7. Feminists often cite the example of European countries, in which employers and the government frequently provide paid maternity leave and subsidized child care, as the model America should be following. We test the validity of that claim and, using examples from real companies, demonstrate the costs of legislation such as the Family and Medical Leave Act, which provides twelve weeks of unpaid leave to deal with family issues. Further, although feminists claim that the European model of workplace policies would help American women, we present data demonstrating that European women are less advanced in the workplace than Americans. Women in European countries work less outside the home rather than more; their unemployment rates are usually higher than men's unemployment rates; and their countries have uniformly higher unemployment rates overall and uniformly lower rates of economic growth.

Professional feminist advocates seem to be either naive or indifferent to the economic costs and consequences of their proposals. They seem not to recognize that when the law confers more benefits, additional costs are also imposed. While working women might hope that those costs come from the employer's pocket, in practice, that rarely happens. More likely, employers will pass those costs on to the public in the form of higher prices. If business conditions do not permit price increases, as has been the case for some years, then additional costs will be distributed among employees in the form of smaller wage increases, a reduced work force, and fewer new hires. If the government requires employers to give women special benefits not offered to men, then employers—however subtly—will become more resistant to hiring women.

After examining the costs of mandatory benefits, we turn our attention to an area outside the workplace where the feminist campaign for statistical proportionality has had disturbing success: college athletics. Chapter 8 explores the history and current application of a piece of federal educational legislation called Title IX. Although the intent of Title IX's creators was to guarantee equality of opportunity, feminists and misguided government bureaucrats have transformed the statute into a weapon for enforcing statistical proportionality in college sports. The result is the elimination of men's sports teams all over the country: between 1993 and 1999 colleges and universities terminated fifty-three men's golf teams, forty-three wrestling teams, and sixteen baseball teams, among others—the vast majority because of Title IX requirements.

In chapter 9 we describe how feminist-inspired policies have resulted in women's being classified by sex in every workplace in the United States that has more than fifteen workers. Employers are required to keep records of how many men and how many women they hire, in many cases divided by job classification. The EEOC can investigate a company at any time, without any complaint filed, to see whether the proportion of women in the work force meets the proportion in the local labor force. If it does not, the commission can assume that discrimination has taken place and can take the company to court, where the firm may ultimately be fined. That possibility has resulted in a quota mentality among personnel departments, which live in fear of an EEOC investigation, and the pressure to hire and promote less-qualified women over more-qualified men.

Unfortunately, contemporary feminists' focus on outcomes has blinded them to the recently more complex, but not necessarily unequal, status of American women. Inherent in many of their discussions is a debate about what kind of society Americans want for themselves. Should all people be held to a single, sex-blind standard, with equality of opportunity rather than equality of result as the guiding force in achievement? Or do women—who, after all, make up more than half the population, who are better educated, who have a life expectancy seven years greater than men, and who have a much smaller percentage on hard drugs and in prison—warrant protected status in the workplace? Do existing preferential government programs assume that women should make certain choices? How do forces *outside* the workplace—cultural and social forces relating to family and personal goals—influence the decisions women make *inside* the workplace and vice versa? By examining those questions, we hope to contribute to the debate over the meaning of equality and success for women in a democratic society.

2

Feigning Discrimination

In 1999 Hillary Rodham Clinton declared at the White House, "We know that women who walk into the grocery store are not asked to pay 25 percent less for milk. They're not asked by their landlords to pay 25 percent less for rent. And they should no longer be asked to try to make their ends meet and their family incomes what they should be by having 25 percent less in their paychecks."[1]

Mrs. Clinton's message, like so many others in our culture, is that American women are shortchanged by a society that denies them the opportunities enjoyed by men. It suggests that since the deck is stacked against women in daily life, they will have to work harder and longer than men to succeed. It reinforces the idea that women do not get a fair shake in the workplace and need special government programs to prosper. And it is plain wrong.

The Victories of Early Feminists
Earlier in the twentieth century, feminists waged a successful campaign to convince the public that women faced entrenched sex discrimination. Those early feminists were right, and today, discrimination against women is illegal. The government enforces antidiscrimination laws, and the courts punish wrongdoers.

It is indisputable that women once faced significant barriers in competing with men in education and employment. As recently as the 1960s, women faced closed doors at some of the most prestigious universities in the nation, such as Yale and Princeton. Most women, when admitted to colleges, majored in a limited selection

9

of subject areas, partly through custom and partly by choice. In addition, help-wanted ads in newspapers segregated jobs by sex and listed different wages for men and women for the same jobs.[2]

But the past decades have brought momentous changes to the lives of American women. Just as earlier generations of immigrants came to the United States and battled discrimination—"No Irish Need Apply" was a phrase that commonly adorned employment listings in the nineteenth century, and quotas or outright prohibitions barred many Jews and Catholics from equal access to colleges and clubs until well into the second half of the twentieth century—so, too, have American women gradually overcome the legal and cultural barriers to equal opportunity that existed just a short time ago.

The working woman has become the rule rather than the exception. Technological advances have shrunk the time required for housekeeping and food preparation and have freed women to pursue other activities. Seismic cultural shifts have also contributed to women's advancement in the public sphere. In earlier decades, the traditional picture of the father was one who rarely engaged in household tasks or looked after children.[3] But many of today's fathers go to supermarkets and are actively involved in rearing their children. By all measures, American women enjoy success and equality of opportunity. They are full citizens capable of making choices about their futures.

Now, women receive over half of all B.A.'s and M.A.'s, as they have done since 1983; they are becoming physicians, lawyers, police officers, and scientists; they are running for elective office and winning at rates equal to those of men; they are starting their own businesses in record numbers; and they are protected from discrimination by a vast web of statutes and regulations. In the United States women have as good a chance at making it to the top as men, if they want to do so. Our free-market, democratic system is the envy of the world. In response to economic opportunity, millions of women apply to immigrate to the United States every year—more applications than to any other country—and other women risk their lives to come here by any means possible, including small boats and clandestine border crossings at night.

Women's Choices

But despite women's success and opportunities, their choices result in fewer women in some areas and more in others. So, since equal opportunity has not led to strict proportionality, feminists deny that equal opportunity exists. In the words of Heidi Hartmann, president of the Institute for Women's Policy Research, and Martha Burk, president of the Center for Advancement of Public Policy, "despite women's considerable progress towards participation as equals with men in society, politics, and the economy, women have still not achieved full equality or their fair share of the benefits of citizenship."[4]

Feminists cannot admit that successful women will often fail to choose the engineering major or the chief executive officer's track. They cannot admit that the reason that fewer women are in the House of Representatives is not that they have a lower success rate when they run—their success rate is the same—but that fewer run. They cannot admit that fewer women than men want to play college sports or work on oil rigs. Instead, they assert that discrimination is responsible for the underrepresentation of women among engineering majors and CEOs. According to Eleanor Smeal, president of the Feminist Majority Foundation,

> [D]espite the gains of the last twenty-five years, women are still far from equality. To this day, women comprise only 3% of firefighters, 8% of state and local police officers, 1.9% of construction workers, 11.8% of college presidents, and 6.2% of board of directors at Fortune 500/Service 500 companies. Without affirmative action, even these paltry numbers would be worse. If women are ever to break the glass ceiling, we should be talking about strengthening affirmative action, not abolishing it.[5]

This is feminism's dilemma: although women's opportunities are now equal, they do not always make the same choices as men. Women's choices frequently result in careers that differ from those of men, sometimes with lower-paying jobs and less career advancement. Eighty percent of women bear children at some point in their lives, and many choose careers to enable them better to combine work and family.

When feminists insisted that women deserved the rights of full citizens, that they deserved the same range of choices about their education and work lives that men enjoyed, then they advanced the cause of millions of American women. But with choice come differences in outcomes, for not all women will choose the same path. Professional feminists expect women to make choices that conform to the organizational agenda. Hartmann and Burk asserted, "In a world free of discrimination and artificial barriers, it is, in our opinion, likely that women and men would choose similar allocations as between work and family, make similar investments in training, and hold similar jobs."[6] When women do not—when women seek job flexibility rather than higher wages or pursue nursing careers or other traditionally female occupations—their "enlightened" feminist sisters label them naive, victims of a false consciousness that prevents them from seeing their own oppression.

A further dilemma for feminists is that acknowledging the true extent of women's accomplishments marks the end of their organizations' raison d'être. Feminism today is not a campaign to end inequality for women. It is a business and a bureaucracy whose mission is as much about organizational survival as it is about securing rights for women. The National Organization for Women and its sister organizations must have an enemy; the new enemy is anyone, male or female, who realizes that women have made it. The feminist battle has evolved from a fight for legal and social equality to a fight for special treatment and affirmative action in education and the workplace, for subsidized child care, for mandated maternity benefits, and for equal numbers of men and women in Congress and state legislatures, in jobs, and on college athletic fields.

Contemporary feminists' embrace of affirmative action—particularly, their habitual use of misleading statistics, as with their presentation of the wage gap—reveals that their agenda is not about securing equality for women but about gaining power and continuing their own institutional existence. Women who challenge the feminists' view of female opportunities open themselves up to a number of charges, the most common being that they are ungrateful beneficiaries of the feminist movement's struggles. They are accused of climbing the ladder constructed by feminists and then heartlessly pulling it up behind them. More often, those who challenge the claims of contemporary feminist organizations—whether on wage discrimination, the import of presidential peccadilloes, or affirmative action—are quickly and conveniently labeled "the backlash" and accused of "cloaking their agenda in false civility while they strip women and people of color of [their] civil rights," as Patricia Ireland, president of NOW, put it in a fundraising letter.[7]

As psychologist Virginia Valian wrote in her 1997 book, *Why So Slow? The Advancement of Women:*

> Most women would . . . aver their belief that all women can succeed on the basis of their merits. But the data are clear: Most women cannot succeed on merit alone. The goal of affirmative action is to create a world in which they can.[8]

And, a few pages later, she wrote that "affirmative action is needed because people tend not to recognize women's merits. If there were no problem, there would be no need of a solution."[9] That is an outdated vision of women's opportunities and a condescending assessment of their capabilities. The train of women's progress has long since left the station, with American women on board hurtling toward greater success. But professional feminists remain on the platform and even claim that women were not allowed to buy tickets for the journey.

Contemporary Feminism Ignores Progress

Women's choices and achievements have not satisfied contemporary feminist organizations. NOW claims that affirmative action is necessary to "right past and present wrongs—like being locked out of opportunities, cheated by an illusion of fairness or judged by subjective standards."[10] Stanford University law professor Deborah Rhode asserted in her book, *Speaking of Sex: The Denial of Gender Inequality*, that "on almost all measures of social, economic, and political status, significant gender inequality persists."[11]

Contemporary feminists extend their vision of equal numbers of men and women even to art museums, where some curators are calling for museums to ensure that half of all art on display is the work of women artists. And modern feminists do not spare the spiritual realm. Hartmann and Burk advocated "neutering patriarchal religions," such as the Catholic Church: "like private clubs that discriminate, tax exemptions should not be provided to religions that discriminate against women, nor should contributions to such groups be tax deductible."[12]

Since American women enjoy a range of opportunities unimaginable just a half century ago, feminists are left with few large battles to fight. There is no modern-day equivalent of the fight for suffrage. Thus, groups such as NOW and the Feminist Majority Foundation pepper their literature with warnings about "stealth discrimination" in the workplace, "hidden curricula" undermining girls in our nation's schools, and sexist behavior that has "gone underground."[13] This is the quandary of any organization that has achieved its goals, such as the relevance of the March of Dimes when a cure for polio was discovered.[14] But the new mission must be reasonable, unlike the new feminist agenda, which drastically changes the philosophy from equality of opportunity to equality of outcome.

Rather than celebrate victory, contemporary feminists need to feign constant defeat, in part so that their services will continue to be needed. Their message has so thoroughly invaded popular culture that it is now taken for granted in the press that women do not receive equal pay for equal work and that they are often short-changed by an educational system that favors men. The media assume that a sexist society confines women to low-paying, low-prestige jobs; that colleges deny them athletic opportunities; and that they require constant government supervision of the workplace in the form of dating regulations, speech codes, and sensitivity training to protect them from the oppressive, sexist, and demeaning behavior of their male coworkers.

Ironically, in that feminist vision of American society, women really do resemble the weaker sex, in need of protection from a host of evils—a society that the original feminists desperately wanted to change. Contemporary feminists thus promote contradictory positions. They say that they are powerful, yet deny past victories. They assert that women are as strong as men when it suits their purposes—such as when they argue that women should hold combat positions in the military—but implicitly deny that idea when it does not—for example, when they call for expanding Title IX regulations to ensure equal representation of women in college sports. The only consistent feature of contemporary feminism is its dogged insistence on the immutability of sex discrimination.

The Feminist Message

The feminist message of women as victims has four characteristics. First, it portrays society as organized around groups, not individuals. Second, it argues that women are oppressed and ignores women's achievements. Third, it proposes that the only remedy for such oppression is government-sponsored preferential programs. Finally, it encourages politicians to change the laws and bureaucrats to interpret laws in such a fashion as to mandate quotas.

The story of group oppression can be seen in the writing of Howard University School of Law professor E. Christi Cunningham. She wrote:

> While women have made significant progress into traditional male and masculine territory, glass ceilings exist because some core male and masculine havens are especially difficult for women to shatter. Title VII has failed to break the glass ceiling because the remaining degree of inequality is essential to the maintenance of male power in the workplace, and, therefore, women's inability to break the glass ceiling persists.[15]

Similarly, the National Organization for Women asserted:

> After more than 200 years of living under the United States Constitution and despite all of the progress we have made, women continue to suffer discrimination in employment, insurance, health care, education, the criminal justice system, social security and pensions, and just about any other area you can name.[16]

Such emphasis on groups obscures the many differences that exist *within* groups and *between* individuals. Absent from the feminists' rhetoric is any discussion of the choices women make about what kind of work they want to pursue and how much of their time they want to devote to it. We live in a society that allows its citizens to pursue many options. Yet contemporary feminists want a society where the government punishes businesses when, as a result of the personal choices women make, less than half of corporate officers are female. Feminists do not want women to have to live with the consequences of the choices they make if those choices conflict with feminist dogma.

In a speech at the National Press Club, Eleanor Smeal called for new legislation putting in place preferential programs for women:

> Women have neither full citizenship nor equality. We must raise not only an equality banner but an equal representation banner. We need a Women's Equality Act which for starters lifts caps on sex discrimination damage awards, extends the statute of limitations, applies to the military, and to all benefit programs including Social Security, Medicare, and Medicaid, and guarantees equality for girls and women in all public education programs, not just those dependent on federal funding. We need a Women's Voting Rights Act that works to solve the underrepresentation of women in Congress.[17]

That feminist message has been widely spread. Practically every school and workplace in America conducts presentations to bring the gospel of oppression to the unenlightened. Impressionable minds are taught about the supposedly sad plight of women in society that can be remedied only by preferences. Feminist groups have succeeded in placing Women's History Month and Take Our Daughters to Work Day on many school and workplace calendars. Similarly, workers grasp the political importance of promoting messages coordinated by employers. Stigma is not placed on those who propose preference programs, but on those who question the practice. To suggest that women are not oppressed is blasphemy in many eyes.

Why does the feminist message of women as victims continue to gain such a credible hearing, and why does it remain the basis for a large part of our public policy?

First, some professional feminists have formed a political coalition with more deserving groups, such as African Americans, to disseminate the view that government assistance is needed. Several interest groups working together have more power than one. Hence, all groups benefiting from affirmative action seem on the side of the feminists. That adds up to the vast majority of the entire U.S. population—everyone except for heterosexual white males—now seeking government help.

Second, Americans want to be fair. They are touched by injustice and want to correct it. Ours is a nation of astounding wealth, and the availability of resources to help others increases the pressure to right perceived wrongs.

Third, we live in a society that has elevated self-proclaimed victims to the level of saints. Making excuses is *de rigeur* and inoculates against criticism. Some may look on a career plateau as a fair reflection of their ability, effort, and career choice; others, however, may find it more seductive to listen to voices that blame outside factors such as the "establishment" or the "patriarchy" for their lack of success.

Feminists have pushed their message forward with an unscrupulous disregard of the facts. They have hijacked the debate about women's progress and vigorously promoted a misguided standard of equality that takes as its measure equal numbers of men and women. If women, who make up approximately half the nation's population, are not half of all college athletes, half of all mathematicians, half of all chief executive officers, half of all bankers, or half of all construction workers, equality of opportunity does not exist. Statistical symmetry is the ruler by which feminists measure women's progress.

Costs of the Feminist Message

Why should anyone care about the claims of the Feminist Majority Foundation or the National Women's Law Center? Most people do not know that those groups exist. But feminist organizations have succeeded in getting laws passed and policies enacted that undermine our economic system. They clog the judicial system with lawsuits based on their ideology. Theirs is a minority campaign that has had disturbing success in the courts and in Congress. The media accept their characterizations as truth. Politicians and businesses, fearful of becoming targets of feminist protest, often lack the courage to challenge their claims.

In 1999 President William J. Clinton and Congress put forth a flood of special legislation aimed at women. President Clinton, Senator Thomas Daschle, and Senator Tom Harkin proposed legislation mandating wage guidelines that would allow government bureaucrats to set salaries for different occupations.[18] The president suggested adding parents to other classes protected by the antidiscrimination provisions of the Civil Rights Act, although mothers would be the primary beneficiaries.[19] In a memorandum to the heads of executive departments and agencies, the president announced that federal government workers should be allowed to take up to three months' accrued sick leave to look after family members. He proposed changes in regulations to allow states to use their surplus unemployment insurance funds—surplus because of economic prosperity—for paid maternity leave.[20] All those provisions represent special preferences for women in the workplace—political pandering to the feminist agenda.

The theme of that agenda is support for special programs for women, ranging from wage-setting for male- and female-dominated occupations, to court-imposed quotas for female hires for businesses that have run afoul of the Equal Employment Opportunity Commission, to quotas for the percentage of women on college sports teams.

Take, for example, wage guidelines or "comparable worth," an idea with which the general public is not familiar but that has been rejected by courts nationwide. With wage guidelines, according to Senator Daschle's Paycheck Fairness Act and Senator Harkin's Fair Pay Act, government bureaucrats set pay scales based on criteria such as educational requirements, skill requirements, independence, working conditions, and responsibility.[21] In fact, that so-called fairness would artificially inflate wages for many workers, particularly women workers. The government, in other words, would engage in making moral judgments about a job's intrinsic worth without regard for the higher wages that other occupations can command in the job market.

In our economic system wages are set on the basis of employer need as well as job description. Wage guidelines thus represent a radical departure from our system's method of setting wages, because jobs with similar descriptions often can command different salaries. Take research positions at universities. In the job market of the new millennium, a university could get all the Ph.D. historians it wanted for $35,000 apiece but would have trouble getting a business professor for $60,000. Yet with the wage guideline calculation, because those jobs share the same title and have the same duties, they should command the same salary. Wage guidelines ignore the *field* of teaching and its current value in the job market as relevant variables. Although ostensibly a program to help women, wage guidelines and their related schemes would ultimately hinder women by making the cost of their labor prohibitive to employers.

Quotas do not always help women—they can also hurt them. One victim of the numbers game was a woman-owned, woman-operated small business, Joe's Stone Crab restaurant in Miami Beach, Florida. In 1997 the Equal Employment Opportunity Commission filed a sex discrimination lawsuit against the restaurant because the owners did not hire female waiters. No women had come forward with claims of discrimination; instead, in making its accusations, the EEOC had used a "commissioner's charge," which allows the agency itself to file a lawsuit. Although Joe's restaurant had demonstrated that from 1991 through 1995 22 percent of its new hires had been women, the court still found the restaurant guilty of "unintentional discrimination" because the available labor pool was 31.9 percent female.[22]

The district court judge prescribed quotas. He said that the restaurant must maintain a percentage of female servers equal to the percentage of females in the larger area labor pool. He took control of the restaurant's hiring practices. The owners had to pay back wages and benefits to four women, two of whom had never even applied for a job but who told the judge that they had considered applying. The restaurant was also required to hire an industrial psychologist to "sensitize" its recruiters, and it must now publish court-approved advertisements of openings in a court-mandated list of publications.[23] As an indication of the absurdity of the district court's decision, the U.S. Court of Appeals for the Eleventh Circuit vacated and remanded the case in 2000, but not before the restaurant had incurred substantial legal fees and undesirable publicity.[24]

Thus has the federal government, from administrative agencies to judges, embraced the feminist mantra that the measure of success should be numerical equality. Affirmative action supporters vehemently deny that they support hiring quotas, but in practice quotas are businesses' only option if they hope to avoid costly litigation. If women do not apply for jobs in numbers equal to their representation in the larger labor pool, business owners will find themselves open to charges of discrimination. Here, then, is an irony of late-twentieth-century feminist logic: a woman-owned, woman-operated business comes under fire for sex discrimination of which no women ever even complained. The revolution, it would appear, is devouring its own children.

Another example also illustrates the harm that quotas are doing to women: in some cases women do not even have the choice of exercising without men nearby. The Women's Workout World chain was sued by the EEOC in the late 1980s for not hiring male employees.[25] The health club argued that women preferred other women rather than men in proximity when working out or undressed, and 10,000 members signed a petition. After seven years of litigation, Women's Workout World settled the case by allowing men to be hired for positions that allegedly would not infringe on women's privacy. The company was required to set aside $30,000 to compensate men who had not been hired.[26] Similarly, in 1997 the Massachusetts Superior Court prevented Healthworks Fitness Center from barring men, a decision that resulted in legislators' passing a law that permitted single-sex exercise clubs.[27]

That has happened because bureaucrats implementing equality of outcomes have distorted laws that were originally put into place to protect individuals; those bureaucrats have focused on group achievements rather than personal rights. Currently, the test of individual discrimination is not how a particular individual has fared, but whether group averages meet a set social goal. Hence, affirmative action, put in place ostensibly to help women, harms them when it is not in the interests of a female restaurant owner to hire precise numbers of women or when women prefer to exercise without men watching. Furthermore, affirmative action casts a veil of suspicion over all women's achievements, since it is not known whether a woman was promoted on her own merits or through affirmative action.

Given the underlying assumptions of affirmative action policy for women, such a turn of events should come as no surprise. Taken to its logical conclusion, affirmative action promotes a vision of society wholly antithetical to that most Americans embrace—one that seeks equality of results rather than equality of opportunity. When voters were asked to assess the validity of preferences for women and minorities, as they were in California and in Washington, they rejected the preferences.[28]

All those proposals reveal a new line of reasoning among modern feminists: it is not enough for employers merely to abide by the law and give women equal access to jobs; affirmative action supporters want the government to force employers to make excessive accommodations for women. As University of Chicago law professor Richard A. Epstein noted in his book, *Forbidden Grounds*, that creates a situation in which self-realization for women is enshrined in law at the expense of businesses.[29]

Conclusion

No one can deny that women once faced substantial hurdles to true equality. The more important question is whether those hurdles remain, and, if so, what should we do? The many protections and preferences feminists call for on behalf of women rest on a particular view of society. Feminists assume that, barring strict oversight by the government, employers will act primarily on their basest prejudices and thus deny women access to education and the labor market. In such a rendering, the success of one's business comes second to the imposition of discriminatory attitudes. According to Nadine Strossen of the American Civil Liberties Union, "[W]ithout affirmative action, women will increasingly be relegated to lower paying occupations and positions, which will adversely affect their whole families."[30]

Modern feminists also claim that affirmative action is necessary because for most of American history, preferences have been given to white men by dint of their sex and race. Why is it wrong, they ask, to push women to the head of the line to help them catch up? Citing the existence of historic privileges provides an especially desirable target for feminists. After all, it is easy to attribute blame en masse to the many men who came before us and worked as doctors, bankers, lawyers, loggers, and businessmen. Many of them are not around to mount a defense. Those who are alive have little desire to debate, particularly if they risk being labeled politically incorrect. But such a focus evades the real question of which barriers to women's advancement exist today.

Preference programs for women now resemble the patent medicines of the nineteenth century. As with all quack cures, the proponents make extravagant claims for their usefulness and issue dire warnings about the evils that will befall the hapless fellow who fails quickly to swallow the magic elixir. But those claims have no substance. Worse, as many patients in the past discovered too late, a cure can sometimes be worse than the disease it seeks to remedy.

We are challenging both defeatism and dependence—defeatism that says that women have failed miserably and a dependence on the government of which feminists should be wary. Earlier in the century the government argued that limiting the working hours of wives and mothers protected women. When the Supreme Court upheld such protective legislation in the 1908 *Muller v. Oregon* case, reformers hailed the decision as enlightened and progressive.[31] Today, such a decision would be soundly criticized, and rightly so, for it prevents women from making their own decisions about how much they want to work.

It is ironic that contemporary feminists have come full circle to promote a similarly protective function for the government. Feminists are enlisting government's power to shield women from supposedly rampant sex discrimination in the workplace or in education. Furthermore, programs to provide women with time off for family purposes, such as the Family and Medical Leave Act,[32] and with paid maternity from unemployment insurance funds, such as the 1999 Department of Labor regulations, preserve the basic philosophy of *Muller v. Oregon.*

Through their rhetoric, contemporary feminists disavow the unparalleled freedom American women enjoy. Their agenda denies women the freedom to choose what is best for themselves and the dignity of knowing that their successes have been earned on merit and not because of their sex.

3

Learning a Lesson: How Women Have Surpassed Men in Education

In 1872 Dr. Edward Clarke, a member of Harvard University's Board of Overseers and a former faculty member in its medical college, told the New England Woman's Club of Boston that women's educational abilities were limited by women's physical characteristics. One year later, he expanded on that idea in a book called *Sex in Education; or, a Fair Chance for the Girls*. The danger of female education, according to Clarke, was that it diverted women's limited stores of physical energy from motherhood and made them "neuralgic and hysteric." He concluded that "the identical education of the two sexes is a crime before God and humanity that physiology protests against and that experience weeps over."[1]

Such sentiments were typical of the times. Earlier generations of women had even less access to education, particularly higher education. Although interest in women's education increased during the nineteenth century and led to the creation of female seminaries such as the Emma Willard School in Troy, New York, founded in 1821, and female colleges like Vassar, which opened in 1865, it was not until the 1870s and 1880s that women began attending colleges and graduate schools in more significant numbers.[2] Those who did had to overcome considerable obstacles, as Clarke's comments attest.

Even as late as the 1960s, education for boys and girls was at times separate and unequal. Although many of the institutional barriers to women's education had crumbled, cultural norms and social expectations still sent the message that certain areas of education were not proper pursuits for women. All children studied reading, writing, and arithmetic, but while boys studied wood shop, girls painted or took home economics. Boys went to dental school; girls went to dental technicians' school. Boys went to medical school; girls went to nursing school. Boys went to law or business school; girls went to secretarial school.

We have come a long way since the 1960s and an even longer way since the days of Clarke. The efforts of several generations of forward-thinking women and men succeeded in removing the formal barriers to women's education in America. Women now receive more than half of all B.A.'s and M.A.'s awarded and almost half of all medical and law degrees, as we show in more detail below. The cultural biases against female education have disappeared. Our society takes as a given that its daughters as well as its sons will reap the rewards of higher education. A woman's pursuit of an education is no longer the cause of hand wringing among Harvard educators.

Education is, however, the cause of much hand wringing among feminists. Organizations such as the National Women's Law Center and the National Organization for Women, as well as education-oriented feminist groups such as the American Association of University Women and the National Coalition for Women and Girls in Education view the country's schools as hopelessly mired in prejudice against women. In a recent assessment of women's educational opportunities, the AAUW could not dispute the overwhelming statistical evidence of women's success. Nevertheless, the organization concluded that "just because girls and women are finally achieving parity or actually exceeding males' past achievements in certain subjects does not negate the subtle gender bias still in operation in our society and in schools that reflect society."[3] Although the alleged bias is, as they say, "subtle," feminist advocacy organizations believe that it is pervasive. By their reckoning it is premature to declare victory over sex discrimination.

Because women have had undeniable success in education, it provides the foremost example of the feminists' dilemma. Women have come so far educationally that, on many college campuses today, they are the dominant sex. Women are matching or surpassing their male peers in test scores and graduation rates, and no one limits women's choices of fields of study. Since few female students are mothers, most women do not have to juggle studying and parenting. Yet feminists are unwilling to see those developments for what they are: a victory for women. Rather, they continue to promote the misguided notion that women are victims of an unfairly biased educational system.

Two forces drive feminists' complaints about education. First, many feminists believe that equality will not be achieved until women make up half of all campus majors. Equal percentages of men and women in all fields is their goal, and they allege that discriminatory social pressure funnels women into some fields of study rather than others. Second, contemporary feminist organizations such as NOW and the AAUW have an institutional stake in promoting the idea that women lack equality of opportunity in education. The pursuit of "gender equity" in education is a booming business, with funds flowing into the coffers of feminist organizations that study it. Unfortunately, the recognition that women have achieved equality would spell the end of a good portion of the budgets of those groups.

Women's educational choices are often not feminists' choices, and in this chapter we examine the distance between the two. We first present the data on women's academic success at the elementary and secondary school, college, and graduate levels. Then, we evaluate feminists' claims of discrimination in education and discuss feminists' gender equity proposals for education.

Breaking Educational Barriers: Evidence of Women's Success

Where is the "subtle gender bias" of which the AAUW speaks?[4] If women are still suffering the effects of past discrimination in education, then we should see evidence of those lingering differences in the current participation and performance rates of men and women. The evidence reveals a markedly different story.

Test Results. Contrary to what feminists would have us believe, measures of academic performance show women overwhelmingly successful in their pursuit of an education. Test scores, for example, show no statistically significant differences between young men and young women. In 1997 the nonprofit Educational Testing Service, which administers the Scholastic Aptitude Test and other standardized tests, released a report that examined test results from more than 400 tests and more than 15 million students. The report's findings document women's educational success.

The authors of the study, Warren Willingham and Nancy Cole, analyzed test results for a large national sample of twelfth-grade students by using seventy-four tests divided into fifteen categories. They found a standard mean difference of .02 favoring women on test performance, an inconsequential difference.[5] The authors also found that nearly all variation in scores occurred *within* the two sexes rather than between them; in most test categories, 99 percent of variation in scores was due to differences within one gender, while only 1 percent was due to differences between genders.[6] Those results are in direct contrast to the popular media perception of girls' needing extra help in school.

Some of the report's most revealing findings dealt with male and female performance in mathematics and science. For many years it has been accepted wisdom that girls do not perform as well as boys in math and science, and many feminist groups such as the AAUW cite that as evidence of discrimination against girls. The facts tell a slightly different story. Girls performed better at mathematical computation, while boys in upper grades performed better at mathematical reasoning. Those who claim that standardized tests discriminate against girls also had to admit that the most persistent gap was not the often-touted one for girls in math and science, but for boys in language and verbal skills.[7]

Similar findings appeared in recent tests made by the National Assessment of Educational Progress. Those tests found no difference between boys and girls in grades four through eight in science performance. The only noticeable difference occurred among high school seniors and then only among the highest-scoring students. In that smaller group boys outperformed girls.[8]

We can make certain generalizations about men's and women's test results. Girls tend to perform better on verbal and language tests, and boys tend to perform slightly better on math reasoning and science tests. A small but consistent tendency exists for girls to perform better on tests that call for open-ended written responses and for boys to perform better on multiple-choice tests.

One reason for those small differences in scoring is different interests outside the classroom rather than differences in innate ability, according to researchers Carol Dwyer and Linda Johnson. On average, boys preferred leisure activities that used math and science skills, such as using personal computers, while girls preferred hobbies such as music, art, or dance classes, some of which enhance verbal skills.[9] Summer camps, where children choose their activities, provide an excellent indicator of boys' and girls' interests outside the classroom. Computer camps are overwhelmingly male, and dance and art camps overwhelmingly female, results suggesting that, on average, boys and girls seek slightly different kinds of activities.

Girls are not neglecting math; on the contrary, data show that girls are taking more math courses than they have taken in the past. Between the early 1980s and 2000, the percentage of girls taking the advanced placement math and science exams steadily increased. While girls constituted 38 percent of students taking the advanced placement exam in calculus in 1985, they represented 45 percent in 2000; similarly, the percentage of girls taking the advanced placement chemistry exam rose from 30 percent in 1985 to 44 percent by 2000.[10] Some researchers attribute that growth not to an increase in girls' interest in math and science, but to the fact that girls are ambitious. As colleges demand more math and science, girls fulfill those academic requirements.[11]

Differential interests in math and science can be seen from data from the Department of Education's National Center for Education Statistics. The data show that twelfth-grade males have far more positive attitudes about math and science than do females. In fourth grade, 69 percent of boys and 70 percent of girls say that they like math, and 68 percent of boys and 66 percent of girls say that they like science. In twelfth grade, however, the difference is substantial for both subjects. Fifty-six percent of boys and 48 percent of girls say that they like math, and 56 percent of boys and 48 percent of girls say that they like science.[12] Such a decline in interest in math and science, evident in the responses of both the boys and the girls, does not provide evidence of discrimination against girls.

Furthermore, although the average scores of boys and girls are similar on achievement tests, boys have a wider distribution of scores. Compared with girls, more boys have high scores and more boys have low scores. When computing averages, those high and low scores cancel each other out, so that averages of the two sexes are equal, and most boys and girls fall toward the center of the distribution, so that they are about equal. We can see that greater dispersion of scores even in fields in which girls on average do better than boys, such as spelling and cognitive reasoning.[13]

But the wider variation in boys' scores results in more boys' being found at the top—as well as at the bottom—of the test range. We can observe those traits early: among a large sample of talented seventh and eighth graders who took the math Scholastic Aptitude Test between 1972 and 1991, there were thirteen boys for every girl who scored above 700.[14] Although only a small percentage of boys and girls are affected, they tend to be the most visible and thus lead to resentment and charges of discrimination. Furthermore, those traits persist into adulthood.

Hence, despite the overwhelmingly positive news about women's and girls' test performance, complaints of gender bias remain a permanent feature of any discussion of standardized testing. In 1996, for example, FairTest, an organization opposed to standardized testing, and the American Civil Liberties Union lodged a complaint with the U.S. Department of Education's Office for Civil Rights. The organizations claimed that the Preliminary Scholastic Aptitude Test was biased against girls and hence violated federal antidiscrimination legislation.

FairTest and the ACLU based their claim on the lower girls' scores on the PSAT. While 60 percent of the students scoring in the top 15 percent of the PSAT were boys, only 40 percent were girls. Since ranking in the top 15 percent is required for students seeking National Merit Scholarships, FairTest accused the College Board (which administers the test) of unfairly denying girls access to college scholarship money. Rather than risk losing federal assistance, the College Board agreed to change the PSAT by adding thirty-nine questions on which girls generally outperform boys and thus deliberately stacked the scoring in girls' favor. That action flies in the face of the principle of equality of opportunity and of all available evidence of girls' ability to succeed without special preferences.[15]

Ironically, FairTest's complaint coincided with a worrisome new educational trend: a decline in the number of boys taking the PSAT, American College Test, and SAT exams in recent years. High school boys are now far less likely than girls to take a college entrance exam, and among lower-income males, the ratio of girls to boys taking those exams is now two to one.[16] That means that fewer boys will be in the college pipeline, and that translates into lower lifetime earnings. Unlike feminists' claims about schools' shortchanging girls, that educational trend received little media attention until 1999.[17]

Degrees Granted. Test performance is not the only area where women's educational success is clearly visible. Just a generation after the end of formal discrimination against women in education, women are receiving high school diplomas and college degrees in greater numbers than men. Ever since 1870, the first year data are available, more than half of all high school graduates have been female.[18] In addition, young women get better grades than young men, both in high school and beyond.[19]

Evidence of sex discrimination at the college level is also hard to find. Women receive more than 60 percent of two-year associate degrees and have received a majority of those degrees since 1978. To critics who comment that associate's degrees are not so marketable as more advanced degrees, the data on bachelor's and master's degrees are heartening: women receive 56 percent of all such degrees awarded, and their percentage of B.A.'s and M.A.'s has exceeded those of men since the early 1980s.[20]

Women are both more likely to attend college and, once enrolled, more likely to graduate than are men. Perhaps the most compelling reason is that the returns from education are greater for women than they are for men: women gain more from college degrees than do men.[21] That is so because a man without a college degree has well-paying opportunities available to him in fields such as construction, timber logging, protective services, or oil drilling, jobs that most women prefer not to pursue, in part because many of them require high levels of physical strength or a high degree of risk.

Some enterprising reporters noted the growing female presence on college campuses in 1999, more than fifteen years after the trend started. They asked, "Where have the men gone?" According to the *New York Times,* "[T]he population of students enrolled in higher education tipped toward women more than a decade ago, and the skew is growing, year by year."[22] That is so even though the United States has more college-age men than women. For example, at the University of Georgia's Athens campus, women represented 58 percent of entering freshmen in 1998–1999 and 60 percent in the 1999–2000 class. To attract more young men, the University of Georgia practiced what amounted to affirmative action for men between 1995 and 1999. The university awarded male students extra points on a "Total Student Index."[23] The university discontinued those preferences in 1999 because of lawsuits.[24]

Graduate school data provide a similarly positive portrait of women's educational attainment. Women have received a majority of master's degrees since the early 1980s. The trend closely tracks women's percentage of bachelor's degrees. Women have also flourished in graduate professional programs. Percentages of first professional degrees (a Department of Education classification referring to degrees conferred in chiropractic medicine, dentistry, law, medicine, optometry, osteopathic medicine, pharmacy, podiatry, theology, and veterinary medicine) awarded to women have grown from a mere 5 percent in 1970 to 25 percent in 1980 to almost 43 percent by 1998. Moreover, individual professional programs in medicine, dentistry, law, and business have large numbers of female graduates.[25]

Women are also catching up to men in earning doctoral degrees. Until the 1970s, the percentage of doctoral degrees awarded to women never passed 15 percent. Yet the contemporary trend in Ph.D. programs is a positive one. By 1998 women were receiving 42 percent of all doctorates, and that number likely will continue to rise. In the humanities, women received nearly half of all doctorates in 1998.[26]

Women still receive fewer doctorates in such fields as economics and engineering. As Shulamit Kahn noted in a study of women in the economics profession, a higher percentage of male undergraduate economics majors continue their studies at the graduate level than do women. In addition, women drop out of economics Ph.D. programs at higher rates than men. Kahn found that "this is a critical point where economics loses women" and noted further that "higher attrition rates of women from Ph.D. programs are not unique to economics, but are seen in other science and engineering fields as well."[27] Other researchers have found a marked preference for women to choose life sciences and for men to choose mathematics or the physical sciences, preferences that cannot be explained by ability as measured by standardized tests.[28] Nevertheless the general trends of women in higher education are encouraging. Test scores, grades, and graduation rates all reveal women's educational success.

Claims of Discrimination in Education

The overwhelming evidence of women's educational success makes it difficult to square the facts with feminist claims. Feminists and other supporters of special preferences for women deny that data on women's achievements are proof of equal opportunity in education. Instead, in a combination of denial and evasion, they offer several justifications for continued government intervention for women in education. First, they say that such intervention is needed to compensate for women's lack of educational opportunities in previous eras. "Disparities and disadvantages for female students continue to be pervasive," the National Women's Law Center notes, "in light of the long history of second-class treatment accorded to girls and women by our nation's educational institutions."[29] The historical record is clear: many women were the victims of discrimination, their educational aspirations often thwarted for more than a century. But the contemporary record of women's achievements is equally clear: women can pursue an education in any field they choose.

Second, feminists argue that government intervention is necessary to ensure the creation of a generation of women who will serve as role models and who will create an "old girl network" to rival the existing "old boy network" in education and in the workplace. Again, past discrimination is offered as the reason for contemporary efforts to give women preferences in education.

But the most frequent complaint from feminists with regard to education is that women are not entering certain educational fields such as math, physics, and engineering at the same rates as men. Examples of that trend are easy to find at any college graduation ceremony, where one will see the engineering majors, predominantly men, walking across the stage to receive their diplomas, followed by the nursing students, almost all women. One might notice that the women exhibit reactions similar to their male counterparts as they exit the graduation stage with degrees in hand: equal doses of pride, excitement, and the exuberance of young people looking ahead to their futures.

But feminists see something else: pernicious sex segregation. "Young women are channeled out of important vocational education opportunities," the National Women's Law Center asserted, and they "remain excluded from or underrepresented in key nontraditional areas of study, such as engineering, mathematics, and physical science."[30] An AAUW publication asked, "Why are women only 16 percent of physics and engineering majors in college? Why are more women not flocking to the more highly paid career of surgeon rather than general practitioner?"[31]

Why indeed? Given women's equal access to higher education, a common-sense answer is that the differences reflect personal taste for particular fields of study. Men are more likely than women to major in engineering, mathematics, or physical science. Women are more likely than men to major in disciplines such as public administration, social work, or communications, as Department of Education figures reveal. Of course, despite those tendencies, women do pursue mathematics and science, especially at the undergraduate level, and men major in social work. Clearly, the opportunities to pursue studies in a male- or female-dominated field exist for motivated individuals of either sex. Male nursing students and female engineering students do exist.

But common-sense answers are not what professional feminists are seeking. Their measurement of women's success is proportionality; they desire equality of outcomes in education rather than equality of opportunity. If women constitute fewer than half of all science or math majors, then discrimination must be the culprit. Of course, if that principle is to be applied equally, then men should make up half of all nursing, dance, and English majors. That standard, as absurd as it is and as stifling to individual self-expression, grows from the way feminists and affirmative action supporters define *equality*.

Those who seek expanded government intervention in education pursue the same end that they do in the workplace, namely, statistical parity between men and women in male-dominated educational fields. For those feminists, equal access is not enough. If an insufficient number of women enter certain fields, then stereotypes about women's and men's abilities will persist, they say. Thus, intervention to "correct" statistical imbalances is required. But providing equal access and opportunities is the law as well as the right thing to do; trying to ensure equality of outcomes is social engineering. We should not confuse the two.

Groups such as NOW, the National Women's Law Center, the AAUW, and the National Coalition for Women and Girls in Education do not view women as making free and informed decisions about their educational training. They see the odds stacked against women in elementary school, high school, and higher education, and from that flows their belief that women, having internalized discriminatory norms, are unfairly pressured to study female-dominated fields. They see women as being persuaded to major in traditional fields such as nursing rather than in math and science.[32] Verna Williams, chair of the National Coalition for Women and Girls in Education, claims that discriminatory harassment keeps girls from succeeding in math and science classes and, thus, that "female students are underrepresented in nontraditional academic and career fields."[33]

Here, we encounter the weapon often wielded in feminist discussions of discrimination: false consciousness. Women may believe that they are freely choosing to become nurses, English majors, or dental hygienists, but in reality they are forced into those lower paying fields by social expectations. Women are "tracked" into such traditional fields of study, as the National Women's Law Center puts it. The passive-voice construction of their claims is deliberate, for feminists do not want to say explicitly what they are pointing out implicitly: that many women have chosen to pursue an education in a female-dominated field. To acknowledge that would be to admit that a good portion of the female population does not share the same values as feminists.

Over the past quarter century, women have moved into many fields that were once entirely male, such as law and medicine. That shows that social expectations have not hindered their progress. Women now earn a good share of doctoral degrees awarded in biology and chemistry, as well as medical and dental degrees. If the social pressures feminists claim prevent women from entering math, physics, and engineering really exist, why do they not apply to law, biology, dentistry, and medicine?

Feminists are correct to make the link between certain fields of education and future financial success. An individual's educational field is a major determinant of expected lifetime earnings. Economists Charles Brown and Mary Corcoran found that the choice of major field of study accounts for a significant part of the male–female wage gap among college graduates. They document the sex-based differences in the kinds of training and skills acquired in schools. Furthermore, they show the considerable influx of women into previously male-dominated educational fields such as business, engineering, physical science, and mathematics since 1968, with no corresponding influx of men into the female-dominated fields of education and nursing.[34] Calculations from their data show that when choices of college majors are accounted for, women make 94 percent of men's earnings.[35]

Brown and Corcoran were equivocal on the implications of that pattern of self-sorting in college majors, but they did admit a possibility not considered by feminists, namely, that students' choices of college majors reflect their abilities and preferences. Students choose to major in fields that interest them and in which they perform well; common sense suggests that programs designed to change women's fields of study may do little to affect the sex-based wage gap.[36] Persuading a woman who is not talented at chemistry to select it as a major will not raise her future wages—it may even lower them by diverting her from a field for which she has greater aptitude and interest.

The latest salvo in feminism's war on education is the high school computer lab, where boys tend to outnumber girls. The AAUW, for example, recently declared that a sizable gender gap exists in the field of information technology. Computer courses have become new "boys clubs," says Janice Weinman, executive director of the AAUW.[37]

Such rhetoric implies that girls are excluded from educational opportunities or that they are socialized to believe that girls should not use computers. Not so. In Fairfax County, Virginia, for example, girls make up 26 percent of the students taking computer science classes, and in Montgomery County, Maryland, they make up half of all computer applications students. Although it is true that more boys than girls enroll in computer programming classes, that situation does not warrant the AAUW's claim that the gap contributes to "a lifetime of lower earnings and lower retirement benefits for a majority of women,"[38] especially since the computer technician field is not one with high lifetime earnings. Given a choice of courses, girls have not flocked to computer science classes in numbers equal to boys. College women have chosen social science more than physical science programs of study. Feminists view those women's preferences as invalid because the end result is an educational landscape that lacks perfect gender proportionality.

Educational Goals of Affirmative Action Supporters

A quick glance at current feminist literature on education reveals a consistent theme. Feminists want the federal government to exercise more control over schools and to issue and follow through on more threats when educators do not meet their standards. Their focus lately has been on Title IX, one of the amendments to the

1964 Civil Rights Act.[39] Title IX of the Educational Amendments Act, passed in 1972, was intended to prevent discrimination based on sex in any educational program or activity that receives federal funds. It was modeled after Title VI of the Civil Rights Act of 1964 and states, "No person in the United States shall, on the basis of sex, be excluded from participation in, be denied the benefits of, or be subjected to discrimination under any program or activity receiving Federal financial assistance."[40]

In 1997 the National Coalition for Women and Girls in Education released a "Title IX Report Card" that measured the successes and failures of the law in its twenty-five year history. The coalition's conclusion? The nation had earned only a C. Verna Williams, chair of the coalition, stated that "the promise of Title IX . . . has yet to be fully realized" and that women and girls still lacked equal opportunity in education.[41] The report card was consistently pessimistic. The highest grade granted was a B+ in the area of access to higher education. In the remaining eight categories the nation received Cs and Ds.

Although such a pessimistic portrait bears little resemblance to the statistical data demonstrating women's educational success, the National Coalition for Women and Girls in Education used its report card to justify making a dozen recommendations for further government intervention in education. The coalition called for increased enforcement and targeted compliance reviews of schools by the Department of Education's Office for Civil Rights and for the office's investigations of "subtle forms of discrimination." In addition, the coalition demanded that Congress continue to fund sex equity programs in schools.[42] Those recommendations raise serious questions, such as what constitutes "subtle discrimination" and who is qualified to adjudge whether it has taken place. Are we to anoint feminist organizations the stewards of the process, as their literature suggests we should?

Although the majority of teachers are female, feminist groups also lack faith in teachers' ability to give girls a fair chance in the classroom. The National Coalition for Women and Girls in Education, for example, urges extensive training of teachers and administrators so that they will learn how to overcome their biases against girls.

The National Women's Law Center is more blunt. It notes that today's educational professionals "were themselves educated at a time when discriminatory practices were the norm."[43] The willingness of those groups to meddle in the educational process suggests a worrisome degree of arrogance—they assume that they have overcome gender bias, while the rest of us, especially teachers, require retraining.

Teacher retraining is the least ambitious proposal gender equity proponents are making with regard to education. In June 2000 President Clinton issued an executive order forbidding "discrimination on the basis of race, sex, color, national origin, disability, religion, age, sexual orientation, and status as a parent" in federally conducted education and training programs and activities. The order describes educational and training programs as including but not limited to schools, extracurricular activities, academic programs, summer enrichment programs, and even teacher training programs sponsored by the federal government.[44] In essence, the executive order is a back-door way of expanding the reach of Title IX, and it has the potential to encourage gender quotas in government educational programs.

That executive order did not appear out of the blue. In June 1999 Clinton had sent a memo to the heads of executive departments and agencies announcing an expansion of Title IX and requesting that each agency draft its own regulations to implement the expansion.[45] Enough executive agencies requested waivers or simply ignored the memo that in 2000, the Clinton administration decided to forgo individual agency implementation and assigned the responsibility to the Department of Justice. Clinton's June 2000 executive order superseded the 1997 memo and gave the attorney general responsibility for drafting the new rules and for making the final determination as to whether a specific program is educational and thus covered by the new regulations.[46]

The potential danger in Clinton's executive order was that if the attorney general decided to interpret Title IX's antidiscrimination principle to mean statistical balancing of men and women, it could be used as a de facto quota in federally funded programs. For example, if the National Aeronautics and Space Administration had an educational and training program for future astronauts where men were the majority of participants, under the expanded Title IX rule, a NASA employee could file a formal complaint claiming that the program discriminated against women. Clinton's executive order could also have created a new vehicle for disparate-impact lawsuits against institutions or businesses that host federal educational and training programs. The executive order applied only to federally *conducted* programs and not federally *assisted* programs. Thus, private businesses involved in joint educational ventures with the federal government were not subject to the expanded regulations. It would, however, have required only another executive order to expand the scope to federally assisted programs. The election of President George W. Bush renders the likelihood of additional executive orders moot.

Such rules bear out the earlier warnings of University of Chicago law professor Richard Epstein, who noted how misinterpretation of Title IX by federal bureaucrats and ideological groups would lead to a "rough proportion of men and women in engineering and science on the one hand, and art and literature on the other, even though, most certainly, far more men are engaged in the former activities, and far more women are engaged in the latter."[47] What that amounted to, in essence, was a denial of choice—the government's refusal to respect the choices of students if those choices resulted in statistical imbalances between men and women.

Such bureaucratic stealth tactics were reminiscent of those feminists employed several decades ago in earlier battles over women's access to education. As Flora Davis, a historian sympathetic to the women's movement, noted in her book, *Moving the Mountain*, feminists kept a low profile during the initial debate on Title IX because they did not want to draw attention to the potential consequences of the program. "If more people understood just how broadly it would affect education," Davis noted, "opposition to Title IX would likely have grown."[48]

Feminists employed similar strategies in the early 1970s to gain passage of the Women's Educational Equity Act, which created a Department of Education program that funds gender equity programs and materials. That enactment is a classic example of how special interests can move legislation through Congress.[49] The act's feminist supporters portrayed the program as small and noncontroversial, much as they had portrayed Title IX.[50] But in practice, the act, which has received successive reauthorization under the Elementary and Secondary Education Act, has become a boon for feminist special interest groups and a major source of misinformation about women's educational opportunities.

Publications produced in compliance with the act rely on research by such individuals as Carol Gilligan, David Sadker, and Myra Sadker. Scholars, including Christina Hoff Sommers in *The War against Boys,* have shown that research to be questionable and misleading. The Education Development Center in Newton, Massachusetts, by far the largest recipient of federal funds under the Women's Educational Equity Act, spends the money producing booklets such as "Gender-Fair Math" and "Gender Equity for Educators, Parents, and Community."[51]

Although the act's funding represents a small portion of the total federal budget (approximately $5 million in 1999), that money has been used to encourage the growth of a gender equity industry— one whose vision of sex-based proportionality has ensnared schools in bureaucratic red tape and lawsuits that waste school districts' already limited resources. The National Women's Law Center, for example, used a 1995 grant to publish how-to handbooks for suing school districts for sexual harassment.[52]

Transforming the Curriculum

Linked to feminists' desire for statistical proportionality in the classroom is an educational curriculum that embraces their particular vision of equality. Feminists, particularly those in academia, have been active participants in the "culture wars" that have been waged on American campuses for the past several decades. In their view, the educational system is hopelessly corrupted by sexism, as Barbara Anne Murphy argued in the *Southern California Review of Law and Women's Studies.* Murphy argued from the dubious premise that sexism is pervasive in society, politics, religion, economics, and education in the United States:

As part of the system of patriarchy, education plays an active role in perpetuating the status quo of unequal social and economic roles of women and men within our society. The educational system perpetuates this status quo through the quality of the curriculum, through the quality of the educational environment, and through subtle discrimination tactics. In effect, the entire country has been operating separate systems for boys and girls despite the fact that they usually share classrooms.[53]

Murphy viewed nearly every facet of the existing educational system as complicit in a patriarchal plot. Textbooks, she said, teach children that women are inferior, lower girls' self-esteem, and perpetuate stereotypes that rob girls of independence. Despite evidence to the contrary, such as the work of Christina Hoff Sommers and Judith Kleinfeld, she argued that teachers ignore girls in favor of boys.[54]

As they do in other arenas besides education, feminists use well-chosen weapons; for example, they speak of "hidden curricula" and "stealth discrimination."[55] In that way they are able to claim that systemic discrimination exists, even in the face of overwhelming evidence to the contrary. Murphy claimed that discrimination against women in education is so inherent and subtle that it is hard to notice and that many girls are not even aware of what is happening to them. To solve the alleged problem, she proposed a complete restructuring of education along feminist principles of equality, with the federal government further monitoring public education so that children can be taught in gender-neutral environments from an early age.[56]

Although they sound extreme, Murphy's views are not even drawn from the most radical end of the spectrum. Since the mid-1990s, academic feminists have stepped up their criticism of college curricula by calling for restructuring along feminist lines. Their goal is the total transformation of the educational system in a way that appears to be gaining sanction in some states.

Writing in the *Women's Rights Law Reporter*, law professor Sharon Sims argued that states should require more teaching of women's history, since traditional history "has had a disastrous effect on women's self-worth" as well as on their ability to develop a "collective self-identity."[57] She criticized a law on women's history that passed in Illinois for failing to include an enforcement mechanism and called for further state intervention to ensure the teaching of history from a feminist perspective.[58]

The goal of those crusaders is to instill feminist principles in students and not to correct historical omissions. Men made much of our country's history. It is a disservice to students to pretend otherwise or to insist, as Sims does, that schools teach the American Revolution "through a women's [sic] eyes."[59] Although teaching our children about the contributions all individuals have made to American history certainly has value, curriculum reformers like those in Illinois have accepted uncritically contemporary feminist ideas about women's supposedly subordinate status in American society.

Feminist efforts at curricular transformation have blossomed at the college level as well. Early in 1997 the New England Council of Land-Grant University Women released its plan for higher education, called "Vision 2000." The vision took as its starting point a contention similar to Murphy's: the idea that an intellectual bias against women infects university life. The authors of the Vision 2000 plan complained about women's purportedly stunted academic future and recommended punitive measures for faculty and administrations that fail to create a curriculum that is "woman-friendly," a descriptor that was never adequately defined. Although the vision's supporters denied it, and although the plan claimed to "ask" faculty for compliance, clearly negative consequences will ensue for those who do not adhere to the vision.[60] For example, the report said that by 2000, faculty members whom students had judged to be noninclusive might be denied faculty prizes, bonuses, or raises. Similarly, Vision 2000 warned that department heads would be held responsible for "improving gender equity" in their subject areas, whatever that means, and compensated accordingly.[61]

As University of Massachusetts professor Daphne Patai pointed out, the Vision 2000 plan tells us far more about academic power politics than about women's educational needs. Women's studies departments at the New England land-grant universities are the most vocal faction supporting Vision 2000, and the proposal includes plans for an autonomous women's studies site to coordinate the transformation of the curriculum.[62] As the Vision 2000 proposal demonstrates, academic feminists, like their mainstream counterparts, ignore the facts about women's educational progress in favor of a storyline that places women in the role of victims in need of government aid. Such a vision is not helpful to women.

Ironically, one of the most recent examples of one sex's denying the other equal access to education was that of an avowed feminist professor denying men the opportunity to take her feminist ethics course. In 1999 iconoclastic Boston College professor Mary Daly refused to allow a male student to attend her class. When college administrators told her that the law required her to allow the man into her classroom, she accused them of being right-wing pawns trying to assert their "white male supremacy." But as college spokesman Jack Duncan pointed out, if a male professor had engaged in similar behavior, the college surely would have been sued. Daly ultimately chose to resign rather than to allow men to attend her course. The degree of praise she received from many in the feminist community reveals the hollowness of feminists' claims about equality in education.[63]

Conclusion

The gap that should concern Americans is not the one that exists between college-educated men and women, but between those who are college-educated and those who have no college education at all. In today's economy, education and training—not gender—are the determining factors for success. We agree with feminists on two counts. First, women should have every opportunity to pursue the educations they desire—as should men. Second, we agree with the conclusion of the National Women's Law Center that "when women move into nontraditional fields, employers have a larger and more diverse pool from which to draw their workforce."[64] But although we agree with those ends, the *means* employed to achieve them must also be just, and it is here that we part company with feminists.

Calls for increased federal government monitoring of the classroom to achieve equity between the sexes is both unnecessary and dangerous, particularly since the measure of equality used in those calculations is an inflexible numerical proportionality rule that is neither realistic nor desirable. Moreover, lurking behind feminists' calls for 50 percent female chemistry classes are two disturbing notions. First is the implicit assumption that women are not capable of making educational choices for themselves and that they are victims of a form of false consciousness that unfairly limits their options. Second is the notion that government bureaucrats, acting as social engineers in the classroom, are the answer to that perceived problem.

As we have seen, the available evidence refutes those claims. Current calls for government affirmative action in education are based on the demonstrably false premise that women are in need of remedial action and protection. Formal barriers to women in education have been removed, and informal cultural barriers continue to crumble. Women who choose to do so can enter previously male-dominated fields of study. Those who choose otherwise are not victims of a sexist society but rather have determined that their ambitions would be best fulfilled in other fields. That women can now pursue a range of educational options and are doing so with vigor and success is the real story of women and education in America.

4

Choosing a Job: From the Kitchen to the Boardroom

Jennifer Simon (not her real name) pursued an educational and professional path that prepared her for a lucrative career in law. After earning her undergraduate and law degrees from prestigious universities, she rounded out her schooling with a master's degree in tax law. She went to work for one major law firm and then another before moving to a job at a government agency. Along the way she married and had two children. By all accounts Simon had achieved considerable professional and personal success and easily could have continued her career as a successful lawyer. Instead, she chose to do something else. Simon decided that she really wanted to be a social worker, so she returned to school to get a degree in social work.[1]

Carly Fiorina dropped out of law school before the end of her first year and had a number of low-paying jobs, including receptionist and teacher, before she went to AT&T as a sales representative in 1980. Expecting to stay at the company for fewer than two years, Fiorina did not even sign up for the savings plan. But after successfully marketing telephone services to federal agencies, she switched to the equipment division, Network Systems, and at age thirty-five became the company's first female officer. Later, she earned praise from industry watchers as group president of Lucent Technology's Global Service Provider Division. In the summer of

44

1999, she was named chief executive officer of the Hewlett-Packard Corporation.[2]

Although those stories are not typical, the experiences of Simon and Fiorina are instructive not only for what they tell us about the unpredictability of contemporary career tracks, but for what they reveal about the limits of preferential programs for women. Government efforts to encourage the hiring of women in previously male-dominated jobs make sense only if employers are systematically denying women entrance into those fields. As the experiences of both Simon and Fiorina reveal, that is not happening. Women who want to become captains of industry or partners in law firms can do so, but many prefer other paths to success and satisfaction.

What preferential programs for women do not take into account is personal choice, the driving factor behind the stories of Simon and Fiorina. Every day men and women make choices—some good, some bad—about their education, their work, and their families. Those choices, such as Simon's to pursue social work rather than law, might not make sense to some people, including many feminists, but they make sense to the people who actually make the personal decisions, including Simon and her family. The ability to make such choices is the hallmark of a free society. The failure to recognize the importance of personal choice is the Achilles' heel of the contemporary feminist agenda.

As the previous chapter illustrates, educationally, women are doing as well, if not better, than men in those fields in which they choose to participate. But how are they faring in the job market? After all, it was not so long ago that women were excluded from many jobs. Are women today able to choose vocations and professions on the basis of their talents and interests, or are certain careers still off-limits to them?

Forty years ago, discrimination in the labor market was an accepted fact of life. Every newspaper in the country had separate classified advertisements—jobs for men, jobs for women, jobs for either sex, and even jobs for couples.[3] As recently as the 1960s, separate pay scales for men and women sometimes existed for the same job, with men earning more. Such behavior was not confined to a few unscrupulous firms but was common practice even among state

and local governments. Although the rhetoric of many contemporary feminists implies that the situation has changed little since
then, the facts reveal the opposite.

A Historical Perspective on Women and Work

Women have always worked. Whether they performed household
tasks, ran family farms, produced goods for sale, or managed stores,
they have participated in the economy throughout American history. That participation was not without restraints or, in some cases,
coercion. Until slavery was abolished, African American women
labored in conditions of often brutal servitude. Legal and social barriers prevented women of all backgrounds from pursuing the same
work as men or from envisioning lives beyond the demands of
hearth and home.

As with Laura Ingalls in the *Little House on the Prairie* series of
books, generations of American women grew up with precise
expectations of what their futures would bring: marriage and children.[4] Many women, such as the fictional Laura Ingalls, did work
around the house or on the farm.[5] Some women even engaged in
paid labor: Ingalls became a teacher to help send her blind sister to
college.[6] Yet, while many women expected to work before marriage,
after marriage, and particularly after bearing children, women were
primarily expected to stay home to manage a household. More
African American than white women worked in paid jobs after marriage, but many also followed the pattern of staying home after
bearing children.

That pattern, repeated over the course of several generations,
doubtless influenced the expectations of American women. Most
white women did not work outside the home after they married,
and unmarried women who did so were often pitied. Indeed, as
recently as the 1940s, the majority of women who worked outside
the home were single.[7] Cultural norms and expectations effectively
limited women's work horizons. Women were also marrying at a
younger age in the first half of the twentieth century. Between 1900
and 1978 the median age of first marriage for women never
exceeded twenty-two years,[8] the typical woman having four years
between high school and wedding vows. Many had fewer.

Since the 1940s, however, changes in culture, technology, and education have caused women's labor force participation rates—the percentage either employed or looking for work—to increase dramatically, from 28 percent in 1940 to 60 percent in 2000. By 2000 the majority of women under the age of sixty-five were in the labor market, with the most dramatic rise among women aged twenty-five to fifty-four; today, three-fourths of those women work outside the home.[9] Paid employment is now the norm rather than the exception for American women.

That pattern of increased employment has been unique to women. In contrast, labor force participation rates for men have fallen from 83 percent in 1940 to just 75 percent today. Although men are still more likely to have paid jobs, the difference has shrunk substantially over the past fifty years. The largest changes have been for older men: between 1948 and 2000, the percentage of men aged sixty-five and over who work dropped from 47 percent to 18 percent.[10]

Such statistics, though revealing of women's dramatic entrance into the labor force, do not give us the whole story. Education played a crucial role in ensuring that a working woman was no longer a contradiction in terms.

Women's educational attainment is linked in two ways to their movement into the labor force. First, as women saw that it was becoming more common and acceptable to work outside the home, they envisioned having decades-long careers rather than jobs that lasted only the few years before marriage. As a result, more women began investing in the skills—including education—that qualified them for higher-paying jobs. Second, as more women acquired such skills, they stayed in the labor force longer to reap the monetary benefits of their investment.

The result is a female work force far more skilled than it was forty years ago. In 1952 almost half the women in the labor force had less than a high school education.[11] In contrast, by 1998 only 9 percent had less than a high school education, and more than half the women in the labor market had attended at least one year of college.[12]

With education and the promise of future careers came delayed marriage and childbearing, though historians are still sorting out cause and effect in this demographic shift. The median age of first marriage has risen by about three years over the past generation, an increase slightly outpacing the increase in education.[13] Later marriage has meant later childbearing as well.

Thus, young women in today's job market are not only more highly educated than their mothers, but they also remain working and childless for a longer span of time. As economist Claudia Goldin has shown in a study of different cohorts of young women, working women now consciously delay childbearing so that they may further develop their careers.[14] Women today are having fewer children as well, in part because of their understanding that they pay an opportunity cost for each additional child in terms of time spent at home.

The greatest change in the expectations of the current generation of American women has taken place with respect to the effect of children on their careers. Women with children, particularly young children, have always been far less likely to work outside the home. Quitting the labor force used to be particularly pronounced among mothers with very young children. Many of those women never rejoined the labor force; others returned when their youngest child went off to school. Given that historical context, the recent increase in labor force participation of married women with children has been dramatic. In 1960 only 19 percent of married women with children under the age of six worked outside the home.[15] In 1999 62 percent did so, and, in addition, 77 percent of married women with children over the age of six worked outside the home.[16]

Mothers have not necessarily moved into the paid labor force as full-time workers. Part-time work offers employees greater latitude in tailoring their hours to fit their needs. Thus, the difficulty involved in balancing work and family commitments has made part-time work an attractive option for women, particularly for mothers. Women have consistently been more likely than men to engage in part-time work, and the proportion of women who do so has remained relatively constant (at approximately 25 percent of the female labor force) during the past few decades.[17] Although 62 percent of married women with children under the age of six work outside the home, fewer than half—only 39 percent—work full-time.[18]

The problems faced by working mothers are different from those faced by childless workers, and they even appear to be different from the issues faced by working fathers. In our society, it is usually the mother who bears the main responsibility for child care. Although 80 percent of women have children,[19] women with children, particularly with young children, are not the majority of women in the work force.

Sixty-one percent of working women have no children at home, and only 16 percent have at least one child under the age of six. Slightly more, 23 percent, have at least one child between six and seventeen years old.[20] Many other mothers work part-time. Consequently, the problems faced by working mothers are not the problems of all working women. Some women have not yet had children or will never have them; others have left their childbearing years behind them; still others have left the labor force.

Choice or Necessity: Why Work?

Why some groups of women work is obvious. Women without another source of income, whether they are single, divorced, or widowed, work to support themselves. After marriage and before children, although the husband may have an income, women work to earn additional income.

The big question is why so many more *mothers* work now than they did previously. It is now the received wisdom that women enter the work force because they have to, and that is certainly true of single mothers. One popular view is that living expenses have increased so much that, unlike families in the 1950s, families today require two incomes to stay afloat. Another view is that women must work to pay an ever increasing tax bill; if taxes were lower, the argument goes, more women would be able to afford to stay home.

But the evidence does not support either hypothesis. With regard to the economic necessity of mothers' working, certainly there are some families for which that is true. But our society is richer than it was in previous decades, when staying home with children was the cultural norm. Families today have larger houses, often two or more cars, as well as multiple television sets, videocassette recorders, stereos, and other consumer goods. Men are retiring earlier, whereas in a time of true economic hardship they would retire later. Both common sense and research suggest that the majority of married women with children work so that they can purchase additional goods that they might consider necessities but that earlier generations surely considered luxuries.

Neither does historical economic evidence uphold the view that tax increases require two workers to share the burden of paying Uncle Sam. Women's participation in the paid labor force has increased steadily over the past fifty years even though tax rates have fluctuated. Tax bills were relatively low in the 1950s, when 35 percent of adult women worked. In 1980, with a top tax rate of 50 percent, 51 percent of adult women were in the labor market. In 1990, with the tax rates markedly lower, 57 percent of women worked. Economic studies show that women's decisions to work are influenced to a great extent by their wages and taxes.[21] The higher the take-home pay, the more women work. Hence, lower taxes would encourage more women to work, not to stay at home. Most working women favor getting rid of the "marriage penalty" (the increase in tax rates as a second earner enters the labor force), because they want more take-home pay, not because they want to quit the labor force for home.

Professor Chinhui Juhn of the University of Houston has shown that the movement of women into the work force between 1969 and 1989 was far greater among those with higher-earning husbands than for those whose husbands earned less. Juhn's findings suggest that it is the attraction of potential earnings, rather than economic necessity, that drew those women in.

Juhn divided men into ten wage-earnings categories, from lowest to highest, and looked at whether their wives were in or out of the labor force in 1969 and 1989. She found that the biggest increase in both earnings and work participation rates came from the wives of high-wage men. The real earnings and the employment of low-wage men declined because of a decrease in the demand for blue-collar workers, part of a structural shift in the U.S. economy. But that was not offset by an increase in work participation of their wives, as would be the case if women were in the work force through economic necessity. As Juhn wrote, "This fact suggests to us that increased market opportunities for women—particularly for highly skilled women—may have played a greater role than husbands' earnings in fueling the acceleration of female employment in the 1970s and the 1980s."[22]

Anecdotal evidence supports that conclusion as well. In her 1997 book, *The Time Bind,* sociologist Arlie Hochschild went inside the corporate world to figure out how and why women juggle work and family.[23] Hochschild concluded that women work because they want to, not as a result of financial need. Moreover, they did not avail themselves of the options provided to them to alleviate their work burdens. The corporation Hochschild examined offered its workers flextime and part-time work, for example, but most women still preferred to work full-time.

Hochschild's rationale for women's labor force participation, however, contrasts with that of Juhn. In her interviews and observations of working women, Hochschild revealed what she considered to be one of the dirty secrets of the work-family struggle: many women eagerly went to the office to escape the alleged drudgery of their domestic lives. They wanted to find relief from tasks such as cleaning, laundry, and shopping and escaped to the office in the evenings to avoid the additional stress of marital tension or problem children. For many of the women Hochschild interviewed, the office had replaced the family and home as the main supportive, affirming institution in their lives.

It is difficult to gauge reasons for working on the basis of survey evidence of a few families within one company, as Hochschild did, and Hochschild's analyis appears to have focused on particularly troubled families. But the message emerging from the data and anecdotal surveys is that women's movement into the work force does not appear to be linked to economic need. Women are working because they find it a preferred use of their time and because paid jobs now seem to carry greater status than the role of housewife and mother. In addition, the lure of material reward presents a compelling reason to work. As our society has become more affluent, more women, rather than fewer, have joined the labor force.

That is evident from standard government data, as well as from the Virginia Slims Opinion Poll, a sample of 2,177 women. In 1974 60 percent of women polled said that they preferred to stay home rather than to work, and 35 percent said that they preferred to work outside the home. In 2000, when the United States was vastly more affluent than it was twenty-five years ago, 44 percent said that they preferred to stay home, and 48 percent said that they preferred to have a job.[24] In the 1950s a mother would have been pitied if she worked outside the home. In the 1990s a woman is often pitied when she stays home with her children. Nevertheless, women's entrance into the work force has not eliminated the challenge of reconciling public and private roles. The ever proliferating literature on the difficulties women face in trying to balance work and family is a testament to the issue's continued impact.

Occupational Choice: Teacher, Logger, or CEO?

In previous eras, American girls grew up knowing that, as women, they would be expected to adopt particular social roles—wife, mother, or perhaps a career in the limited range of professions or jobs open to them. Earlier generations took it as a given that certain occupations were male or female. Many teachers, nurses, and librarians were female. Policemen and firemen were male, as were bankers and mayors. Occupational stereotypes were a fact of life, since so many jobs were off-limits to women, either legally or de facto through social pressure. Today, we have "police officers" and "firefighters" rather than police*men* or fire*men*, and the effect of those changes has been far more than semantic. Within the space of a generation, occupations that were previously almost exclusively male, such as lawyers, pharmacists, and physicians, are now pursued by men and women. Even corporate America, once a bastion of male executives, is being transformed. To cite just three examples, Shelly Lazarus, chairman and chief executive officer of Ogilvy and Mather Worldwide, Heidi Miller, vice chairman of Marsh Inc., and Andrea Jung, chief executive officer of Avon Products, have all made it to the upper echelons of the business world. Their success belies the claim that women cannot succeed in male-dominated fields.

Shelly Lazarus received her M.B.A. from Columbia University in the late 1960s, a time when only 3 percent of all M.B.A.'s awarded went to women. After she had spent two years with the Clairol Corporation, Ogilvy and Mather, an advertising giant, recruited Lazarus, and she has been with the company ever since. Over the course of her more than twenty-five years with the company, Lazarus has progressed steadily through the ranks, ultimately becoming CEO in 1996. Lazarus's ascent was the result of determination and an excellent business sense. In 1991, with Oglivy and Mather losing business, Lazarus engineered a successful turnaround by winning such clients as American Express, IBM, and Kodak. By the end of the decade she was responsible for 377 agencies in ninety-seven countries.[25] Lazarus took a common route to the top of the business world: M.B.A., at least twenty-five years with the same company, and lots of hard work.

Heidi Miller, now vice chairman of Marsh Inc. and previously chief financial officer of Priceline.com and chief financial officer of Citigroup, the world's largest financial company, took a different path. Miller is six years younger than Lazarus and earned a Ph.D. in Latin American history from Yale University. Afterwards, she worked for thirteen years at Chemical Bank in various positions, including managing director of emerging markets, loan officer, and manager of an equity portfolio. From there, Miller navigated the intricate maze of mergers in the banking industry; she worked first at Primerica in 1997 as senior vice president for planning and assistant to the president, Jamie Dimon. She then became chief credit officer and risk manager for Smith Barney and later chief financial officer for Travelers Group (which became Citigroup when it merged with Citicorp in 1998). In 2000 she left the prestigious Citigroup position to take a gamble with the smaller Internet upstart, and she subsequently joined Marsh & McLennan Cos. as vice chairman of its insurance brokerage division.[26]

Andrea Jung, born in 1958, is another example of a famous businesswoman with a liberal arts degree. Instead of pursuing a business degree, she majored in English literature at Princeton University. After that, she embarked on a career as a buyer for Bloomingdale's. Working her way through the retail clothing industry, Jung held positions with I. Magnin and Neiman Marcus. When Jung eventually joined Avon Products, Inc., in 1994, her goal was to rejuvenate the Avon image around the world. Her success in doing that earned her the chief operating officer's spot in 1998 and the CEO's office in 1999.[27]

Fiorina, Lazarus, Miller, and Jung all took individualized routes to the top of corporate America that often combined nontraditional educational experience with lots of practical work in varied jobs. They all also managed to combine children with career and showed that, with organization and hard work, it is possible to have both. Shelly Lazarus has three children, Heidi Miller and Andrea Jung have two each, and Carly Fiorina has two stepchildren. In an interview Miller said, "It's very powerful to walk into those meetings with a pregnant belly. Men were so nervous that my water would break right there that I could hurry them to get things done."[28] On another occasion she said: "Those who are most successful are extremely flexible and able to grasp complex issues quickly. You must also have strong people skills and be able to work effectively at all levels of the company. And, unfortunately, you must also be willing to work long hours."[29] That recognition of the effect of individual choices—and the necessary trade-offs all men and women must make—stands in stark contrast to the claims of many feminist groups, which continue to see women as victims of discrimination in the workplace.

The former patterns of open discrimination against women have ended. Today, businesses that overtly discriminate against women, such as Mitsubishi Motors or the U.S. Information Agency, are heavily penalized for their violations of the law. And no business that has barred women from applying for jobs gains a sympathetic hearing in the country's courts.

The fundamental issue with regard to job choice is this: We should not assume that women will always choose the same jobs as men. When a woman who anticipates having children makes a career decision, her choice may be influenced by the expected effects children may have on her capacity and interest in full-time work, for example. Flexible hours and jobs that can be interrupted for intervals of months or even years are parts of careers that are most compatible with motherhood. Admitting that some women prefer a combination of more family time and a less challenging career is anathema to radical feminists, but that shows how far removed they are from the situations or values of women who do not identify with feminists' radical goals.

Perhaps the most challenging careers for working mothers (usually women ages twenty-five to forty-five) are those that have the following characteristics: intensive and uninterrupted investments in education and work, long and unpredictable hours, and major career hurdles early in the career. Jobs with those characteristics, such as practicing law in a major firm, practicing in certain fields of medicine, or working in investment banking or corporate management, require uninterrupted commitments of sixty hours a week, year after year. With such professional demands, raising children is difficult, although the examples of Shelly Lazarus, Heidi Miller, and Andrea Jung demonstrate that with high amounts of energy and organization it can be done.

Professional school programs virtually closed to women a generation ago are now easily accessible. But earning professional degrees presents many women with a difficult dilemma: pursue a challenging and rewarding career but face substantial obstacles to having a family, or pursue a less demanding career path that allows greater flexibility for a family.

For most professional school graduates, regardless of sex, success in a competitive career in the corporate world is a one-way street. One can pursue those challenging careers only by working consistently. A pause, even momentary, leaves one hopelessly behind, passed over in the frenzy of others pursuing the same goal. Many men pause for a variety of reasons—personal and professional—and are left behind. Even more women pause for the same reasons, and many more pause to have children. The net result is that while women are approaching parity or have exceeded men in professional school degrees, many women eschew the most challenging career paths.

The Harvard Business School classes of 1973 and 1983 provide a compelling example of the trade-offs that women face. Of the thirty-four women who graduated in the class of 1973, 70 percent were still working in 1998.[30] For the 189 women in the class of 1983 the percentage was almost identical—67 percent.[31] Not all those who have left the labor force have done so for family reasons, but the percentages are far lower than for the male graduates—and, more revealingly, are consistent over the span of a decade.

Even for the top graduates of the best professional schools, such as Harvard Business School, only a few from each class reach the pinnacles of professional success. It is a fact of life that most companies are pyramid-shaped, with fewer positions at the top than at the middle or lower levels. Men who fail to make it to the top attribute the disappointment to the competitive market or to a career that has peaked. But for women, the explanations given are often different: contemporary feminists, for example, cite the "unfairness of the system," the "glass ceiling," or "discrimination" as reasons. Choice or career realities never enter their equation—a remarkable omission, given the reality of women's experiences in the working world.

Making It on Their Own: Women in Small Business

If feminist groups overlook career realities in assessing women's workplace opportunities, they also ignore another thriving community that challenges the image of women as victims: female entrepreneurs. A generation ago, women-owned businesses were exceptional. Aside from family-owned proprietorships in farming and retail trade, few women owned independent businesses.

Today, women-owned businesses are proliferating. According to the National Foundation for Women Business Owners, 9.1 million of them in the United States employ 27.5 million people and generate over $3.6 trillion in annual sales. Between 1987 and 1999, the number of women-owned businesses more than doubled. Women also own 3.5 million home-based businesses, employing 14 million people, mainly in service-oriented industries such as consulting and finance. More than half of all women-owned businesses start at home.[32]

What motivates female entrepreneurs? In 1998 the research organization Catalyst and the National Foundation for Women Business Owners surveyed female small business owners to ask them why they started their own businesses.[33] The overwhelming response was the desire to become entrepreneurs—the idea that they could make it on their own—rather than discrimination.

Most women took the leap because they had a good idea or an entrepreneurial dream that they wanted to fulfill. A majority of the women entrepreneurs surveyed also cited unquantifiable rewards such as being one's own boss.

Many women business owners also value the flexibility their own business provides. Marilyn Carren of Venice, California, started her home-based photography business after the birth of her child. "I'm working as an artist, I have respect, I'm raising my child, and I don't have a boss," Carren happily remarked.[34] For many women, particularly young mothers, the flexibility of home-based work is appealing. With the growth and ease of technology, those businesses are also able to reach a far wider range of potential customers than they could just ten years ago.

Similarly, in the profile of the 189 women of the Harvard Business School class of 1983 mentioned earlier, writer Anne Faircloth noted that "[f]irst and foremost, the women of the class of '83 are entrepreneurs."[35] For example, Rysia de Ravel runs a conference-call-services company; Robbin Steif founded a gift company called Send Me No Flowers; and Tanya Styblo Beder's Capital Market Risk Advisers helps clients stay out of financial trouble.

Government Advantages to Women-Owned Businesses. Women-owned businesses are given substantial advantages in government contracting, including preferences such as those given to racial and ethnic minorities. Despite court decisions, such as the *Adarand* decision, declaring such preferences presumptively unconstitutional, those special preferences and affirmative action programs continue.[36] For example, the U.S. Small Business Administration notes on its Web site that "we implement many initiatives that help increase the share of federal procurement dollars awarded to Women-Owned Small Businesses." The Federal Acquisition Streamlining Act of 1994 sets a target that women's participation should be 5 percent of the total value of all contracting and sub-contracting awards in any year, and the SBA is "working to establish aggressive goals and to develop meaningful initiatives . . . to ensure that these goals are achieved."[37]

As we discuss in greater detail in chapter 9, individual agencies are developing systematic approaches for increasing the share of women-owned small businesses in their contracts. Most cabinet agencies have published individual memoranda of understanding on their Web sites in which they describe their efforts. Those include appointing an individual women's business advocate; having women business enterprise days; and collecting and promulgating data on women-owned small businesses to give to contractors. Certain federal agencies, such as the Department of Transportation, the State Department, the General Services Administration, the Treasury Department, the Defense Department, and the Department of Labor, provide awards to those in charge of procurement "to recognize the buying activity that is the most successful in promoting and awarding WOSB contracts and subcontracts."[38] The Department of State "includes the achievement of departmental socioeconomic contracting goals, including the five percent WOSB goal, and the efforts made towards the goals, in the performance plans of . . . procurement managers."[39]

The surge in the number of women-owned small businesses contradicts feminists' views that such businesses need special help, because the vast majority of such businesses do not receive preferences in government contracting and exist on their own without them. Paradoxically, feminists often point to the growth of small businesses as proof that more preferences are needed. They argue that women start small businesses because they are driven from male-dominated corporations by discrimination. If corporations were friendlier toward women, the argument goes, then women would not need to leave to start their own companies.[40]

Some women who started their own businesses are now familiar household names. Although atypical, Martha Stewart and Oprah Winfrey are living proof that women do not need preferences to reach the upper ranks of corporate America. Stewart started out with a catering business and how-to books on entertaining, expanded into magazine publishing and television, and is now chairman and CEO of Martha Stewart Living Omnimedia, a vast empire that pulls in approximately $1 billion in annual sales.[41] Winfrey is chairman and CEO of Harpo Entertainment Group.

Twenty-two million Americans and millions of others around the globe watch her TV show every day, and her book recommendations produce bestsellers.[42] Those women owe their success to hard work, determination, talent, and vision—not to government programs.

Occupational Segregation—The No-Choice Movement

The toppling of the barriers that used to bar women from job opportunities seems not to have brought much recognition from feminist groups. Rather, they still focus on a perceived enemy: occupational segregation—the tendency for women and men to cluster in particular jobs, such as secretarial work or nursing on the one hand and truck driving or mining on the other.

The "women's right to choose" rhetoric that suffuses the feminist position on abortion is nowhere to be found in their discussions of occupational segregation. Instead, feminists assert that women evidently lack the ability to choose jobs for themselves. According to that view, they do not choose certain careers based on their personal preferences, qualifications, and future plans; instead, they are forced into certain types of jobs. Feminist commentators speak of "authentic" and "inauthentic" choices for women—the latter referring to options women pursue as a result of social pressure or discrimination.[43]

Feminists claim that women toil in a "pink-collar" ghetto—referring to those jobs that require less educational training and offer fewer opportunities for upward mobility.[44] Even when feminist groups concede that an element of choice is involved in women's occupational stations, they still describe women as victims of intolerable workplace situations. For example, Stanford University law professor Deborah Rhode argued that women are "trapped in part-time positions."[45]

And that is not merely a rhetorical campaign. Feminist special interest groups frequently deploy statistical evidence of occupational segregation to justify government intervention in the workplace. Of course, certain male-dominated occupations such as postal carriers, garbage collectors, and airline pilots are examples of professions that allow free time either during the day or between shifts like many pink-collar jobs. Yet it is never suggested that workers in those occupations choose "blue-ghetto" jobs—which are the male equivalent of the pink-ghetto jobs. Why not? Because feminists assume that occupational choices are the result of discrimination rather than personal preference. They want the government to interfere in the labor market to correct the perceived imbalance.

Feminists criticize society, rather than individual women, for occupational segregation. Women are not faulted by feminists for majoring in English or women's studies. Yet feminists argue that pressure from society keeps women away from math and science studies and from applying for jobs as firefighters or surgeons. It would be more logical for the feminists to call on young women to major in math or to choose the surgical specialty.

Nothing prevents women from choosing the surgical specialty. For instance, Beth Dollinger graduated from medical school in 1981 and became an orthopedic surgeon at a time when few women were entering that field. She was attracted to it because she liked using the tools that were used for the surgical procedures. Dollinger has a busy practice in Elmira, New York, and reported that she was not pressured to avoid surgery and that no patient has avoided her because of her gender. She is happily married and has three children.

When asked why more women do not choose surgical specialties, Dollinger attributed their decision to a lifestyle choice rather than to social pressure. Not only is the residency longer, but the work is less predictable, and surgeons generally continue to see patients on whom they originally operated, a factor that reduces flexibility. Dollinger is regularly called in the middle of the night to treat emergencies, and she always assures patients that they will see her, rather than another surgeon, throughout their treatment. That relationship differs from such specialties as family practice or pediatrics, popular with women, where patients frequently see different physicians within the group practice.[46]

Women's occupational segregation has at times proven to be advantageous, a buffer against serious economic change. During the Great Depression of the 1930s, women's labor force participation rose slightly (from 24 percent in 1930 to 25 percent in 1940), as men's participation declined. Furthermore, the industries hardest hit by the depression—the automobile, steel, and construction industries—were predominantly male, while those that were less affected and recovered more quickly—lighter manufacturing and clerical work—had a higher percentage of female workers.[47]

That trend continues in the contemporary labor market. The top two economic sectors expected to grow significantly between 1990 and 2005 are female-dominated occupations: service and retail trade, finance, insurance, and real estate.[48] For many women workers, the "pink-collar ghetto" will be a boon—not the bane that feminists claim it is.

Yet, despite their growth potential, female-dominated occupations command lower pay than male-dominated occupations for several reasons. Female-dominated occupations usually require less work experience and training. They also entail less risk of physical harm. In general, jobs in the "pink ghetto" have the following characteristics: flexibility, physical safety, indoor location, low risk, no demands to relocate, and contact with people. They also require skills that deteriorate at a slower rate and thus allows greater freedom for women to move in and out of the work force.

One of the more absurd claims made by feminists is that discrimination is rampant in those occupations that still have fewer than 10 percent of female workers.[49] Many of those occupations are risky and require substantial amounts of physical strength—mining, timber logging, construction, firefighting, and welding and cutting. Others, such as truck driving and railroad transportation, call for odd hours of work. Women who want to pursue those paths can and do, but for the average woman, dangerous jobs or jobs with long or inconsistent hours have not been appealing. To take the average woman's preference for certain kinds of jobs as evidence of discrimination suggests that women are somehow incapable of making their own choices. Government initiatives aimed at "encouraging" women to pursue such jobs are a form of wishful social engineering.

Unfortunately, such programs exist throughout the federal government agencies. The Department of Labor is home to the "Nontraditional Employment for Women" program, which in the 1990s awarded $1.5 million in grants to several states "to train and place women in nontraditional career fields."[50] In 1998 the Labor Department gave another million dollars in grants to labor unions to support "apprenticeship programs and nontraditional occupations" for women.[51] Those programs—pursued at taxpayers' expense—seek to solve a problem that exists only because of women's choices in school and in the workplace.

Occupational segregation is not just visible in low-wage jobs but can be seen in high-paying fields also. In 1998, for doctors under the age of thirty-five, 62 percent of obstetricians/gynecologists were female compared with 1 percent of neurosurgeons.[52] In law few women are litigators, but many women practice in the field of estates and trusts.[53] With the movement of women into many diverse fields, it is stretching the imagination to say that women are prevented from being neurosurgeons and litigators, two specialties that call for aggressive, driving personalities. That is just another indication that women and men make different choices when faced with the same opportunities.

Conclusion

Today, qualified women can participate in all occupations and professions. The law protects their right to do so. Little if any evidence exists to support the notion that women need additional intervention by the government to move into certain kinds of jobs. The examples of Jennifer Simon and Carly Fiorina cited at the beginning of this chapter illustrate the extent to which educational achievement cannot guarantee career achievement, measured in conventional terms of money and status. Simon, with her two law degrees and initial jobs in tax law, could have continued in those more lucrative professions. Instead, she changed careers and is training to become a social worker—a job that pays substantially less than tax law and that is in a female-dominated profession. Fiorina dropped out of law school and floated around in different lower-level jobs before working her way to a top position at Lucent Technologies and later to the CEO's office at Hewlett-Packard. The experiences of those women and millions of others reveal the power and consequences of individual choices. The laws and institutions of a free society exist to protect those choices, not to dictate what they should be.

5

Mythical Problems and Solutions: Wage Gaps, Glass Ceilings, and Incomparable Worth

Newspapers and television news often use the terms *wage gap* and *glass ceiling*. Feminists cite the existence of the "gap" and the "ceiling" as a rallying cry to urge the government, unions, and employers to expand preferences for women in the workplace. The "wage gap" and "glass ceiling" are alleged evidence of inequality between the sexes that supposedly dwarf all other forms of inequality. The wage gap comes with a solution—government-mandated wage guidelines for different jobs, known as "comparable worth" or "pay equity" by their proponents.

Not everyone has the same income, and it would be surprising if everyone did. Some people earn more because they are smarter, they work harder, they work more hours during the day, they have spent more time in school, they take more financial risks, they are willing to work during unusual hours, or they work in dangerous or unpleasant jobs. But those wage gaps are not the ones at issue. The "wage gap" cited by the popular press is the average annual pay of all full-time working women compared with the average pay of all full-time working men—in 1999, seventy-three cents on the dollar. To feminists, gender is the only reason for the wage gap. Education, number of children, and time spent in and out of the workplace are not considered as relevant explanations, because they

63

are not supposed to reduce women's wages. Why are the media only concerned with gender, when many other factors affect wages?

The same reasoning holds with the glass ceiling. That image is used to suggest that women face an invisible barrier that keeps them from rising to upper levels in corporations. Interestingly, only women hit glass ceilings, not men, although organizations are pyramid-shaped, with fewer managers than workers, and not everyone can get to the top. As noted in chapter 4, when a man reaches his maximum level in a company, people say that he has peaked, and they think no more of it. In contrast, when a woman gets as far as she is going, she is described as having struck a glass ceiling. Why?

The answer is that to justify large-scale government intervention in the workplace on behalf of women, feminists must vigorously maintain an arsenal of purported evidence of women's inequality, despite other perfectly reasonable explanations for the occurrences. Hence, the concept of wage gaps is most frequently deployed as an example of women's subordinate status to justify replacing the current U.S. economic system of wage compensation with government earnings guidelines.

In chapters 3 and 4 we show that women have moved into many previously male-dominated educational fields and professions. Those that are still male-dominated, we argue, are that way because fewer women than men choose to go into them—mathematics and engineering or construction and oil-drilling. We conclude that no systematic discrimination against women exists in education and in job choice. This chapter examines whether outside forces indeed exist that limit the wages of women—but not men. The question is important, for if one can show that wage gaps and glass ceilings are caused not by discrimination but are the natural result of free choices men and women have made in the workplace, then the foundation of special preferences for women collapses. Even if some degree of discrimination does exist in the workplace, it does not follow that preferences are the most efficient solution for fighting discrimination.

In a speech delivered in 1996 at the University of North Dakota, evocatively titled "Women's Rights under Siege," the American Civil Liberties Union's Nadine Strossen warned that the gains in education and in the workplace that women have made in the twentieth century are transitory, capable of being whisked away in the absence of government intervention. Strossen has little patience for those who dispute that gloomy portrait, and she argues that those who criticize affirmative action are themselves examples of the "stereotyping and injustice that continue to plague this country."[1] She herself offers no evidence to prove that, without special preferences, women's gains in education and the workplace will disappear.

Similarly, law professor Mary K. O'Melveny, pointing to the often cited statistics produced by the 1995 U.S. Department of Labor's Glass Ceiling Commission Report, claimed that women still face pervasive discrimination in the workplace: "There is simply no other explanation for the fact that women are largely found in the lowest paid jobs, at the lowest rung of the career ladder, marginalized in their efforts to advance, and treated less favorably than their comparably situated male colleagues in every respect." Only by more widespread use of affirmative action, she concluded, "can we change this depressing picture."[2]

That picture is indeed depressing, but not for the reasons cited by the feminists. It is depressing because it is incorrect, because it relies on misleading statistics to justify preferential treatment for women in the workplace, and because it devalues women's choices. A careful assessment of the evidence reveals a very different situation, one that provides a more complex but more reasonable explanation for observed differences between men and women in the workplace. It demonstrates that women have achieved equality of opportunity in the workplace, but that many make choices about work and their personal lives that result in lower wages and lower rates of advancement.

Feminists do not suggest that the way for women to earn salaries comparable to men's is by spending more time in the work force. Rather, they argue that women should not be penalized for the time they take out of the work force to have and rear children, so employers should give them the same wages as if their tenure had not been interrupted. According to Department of Labor statistics, women's full-time average hours of work, including time taken for maternity leave, were 92 percent of men's in 1999.[3] As Susan

Bianchi-Sand, then–executive director of the National Committee for Pay Equity, said, "Yes, women leave at 5:00 p.m. to go home and look after their children. But they're still working, just not for their employers. Why should they get paid less?"[4]

What professional feminists are calling for is a complicated, government-managed and contentious system of setting pay scales, one with some of the characteristics of the central planning practiced under Soviet-style socialism. Employers would be required to subsidize women, but that could be changed to whatever groups the government currently favors. Using the power of government to legislate higher wages moves the United States inexorably to the socialist systems once employed by Eastern Europe.

The Wage Gap

In 1820 women's average annual earnings were one-third of men's. That figure rose to 54 percent by the end of the nineteenth century.[5] Women's average annual earnings continued to rise relative to men's at a slower pace during the twentieth century and reached 60 percent in 1980 before making a significant jump to 72 percent in 1990. In 1999 average annual full-time wages of women were 73 percent of those of men.

Accounting for time worked in a year reduces average wage gaps. A comparison of 1999 average weekly earnings from the U.S. Department of Labor yields the result that women's pay is 76 percent of men's—rather than 73 percent for annual earnings. This is so because women work fewer weeks in a year than do men. More dramatically, the Department of Labor's hourly earnings comparison shows that women's pay is 84 percent of men's, up from 82 percent in 1998 and 65 percent in 1980. Hourly wages are a better measure of comparison than weekly or annual wages, because they take into account the number of hours worked in a year. Women work fewer hours than men—one reason for the lower average annual wage figure.

The difference between men's and women's average earnings exists because of major variations in factors such as hours worked, education, age, part- or full-time status, experience, number of children, and, perhaps most important, consecutive years in the work force. Combining all those factors, we get the statistic that women's average annual earnings are 73 percent of men's. But that statistic, although accurate, says nothing about the equity of an individual woman's salary versus the salary of an individual man with the same job. On average, men have been in the labor force for longer periods of time and, as discussed in chapter 3, they have had more training in higher-paying fields such as engineering, math, business, and computer science.

Wage calculations that account for the factors listed above produce *adjusted* wage gaps, which are far lower than average wage gaps. When economists look at adjusted wages, the wage gaps that they calculate are far smaller than 73 percent, with many studies ranging from 88 percent to 99 percent.[6]

A number of reasons exist for the difference between average and adjusted wages. For example, consider the effect of full-time hours worked on wages. Just because average wage gaps compare full-time workers does not mean that all workers work equal numbers of hours. Working full-time can mean any number of hours per week above thirty-five, and sometimes less than that, if a full-time job (such as teaching) encompasses fewer than thirty-five scheduled weekly hours. So the comparison of full-time women's wages with men's can compare people working thirty-five hours a week with those working sixty hours a week. If a man and a woman each work forty hours a week at a company for $10 an hour, but the man chooses to work an additional eight hours a week overtime (paid at one and a half times his wage rate), the woman would make $400 and the man would bring in $520. Her wages would be 77 percent of his—not because of discrimination but solely because she had not volunteered to work overtime.

Educational background is another crucial factor influencing wages. As noted in chapter 3, women have received more B.A.'s and M.A.'s than men since the early 1980s, so they are obviously not discriminated against as students in higher education. Data show that women get better grades and have average scores on standardized tests that are similar to those of men. But evidence shows that many women prefer not to study math and the physical sciences.[7] The vast majority of physics and engineering graduates are male, and a majority of communications and public administration graduates are female.[8] Yet physics and engineering can pay substantially more.

No laws or regulations prevent women from choosing to major in higher-paying fields, and their decisions to pursue degrees in communications or public administration—or literature or women's studies—are not due to discrimination. Failing to account for educational field in wage gap measures is similar to comparing an eminent history professor with an outstanding business executive—historian Barbara Tuchman versus Martha Stewart. Both are equally talented, but they have chosen different fields.

Another factor neglected in measures of the gap between average wages is the age of the men and women in the work force. Men have worked in great numbers for a longer period of time than women, so there are far more working men in their fifties and sixties than there are women. And since those in their fifties and sixties are usually at the peak of their professions, there are more highly paid men than women.

Tenure and experience are two of the most important factors in explaining the wage gap. According to the U.S. Bureau of the Census, women on average spend a far higher percentage of their working years *out* of the work force than men.[9] As demonstrated empirically in economic studies, this means that when women return to the workplace, they will not earn as much as their male or female counterparts who have more uninterrupted experience in the workplace.[10]

In many studies, when such relevant factors are considered, the wage gap virtually disappears. Women without children and with similar levels of education and experience earn as much as their male counterparts. Data from the National Longitudinal Survey of Youth, which provides detailed education and workplace information for individuals, show that among people ages twenty-seven to thirty-three who have never had a child, women's earnings are close to 98 percent of men's.[11] In another study using the same data set comparing mothers and childless women with similarly educated men, mothers with the same education earned 75 percent of the men's earnings while childless women earned 95 percent.[12] The divergence can be attributed to differences in choices of hours and occupations.

Some studies use another information source, U.S. Bureau of the Census data on men and women in different occupational categories, to measure wage differences. That data source can also be used to estimate the different productivity of men and women and compare those measures with wage rates. Those studies conclude that women earn in the range of 88 to 99 percent of men's wages, depending on the industries analyzed.[13] For example, University of Maryland professor Judith Hellerstein found that women in the banking and the miscellaneous products and plastics industries made 99 percent of what men earned.[14] Those studies account for some differences, such as occupations and hours worked, but they are unable to capture such details in the National Longitudinal Survey as numbers of children, field of education, or, in some cases, precise job descriptions.

Those numbers are far above the average seventy-three cents on the dollar wage ratio trumpeted by feminists. No serious academic study concludes that, all factors accounted for, women are paid only seventy-three cents on a man's dollar.

As we noted, 80 percent of women bear children at some point in their lives, and many economic studies document the link between increased numbers of children and lower average earnings. Economists David Neumark and Sanders Korenman have published several articles analyzing the effects of marriage and motherhood on wages. They find that although marriage does not lower wages, having children does. The more children, the lower the earnings, all other factors equal.[15] Different explanations exist for that phenomenon. First, children may take time away from women's careers, both in terms of the time taken to bear children and the time put into work afterward. Second, women who invest in education to qualify for high-paying jobs—who go to the trouble of training to become a lawyer or a doctor, for example—choose to work and reap the returns from that education. They may delay having children, have fewer of them, or have none at all.

Some would say that there is a third explanation, namely that employers discriminate against women who have children. As a result, mothers are paid less for the same work or are forced into positions of lower responsibility or pay. Ostensibly for that reason, President Clinton issued an executive order in 2000 forbidding discrimination against parents in hiring, pay, and promotion in the federal government.[16] But if employers were antichild, why would they not discriminate against fathers also? Furthermore, if employers have the power to discriminate against mothers (or fathers), why stop at seventy-three cents on the dollar? Why pay mothers more than the minimum wage? We do not see that happening, because employment is a willing contractual agreement between two parties rather than an abuse of power by one party over another.

Some feminists offer a slightly more nuanced view of the wage gap. Their evidence for wage discrimination centers on something called the "unexplained statistical residual." In other words, in some studies comparing male and female earnings with all possible factors controlled, a difference remains. Feminists take the remaining statistical difference between men and women as prima facie evidence of discrimination.

But that residual is not in fact evidence of anything except the vagaries of statistical analysis. If similar statistical analyses were performed on groups of white men, for example, an unexplainable residual would also be found. Should we assume that unexplained differences in wages among white men are the result of discrimination?[17] As economist Victor Fuchs has argued, "[I]t is a huge leap from the conclusion that sex has a major effect on earnings to the inference that *employer discrimination* is the major source of the wage differential."[18] Yet that is exactly what feminists have been arguing for years.

Parts of the residual can be explained by what economists Solomon Polachek and Claudia Goldin have described as "different expectations of future employment" or "human capital investment."[19] In other words, since most women have children, they plan their careers accordingly and often seek employment in fields where job flexibility is high and where job skills will deteriorate at a slower rate. That allows them to move in and out of the work force with greater ease or to shift from full-time to part-time work, if they so choose.

Although study after study has demonstrated the unambiguous, common-sense relationship when hours worked, education, experience, and numbers of children are compared with earnings, groups such as the National Committee on Pay Equity insist on focusing on average rather than adjusted wage gaps. They regularly launch media stunts such as the March 1997 "Ask Your Boss for a Raise Day" or the April 1999 and May 2000 "Equal Pay Day."

In 1999 feminists, saying that in 1998 women earned seventy-four cents on a man's dollar, celebrated Equal Pay Day on April 8 and gave out cookies with a quarter removed. On that day, they said, 27 percent of the year had passed, so women had caught up to men's earnings in the prior calendar year. In its organizational literature the National Committee on Pay Equity encouraged stores to sell drinks for one dollar to men and seventy-four cents to women and to give away fake dollar bills with holes in them to represent the wage gap.[20] During the same year at a press conference at the Russell Senate Office Building on Capitol Hill, Senator Patty Murray and Representatives Eleanor Holmes Norton, Rosa DeLauro, and Carolyn Maloney charged, "We know that American women still earn about 75 cents for every dollar earned by men. And we know that this wage gap shortchanges not just women but the families who depend on them."[21]

In 2000 the National Committee on Pay Equity used a different media tactic. To further dramatize the alleged problem, they said that the difference in women's and men's average annual salaries ($9,483) represents 37 percent of women's actual salary ($25,862), so Equal Pay Day should fall on May 11, when approximately 37 percent of the year had passed. Feminist groups asked women to carry red handbags to show that women's pay was "in the red."[22]

The Institute for Women's Policy Research, another group that produces wage gap statistics, claimed that women collectively lost $200 billion in wages per year owing to pay inequity.[23] In 1999 the organization joined the AFL-CIO to release a report entitled *Equal Pay for Working Families: National and State Data on the Pay Gap and Its Costs*. The report again propounded the fiction that, in 1998, women were paid only seventy-four cents on a man's dollar in the United States as a whole and presented data for women's earnings in individual states. In Louisiana, for example, women's earnings were supposedly 67 percent of men's, whereas in the District of Columbia women earned 97 percent of men's wages. In addition, the report looked at the percentage of men and women working in different industries and concluded that "America's working families lose a staggering $200 billion annually to the wage gap." That meant that employers should have paid women $200 billion more.

The joint study calculated the cost of alleged "pay inequity" caused by the predominance of women and men in different occupational categories. The study compared the wages of workers in female-dominated occupations with those in nonfemale-dominated occupations. The workers had the same sex, age, race, educational level, marital and parental status, and urban/rural status; they lived in the same part of the country and worked the same number of hours; and they worked in firms of the same size in the same industry. The study concluded that women were underpaid by $89 billion per year because of occupational segregation. Without sex, race, marital and parental status, and firm and industry variables, that figure rose to $200 billion per year.

The study boasted an impressive list of variables, but it left out two major factors. First, it omitted the type of job and stated in a footnote that "no data on the content of the jobs (the skill, effort, and responsibility required by workers who hold them nor the working conditions in which they work) are available" in the data set used. Second, the study excluded the field of education pursued. It is meaningless to say that the earnings of a man or a woman with a B.A. in English should be the same as the earnings of a man or a woman with a B.A. in mathematics. So the study compared workers without regard to education or type of work: secretaries with loggers, bookkeepers with oil drillers. Such numbers do not present an accurate estimate of wage gaps.

Why do those feminist and other organizations offer the public such blatant untruths? One explanation is that they have a stake in maintaining a thoroughly skewed view of women's wages. Doing so provides them with ammunition to lobby for government regulation of wages (a subject we discuss later in this chapter) and increased hiring of women in predominantly male occupations. If those organizations admitted that differences in wages between men and women were due to differences in education, seniority, and time in the work force, they would not be able to perpetuate the women-as-victims mythology that draws in organizational dues and pays their leaders' salaries. In short, an accurate view of the wage gap would reduce their organizational power.

The Glass Ceiling

In 1998 Sheila Wellington, president of the research organization Catalyst, said that women at the top of corporate America face "a formidable obstacle."[24] But Catalyst's own surveys suggest a different metaphor: a "leaking pipeline." Women, Wellington conceded two years previously, continue to leave their jobs in the corporate world to pursue employment elsewhere, including in businesses they themselves start.[25] Herein lies the crucial oversight by those who claim that a glass ceiling is holding back American women: women's own choices and decisions about their careers are never factored into the equation.

A Fortune 500 company, sued for sex discrimination because of its low number of female managers, commissioned a study to try to find out why its managerial work force was imbalanced. The results? The disparity was a result of "differences in behaviors and attitudes of male and female clerks—differences the company and its policies had no part in producing." Those differences were significant: women were less willing to work long hours or to relocate, and nearly half the women voiced a preference for part-time work.[26] Such preferences affect an employee's chances of advancement in corporate America. Relocating is a route to future promotions because it gives employees additional experience in different parts of the corporation. Employees who work long hours are more valuable to their firms and are more likely to be rewarded with a promotion. In chapter 3 we show how women's educational choices affect earnings, and in chapter 4 we describe how women's choices of jobs influence their progress in the workplace. We also cite government data that show that men work more hours, on average, than women and that they spend more consecutive years in the work force, another important determinant of future promotions.[27]

Women's choices were also overlooked by the nation's Glass Ceiling Commission, which in 1995 released a lengthy report called *Good for Business: Making Full Use of the Nation's Human Capital*.[28] The title of the commission prejudged the results before the research was even begun, not to mention completed. While the commission admitted that certain qualities characterize the people—male or female—who successfully scale the executive ladder, they focused most of their attention on the outside forces that supposedly prevent women from getting ahead in the workplace.

The commission concluded that the key factor preventing women's advancement was prejudice, although it offered no data to show that discrimination existed. The report cited no cases of more-qualified women being passed over in favor of less-qualified men. The commission did accuse white men of thinking that women were not suited to managerial ranks, although it presented no evidence that such attitudes were common in the business world.[29]

The commission's report also downplayed the significance of the pipeline theory, one of the more reasonable explanations for the smaller number of women in the boardroom. Typical qualifications for senior management positions include an M.B.A. and approximately twenty-five years of work experience. A cursory glance at labor force participation rates from the past fifty years reveals that the pool of women who meet those qualifications—the qualified labor pool—is small. Furthermore, in 1970 only 4 percent of all M.B.A.'s granted were awarded to women, and in 1975 the number stood at 8 percent. Yet the commission's report did not analyze the success or failure of women in the qualified labor pool; instead, the report compared the number of women in the *total labor force* with the number of women in senior management positions and came up with a shockingly low number to incite the public: 5 percent.

The Glass Ceiling Commission concluded that, without discrimination, every industry would "have the same proportion of the work force population as their respective populations' representations." In plain English, that means that since the percentage of the work force that is female is 46 percent, then every industry, from mining to retail to services, should contain approximately 46 percent women in the absence of discrimination. But that claim of equal numbers is patently absurd, since it assumes that men and women have no particular preference or dislike for certain professions. That claim has been disproved for education also, as discussed in chapter 3.

In the American workplace today, if a ceiling on advancement exists, it is gender-neutral. Any such ceiling affects both men and women; it prevents those who choose to devote more time to their personal lives from advancing at the same rate as those who devote more uninterrupted time to the workplace.

Disparate Impact

The disparate numbers of men and women in top corporate positions are at the root of the glass ceiling issue. They are also relevant to a lesser extent at lower- and middle-income levels, where calls for proportional representation undergird the larger arguments for preferential programs for women. Feminists vehemently deny that they favor the use of quotas in hiring, but they advocate "hiring goals that encourage diversity by rewarding managers whose work forces include employees from backgrounds that are roughly [equivalent] to workers available in the relevant labor pool."[30] Although such a proposal may sound innocuous to some, in practice it has serious consequences. The Equal Employment Opportunity Commission, the government agency charged with enforcing the nation's antidiscrimination laws, frequently brings suits against firms on the grounds that they do not hire women in proportion to their representation in the labor pool. Those suits make heavy use of the theory of "disparate impact," which holds presumptively illegal "a facially neutral rule or practice of the employer [that] has a disproportionate impact on one sex."[31] In other words, if an employer decides that a worker has to be able to lift heavy serving trays (as in the case below) and that because of that rule more men than women are hired, the employer could be found guilty of discrimination on the grounds of disparate impact. Such suits can involve prolonged litigation, and the courts find many businesses guilty.[32]

Such suits can be brought even when no woman has complained of discrimination. One of the most arrogant assumptions of some modern feminists is that American society is so sexist that the EEOC must ferret out discrimination even when no woman has complained of unequal treatment. That assumes ignorance on the part of American women because, if the EEOC is required to find discrimination in places where women themselves have not found it, then most women must be unaware of the supposed sexism that surrounds them. To say that women would be loathe to sue employers ignores the litigious nature of life in the United States, where people sue for the most trivial of reasons.[33]

For example, as we noted in chapter 2, the EEOC filed a sex discrimination lawsuit in 1997 against a woman-owned and woman-operated family restaurant, Joe's Stone Crab in Miami Beach, Florida, on the grounds that the restaurant discriminated against women when it hired servers. No woman had filed a grievance against the restaurant, but the EEOC used its power to file a lawsuit without a complaint, called a "commissioner's charge," and charged the restaurant with discrimination on the basis of the theory of disparate impact. Although Joe's restaurant had demonstrated that 22 percent of the servers that it hired between 1991 and 1995—the years leading up to the trial after the EEOC announced its investigation—were female, the U.S. district court ruled that since the available women in the labor pool constituted 31.9 percent of potential employees—a surprisingly detailed estimate—Joe's was guilty of discrimination. The court also condemned the practice of allowing subordinates to hire employees. The Supreme Court has noted in another case that an employer can be held liable for discrimination by delegating "employment decisions to those employees who are most familiar with the jobs to be filled and with the candidates for those jobs" if those employees discriminate against certain classes of job candidates.[34]

The court ruled that before 1991, only a few women had applied to the restaurant to be servers because of Joe's reputation for hiring men only. According to the court, Joe's should have placed advertisements in local newspapers and used its hiring meetings to spread the word that this was not true. The restaurant had always had women servers.

Joe's Stone Crab was required to pay back wages plus interest to four women, two of whom had never applied for a job at the restaurant. The restaurant was ordered to pay $71,149 plus interest to Catherine Stratford, who was apparently planning to apply to work at Joe's in 1990. She did not do so because she had heard from two sources that Joe's did not hire women. She did, however, apply the following year but was not hired. According to the court, that was the result of discrimination. The court determined that, barring discrimination, she would have been hired in 1990 if she had applied and would have worked through 1995, and thus she was entitled to back wages.

Carol Coyle, who applied for a job in 1991 but was rejected, was awarded $15,313 plus interest because the court determined that she was not hired because of sex discrimination. Her payment is the difference between the amount the court calculated she would have earned at Joe's and the amount she actually earned working for another restaurant.

The court awarded $35,230 plus interest to Raquel Munoz and $32,513 plus interest to Teresa Romanello, who allegedly both considered applying for a job at the restaurant but did not do so because of its reputation. The court determined that those women would have been hired in 1989 in the absence of discrimination if they had applied.

In addition to the payments, the selection of future employees was to be strictly monitored by the court and the EEOC until January 1, 2001. All potential hires had to be told that their employment was conditional on the approval of a court-appointed monitor. The restaurant had to pay for a "criterion-related validation study of the evaluation criteria" used to hire servers, a study conducted by an industrial psychologist. The restaurant was required to advertise for a defined period of time in specified newspapers, interviewers had to be trained by an industrial psychologist named by the court, and a court-appointed monitor had to attend the interviews.[35] In 2000 the U.S. Court of Appeals for the Eleventh Circuit vacated and remanded the district court's decision. The restaurant does not know whether a new trial will take place.[36]

The *Joe's Stone Crab* case is not the first of its kind. Such aggressive targeting has been going on for more than ten years, at great cost to American business. In 1987 Thomas Maggiore, owner of two

Italian restaurants in Phoenix, Arizona, faced a similar charge. In Maggiore's case, since no women came forward with discrimination claims, the EEOC placed advertisements in local newspapers to seek potential female victims. In the end, Maggiore settled with the EEOC and spent almost a half million dollars of his own money and wasted countless hours in the process.[37] In another well-known example, Sears, Roebuck & Co. spent years fighting the EEOC's charges of sex discrimination, again without any complaints from workers, before finally winning the suit in 1988.[38]

Another EEOC tactic is to launch lengthy and expensive audits of businesses that it suspects are discriminating against women. Although those audits do not always result in the EEOC's bringing formal charges of discrimination against the business, they always result in businesses' having to divert funds and resources—sometimes for several years—in an effort to rebut EEOC claims.

Wage Guidelines

Feminists' desire to have employers pay the costs of women's personal decisions has encouraged a new, dramatic effort: a call for bureaucratic wage guidelines in the workplace. It is already illegal to pay unequal wages to equally qualified men and women who do the same job, but wage guidelines, called "comparable worth" in the 1980s and renamed "pay equity" in the 1990s to make the guidelines more appealing, move beyond existing law. Supporters of pay equity propose equal pay, not for equal work, but for different categories of jobs on the grounds that it is unfair that some predominantly female occupations are paid less than some predominantly male ones. Hence, feminists say that not only should pay be equalized among jobs, it should also be equalized among occupations.

Wage guidelines made their first appearance on the public policy scene in the 1980s and were rejected by the courts as a requirement for states' compliance with nondiscrimination laws, most notably in *AFSCME v. Washington*.[39] Guidelines rest on the assumption that some value system exists that, without sex discrimination, would ensure that teachers earned as much as truck drivers or nurses as much as garbage collectors. Supporters of wage guidelines challenge not how the market functions but its justice. They equate economic measures of worth, such as earnings, with moral questions, such as the "value" of a certain type of work to society and how that is translated into wages.[40]

As numerous students of the issue have shown, wage guidelines propose an "objective" measurement of a job's worth by examining factors including mental demands, working conditions, and the knowledge or skill required to perform a task. It quickly becomes clear that those assessments not only favor traditionally female occupations over male ones, but also favor education and white-collar jobs over manual, blue-collar work. Neither experience nor risk, two factors that increase men's average wages relative to those of women, is generally included as a relevant job-related criterion. Ninety-two percent of workplace deaths are male, a statistic that demonstrates how much more dangerous men's jobs are than women's.[41] Some of the difference between men's and women's average wages reflects the increased danger of men's jobs, and if risk is omitted in wage guideline systems, there will be shortages of candidates for such jobs.

Wage guidelines underwent a renaissance in the late 1990s because feminists realized that, with women's choices influencing the average wage gap, the only way to eliminate such a gap was to mandate equal pay for different jobs. In 2000 President Clinton announced a $27 million so-called Equal Pay Initiative, saying that women "only get to take home three out of every four paychecks" and that "the average woman has to work, therefore, an extra 17 weeks a year to earn what a similarly qualified man in the same kind of job makes."[42] He advocated passage of Senator Tom Daschle's Paycheck Fairness Act, which calls for voluntary wage guidelines: "The guidelines . . . shall be designed to enable employers voluntarily to compare wages paid for different jobs to determine if the pay scales involved adequately and fairly reflect . . . [these] requirements for each such job, *with the goal of eliminating unfair pay disparities between occupations traditionally dominated by men or women*" (emphasis added).[43] In other words, going far beyond current law, the Office of Federal Contract Compliance of the Department of Labor could decide that administrative assistants should be paid as much as oil drillers, and teachers as much as construction workers.

The Paycheck Fairness Act could be a backdoor way for a president to impose wage guidelines on American business. Those guidelines are described as "voluntary,"[44] but there is nothing to prevent a president from issuing an executive order forbidding the federal government to do business with companies that do not adopt the standards. Since courts have declared that nothing in existing sex discrimination laws requires employers to use wage guidelines in setting wages, passage of the Paycheck Fairness Act would give the president the opportunity to put the guidelines in place through regulation.

But Senator Daschle's voluntary wage guidelines are not enough for the feminists. The NOW Web site asserts:

> The Paycheck Fairness Act is very limited in that it expands the availability of damages under the Equal Pay Act of 1963 (which affects only jobs that are nearly identical), develops fair pay guidelines that would be voluntary for employers, and prohibits employers from retaliating against their own employees who inquire whether their own pay is fair.[45]

NOW calls for passage of Senator Tom Harkin's Fair Pay Act. That act

> would prohibit employers from paying lower wages to men (working at jobs held predominantly by women) than they would pay men (in predominantly male-held job categories) if those jobs are equivalent in value to the employer. This is an approach which overcomes several of the persistent obstacles to pay equity—that is, many jobs are equivalent but not identical.[46]

Under Senator Harkin's bill, employers would be required to determine which jobs are equivalent and each year present to the EEOC a report that shows wages paid to all employees by sex, race, and national origin in each job classification.

Such wage guidelines have not worked in many locations in which they have been tried. Minnesota, the United Kingdom, and the province of Ontario, Canada, provide three separate examples showing the limitations of comparable worth systems. Comparable worth is ultimately an exercise in setting wages. Bureaucrats and tribunals attempt to get the right wage for the right job by using wage evaluations or courts to set prices. The exercise of setting those prices is itself extremely complex and time-consuming, as we show below.

Wage guidelines not only tamper with wages among occupations but also within occupations and often reward new employees over experienced employees. In some instances, under wage guideline programs, line employees are compensated more highly than their supervisors, an unstable situation with obviously perverse incentives. Who would want to be promoted into a lower-paying job? Many jurisdictions have had to tinker with the wages recommended by comparable worth formulas to retain key workers, such as supervisors.

Minnesota. The Minnesota state government implemented wage guidelines in the 1980s after passage of the State Employees Pay Equity Act of 1982 and the Local Government Pay Equity Act of 1984.[47] No other state has wage guideline laws that cover both state and local government employees. Wages were set by using evaluation forms filled out by employees, who detailed their job descriptions and required qualifications. The more complex the job and the higher the educational qualifications, the higher the salary. According to Faith Zwemke of the Minnesota Department of Employee Relations, the program's success was demonstrated by the reduction in the wage gap from seventy-four cents to eighty-seven cents over the period 1982 to 1997.[48]

One major drawback of the Minnesota system when it was set up was that it relied on employee descriptions to calculate salaries. The lengthier the job description, the more likely it was to deserve a higher salary, so the system rewarded employees who were more verbose than their colleagues. Naturally, that led to dissatisfaction and complaints. The largest Minnesota county, Hennepin, processed some 3,500 appeals of 10,201 job evaluations for employees. That not only took much effort but led to ill-will and poor morale among employees as certain jobs were judged worthy of higher pay than others.[49]

Other facets of Minnesota's system led to ill-will as well when a comparable worth system was put into place. Under such a system, the state government raised the pay of female-dominated groups of workers—defined as those with more than 70 percent female employees—on the theory that discrimination caused wage disparities. If a group was 69 percent female, however, the state did not raise the wages of those employees because it considered pay differences to be due to factors other than discrimination. That resulted in some employees' being unwilling to accept promotions because supervisory positions were often not female-dominated, so they were not subject to wage guideline pay increases. Hence, accounting supervisors, who held bachelors' degrees in their fields ended up getting paid less than accounting technicians, who were less skilled.[50]

Further, as some employees change jobs, job classifications can move from balanced to female-dominated and back again. Minnesota has a policy of sticking to original job classifications, however, so job classifications that recently became female-dominated do not qualify for wage guideline increases.

A central problem of comparable worth systems is that wages are sometimes set too low to attract workers. At times that was clearly the case in Minnesota, where state wages for nurses and computer programmers have at various times been set substantially below the prevailing private market wage. The result was predictable: the state had few applicants and many vacancies for nurses and computer programmers. Moreover, the situation was unstable as nurses and computer programmers previously hired by the state began to flee for higher-paying jobs in the private sector.

The state is, however, permitted to pay male-dominated positions more to offset shortages caused by low wages. At the same time, it is not acceptable to pay female-dominated positions less because they are available for lower wages in the private sector. That has the effect of raising all wages in state government, which are paid for by higher taxes in the state. Minnesota's employees are among the best paid in the nation, so the state clearly has set a policy of spending more on employees' salaries. Taxpayers in other states, however, may be less willing to fund such a program.

The reduction in the wage gap for Minnesota state employees between 1982 and 1997 is not necessarily due to its wage guidelines program, because all women's wages rose during that period. It is possible that female wages would have risen even faster during that period if wage guidelines had not been in place: taxes on residents would have been lower, and the funds could have been used for private investments that would have stimulated economic growth and raised women's wages through the private sector.

United Kingdom. Unlike Minnesota, in the United Kingdom wage guidelines apply to both private- and public-sector employees. The right to bring a complaint in the U.K. system originates from two legal sources. First, Article 119 of the Treaty of Rome called on each member of the European Community (now the European Union) to maintain the principle of "equal pay for equal work." The European Court of Justice ruled that the principle applies to all individual countries in the European Union, without having to be ratified by each. Second, the United Kingdom had its own Equal Pay Act of 1970, which was fully implemented in 1975. Men and women had to receive the same pay when they did similar work.

The U.K. system works as follows. Any employee who considers his salary to be unfair is allowed to complain to a three-person court-appointed tribunal, which then evaluates his claim. The evaluations are supposed to be completed within three months, but the tribunal never meets that timetable. The process involves experts on both sides of the case who argue over the merits of the different skills required to perform the job. With such a system, no adjustments are made until a complaint is filed. That provides an incentive for employees to complain.

In the landmark case of *Hayward v. Cammell Laird Shipbuilders Ltd.,* the first to compare different occupations, a female cook in a shipyard complained that her work was equal to that of male painters, carpenters, and insulation installers. The case was filed in 1984, and the final ruling was made in 1988. The independent expert concluded that the painter and the carpenter rated above the cook on responsibility demands because they had to work with more costly tools. But the cook rated above the others in planning and decisionmaking demands because she had to make a daily deadline. In the end, the jobs were declared of equal value, and the cook's wages were raised—to such a degree that she was paid more than her supervisor, whose salary had to be increased in turn.[51]

Similarly, in 1986 Pamela Enderby, who worked for the National Health Service, sued for higher wages on the grounds that her work as a speech therapist was of equal value to that of men working as pharmacists and clinical psychologists. Speech therapists, primarily women, are paid about 60 percent of what psychologists, primarily men, are paid. Although Britain's Industrial Tribunal dismissed the claim, the court of appeals sent the case to the European Court of Justice, which ruled that it could proceed.[52] The case was not resolved until 1998, almost twelve years later.[53]

The U.K. system presents additional complexity because of the interaction of national and EC laws. Court cases can take years to decide. With a complaints-based system in place, employers have even more incentives to avoid hiring women since they can be the potential subject of lengthy and costly litigation.

Canada. Canada has had wage guidelines since the Canadian Human Rights Act was passed in the mid-1970s. The act provides an excellent example of the havoc that a comparable worth system can wreak in the economy. Salaries are set according to strict pay scales, which seem to be far from market wages. In 1999 courts ruled that the government had to pay billions of dollars in back pay to underpaid federal workers to settle "pay equity" suits. The 230,000 mostly female federal workers employed by the Canadian Treasury Board were due to receive Can$30,000 each, at a cost of about $3.6 billion, or $200 per Canadian taxpayer.

But that huge settlement did not end the discontent. In a letter signed by twenty women in the *Ottawa Citizen,* secretaries protested that they were not awarded as much as clerical workers:

> We agree wholeheartedly that senior secretaries have been left out in the cold and have been treated unfairly in the pay equity agreement. The pittance that SCY-03s are receiving in pay equity (a little over $8,300 with interest) is an insult compared to the amount awarded to their clerical counterparts (CR-04s) who will be receiving close to $48,000 with interest.[54]

Other Canadian employees working for other branches of the federal government, such as the Canada Customs and Revenue Agency and the National Research Council, were not covered by the settlement and prepared their own "pay equity" suits.[55] In 2000 health care workers won a $45 million settlement.[56] Canadian flight attendants sued on the grounds that they were paid less than male-dominated ground and flight crews.[57] Since "pay equity" applies only to workers within the same establishment, airlines argued that ground and flight crews are part of another establishment because they are subject to different bargaining units and contracts.[58]

Similarly, Bell Canada, the largest local exchange telephone company in Canada, confronted large comparable worth claims, primarily from operators and clerical workers. Despite operators' being paid Can$19.50 an hour, the Canadian Telephone Employees Association sued because the operators' pay was lower than that of predominantly male technicians. The union won the case, and in July 1999 the Canadian Supreme Court ruled that the case must be heard before the Canadian Human Rights Tribunal. The case was still not settled by the spring of 2001.[59]

Bell Canada contracted with Excell Global Services of Arizona to provide some expansion of future operator services and thereby to avoid the most onerous of Canadian comparable worth laws. Thus, while operators at Bell Canada may have at least briefly had higher wages than they would have had under a completely free labor market, Bell Canada will create fewer jobs in Canada than otherwise.[60]

Feminists frequently deny that they support a centrally planned economy. What they want to do, they say, is to correct a flaw in the labor market that exists because of discriminatory attitudes about women workers. But wage guidelines are not only the first step toward central planning—they are central planning. If the law sanctions meddling with the market for wages to achieve "gender justice," what will prevent other groups in society from demanding "more equitable" distribution? The wage gap between married and unmarried men (estimated at 60 percent in the early 1990s) is far higher than even the inflated figures of the male–female wage gap. Do unmarried men also deserve wage guidelines?[61]

Ironically, although the stated intention of those proposals is equality, their underlying assumption is that women cannot make their own way in the labor market. A sexist society, the argument goes, compels women to work in certain fields. Since employers pay more for male-dominated fields, the government should rectify the imbalance. That argument flies in the face of the premise that supposedly undergirds feminism—that a woman is just as capable of standing up for herself in the workplace as a man. Opponents of comparable worth and related proposals, feminists say, "fear the greater autonomy for women that higher female wages might mean in terms of family dynamics."[62] Through their support of wage guidelines, feminists discourage women from moving into higher-paying occupations.

But wage guidelines work against women's interests, as the Bell Canada case shows. If employers had to raise the wages of women above their productive rate, fewer would be hired. Schemes such as comparable worth, which purport to help women in the work force, could very well end up limiting their opportunities.

Conclusion

Many factors influence women's status and pay. Decisions about balancing work and family life and about priorities and definitions of success affect women's compensation. The free exercise of choice for which the feminist movement initially fought does not produce equal average male and female wages nor equal numbers of men and women in the boardroom. Nor should we expect it to do so. The outcry raised by feminists is so vehement because they will not accept that women's definitions of success are not always centered on climbing the corporate ladder or earning the highest salaries.

Since feminists do not like the choices some women have made, they argue that women should be immune from the consequences of those choices. Citing evidence of wage gaps and glass ceilings, feminists call for further government intervention in the workplace. If men and women do not naturally distribute themselves proportionally in the workplace, they say that discrimination must be the reason and that the government should adjust the proportions.

But feminists fail to consider both the viability and the desirability of that kind of government intervention. As writer and scholar Dorothy Sayers commented over fifty years ago, the leaders of the women's movement, no matter how well intentioned, often lost sight of the obvious: "When it comes to a *choice,* then every man or woman has to choose as an individual human being, and, like a human being, take the consequences." Sayers presciently warned her readers that feminism's insistence on discussing every social problem in terms of categories of sex was dangerous because, as with all categories, "if they are insisted upon beyond the immediate purpose they serve," they will only "breed class antagonism and disruption in the state."[63]

An inherent danger also exists in feminists' reliance on the government to implement their goals. Early in the twentieth century, during the Progressive Era, reformers such as Florence Kelley of the National Consumers League initiated campaigns to limit the working hours of women who were wives and mothers. The reformers were successful, and the government passed laws to protect women in the work force. In 1908 in *Muller v. Oregon,* the Supreme Court upheld the constitutionality of one of the laws that limited the number of hours women were allowed to work. The Court's reasoning was that "women's physical structure and the performance of maternal functions place her at a disadvantage" and that "this difference justifies a difference in legislation and upholds that which is designed to compensate for some of the burdens which rest upon her." At the time, reformers hailed the decision as enlightened and progressive.[64]

Today, such a ruling would be soundly criticized—and rightly so—for it prevents women from making their own decisions about how much they want to work. Contemporary arguments for preferential programs for women, however, promote only a slightly different and similarly aggressive, protective function for the government. Rather than use the government to protect women from themselves by legislating the number of hours that they are allowed to work, feminists enlist the government to protect women from supposedly rampant sex discrimination in the workplace.

Many men and women, but more women, decide that the price of achieving the highest salaries is not worth the rewards. According to Gail Wills, who left a large accounting firm to start her own business in Grand Prairie, Texas, "The leap from manager to partner was going to require a lifestyle change. I wasn't willing to give up nights and weekends to hobnob to make the connections the firm would need."[65] Women such as Wills are not victims. They are making informed choices about their future. As a result, we see a higher percentage of men in certain top positions. But feminists want the government to protect women by using its power to insist on a certain level of female representation in the workplace, regardless of effort and qualifications. They are advocating the use of government to engineer equality of outcome, rather than to ensure equality of opportunity.

One historian, writing about the *Muller v. Oregon* decision, noted that "once codified, the notion of female weakness and dependence embedded in the laws and the court decisions was difficult to extirpate."[66] Indeed, it took decades of struggle by women's movements to achieve equality of opportunity for American women. Preferences for women in the workplace are in danger of promoting a similar dependence for women—a dependence on the government that, in the face of women's obvious achievements, is unnecessary.

6

No Laughing Matter: Sexual Harassment

The entrance of women into the work force during the past few decades has produced a gradual yet profound revolution. It has sparked new debates over wages and career advancement, sex discrimination, and the social impact of women's participation in previously male-dominated fields of endeavor. The effects of the revolution have been largely positive, and women today, by and large, enjoy equal opportunity as they pursue their goals. But change of that magnitude inevitably brings disruptions. It is in that context that the problem of sexual harassment on the job is best understood.

For better or worse, American women are spending more time than ever before at the office. Although some workers experience harassment on the job, many more meet their future spouses there. The workplace now serves as the site for a large part of our social interaction—whether in the form of friendships, romances, or animosities. It is not surprising that the introduction of women into some workplaces has led to tensions. Employers and employees are still figuring out how to navigate those waters, and they look to the law to guide them. They want to know how to determine when behavior is harassment and when it is misguided romantic interest; employers question whether they can and should monitor the personal relationships and behavior of their employees.

The vast majority of American businesses do not become involved in sexual harassment suits. Only 15,000 people, or .02 percent of the female work force, filed sexual harassment complaints with the U.S. Equal Employment Opportunity Commission in 1999.[1] That is the lowest number since 1994.[2] Although the number of sexual harassment complaints the EEOC received more than doubled between 1991 and 1999 (from 6,883 to 15,222), the percentage of complaints found by the EEOC to have "no reasonable cause" has also risen steadily. In 1999 the EEOC determined that 44 percent of the charges filed were wholly without merit. In other words, after investigating, *the commission could not substantiate the claims of nearly half the complaining parties* and determined that no reason existed to believe that discriminatory harassment had occurred. Only 23 percent of all charges filed in 1999 were found to be meritorious allegations.[3]

Despite those data, a perception, perpetuated by the media, exists that sexual harassment is a major problem, and sexual harassment law and policies have generated a great deal of uncertainty. Numerous rulings by state and federal courts and countless political and social commentaries on the subject have appeared, but the public has yet to reach a consensus on what sexual harassment is and how best to handle it.

This chapter assesses the current state of sexual harassment law and questions whether the response to the problem of sexual harassment has been reasonable and effective. Have employers' sexual harassment policies, federal regulations, and lawsuits succeeded in deterring and preventing harassment? What roles have feminist ideologues and special interest groups played in the campaign to end sexual harassment in the workplace? Finally, what benefits and costs have accrued to businesses and to society as a whole as a result of sexual harassment law? What would work better than the current system?

What Is Sexual Harassment?

In 1974 the first known sexual harassment lawsuit, *Barnes v. Train,* was a clear-cut case of sexual extortion: a woman working as a payroll clerk at the Environmental Protection Agency lost her job after refusing repeated demands from her boss that she submit to a sexual affair. Although a federal district court initially denied her claim that she had been the victim of sex discrimination, an appeals court ruled for Barnes, awarded her back pay, and confirmed that Title VII of the Civil Rights Act of 1964, the country's major piece of employment discrimination legislation, protected workers from such demands.[4]

Although the *Barnes* case and a few others were making their way through the courts in the mid-1970s, a fully articulated legal theory of sexual harassment as sex discrimination did not appear until the late 1970s. Catharine MacKinnon's *Sexual Harassment of Working Women* forever embedded the term *sexual harassment* in the legal lexicon. Her work and the guidelines on harassment issued by the EEOC in 1980 laid the groundwork for contemporary sexual harassment law.[5]

MacKinnon's work has had an enduring impact on how we understand sexual harassment. Like the court in the *Barnes* case, MacKinnon argued that Title VII of the Civil Rights Act of 1964 provided protection against harassment. But MacKinnon went further than the court in her legal reasoning. She claimed that that protection is necessary because sexual harassment is linked to women's subordinate social status and lack of economic power. "To the extent that women and men are not similarly situated sexually," she said, "the reason is pervasive social inequality. It is not biological difference or personal choice." Because of that inequality, MacKinnon argued, expressions of sexual harassment were a form of sex discrimination on a par with the refusal to hire women or the payment of unequal wages because of sex. "Economic power is to sexual harassment as physical force is to rape," she wrote in an often quoted aphorism.[6]

The basis of MacKinnon's legal theory is that sexual harassment is not merely an unfortunate byproduct of women's entrance into the workplace. Rather, it is another expression of women's enduring subordination. MacKinnon succeeded in changing the way sexual harassment was understood; her analysis shifted the focus from individual episodes of bad conduct to the supposedly intractable subordination of women. As with "patriarchy," feminism's ubiquitous villain, that interpretation of sexual harassment makes it a permanent fixture of a supposedly male-dominated society, immune to eradication until society itself is thoroughly restructured along feminist lines.

In practical terms, MacKinnon's work encouraged a new generation of feminist theorists to use sexual harassment law to reinterpret employment discrimination law so that it conformed to their ideological vision. As they have done with other areas of discrimination law, feminist legal theorists have used that interpretation of sexual harassment—which unfortunately has also received the imprimatur of many courts—as a vehicle for furthering their particular ideological goals, whether they be statistical parity in the workplace or offices that abide by feminist-approved codes of conduct.

MacKinnon's was not the only early interpretation of sexual harassment. In 1980 the EEOC issued guidelines for sexual harassment. The current version of those regulations states:

> [U]nwelcome sexual advances, requests for sexual favors, and other verbal or physical conduct of a sexual nature constitute sexual harassment when (1) submission to such conduct is made explicitly or implicitly a term or condition of an individual's employment, (2) submission to or rejection of such conduct by an individual is used as a basis for employment decisions affecting such individual, or (3) such conduct has the purpose or effect of unreasonably interfering with an individual's work performance or creating an intimidating, hostile, or offensive working environment.[7]

The guidelines distinguish between two forms of harassment: "quid pro quo" harassment—literally, "this for that" or "provide me with these favors or lose your job"—and "hostile environment" harassment. The former, as in the *Barnes* case, is sexual extortion, and most people agree (as do we), that Title VII should protect employees from quid pro quo harassment. Questions about the definition and scope of hostile environment harassment, on the other hand, have bred considerable confusion in the courts and in the workplace and ultimately have had a more significant impact on the American workplace than quid pro quo harassment law. Early sexual harassment lawsuits tended to be quid pro quo cases, but by 1994 85 percent of the sexual harassment claims filed by women with the EEOC were hostile environment claims.[8]

Although the EEOC's guidelines provided standards for determining whether hostile environment harassment had occurred, such as whether behavior "unreasonably interfered" with a person's ability to work, those guidelines were vague enough that the details had to be sorted out through litigation. In 1986 in *Meritor Savings Bank v. Vinson,*[9] the Supreme Court first established that hostile environment harassment was actionable under Title VII.[10] The court agreed with the plaintiff that her supervisor's pattern of harassing conduct was a form of sex discrimination, despite the fact that she had not suffered a measurable economic loss due to his actions. The case put hostile environment harassment on the legal map, but it did little to clarify what kinds of behavior constituted creation of a hostile work environment.

At the same time, as is frequently the case, lower courts were reaching different conclusions on the basis of similar evidence. That same year, for example, in *Rabidue v. Osceola Refining Co.,* the Sixth Circuit ruled that the vulgar language experienced by the plaintiff did not warrant a claim of discrimination. Title VII's intent, the court opined, was not to "bring about a magical transformation in the social mores of American workers."[11]Although sexual harassment law was being applied in an increasing number of hostile environment cases, little consistency was apparent in *how* the courts applied the law, and a great deal of confusion existed about what a hostile environment was.[12]

The 1990s brought heightened scrutiny to the issue of sexual harassment. After an initial surge in filings with the EEOC from 1980 through 1984, the number of sexual harassment complaints had leveled off. A second surge of complaints hit the EEOC between 1991 and 1994 and is usually attributed to the publicity surrounding law professor Anita Hill's testimony at Clarence Thomas's Supreme Court confirmation hearings in 1991. In fact, it is more likely that the surge was due to Congress's passage of the Civil Rights Act of 1991. Contained in the new Civil Rights Act were provisions allowing plaintiffs in sexual harassment cases to sue for compensatory and punitive damage awards and to request jury trials.[13] Thus, sexual harassment plaintiffs had gained the opportunity to pursue large damage awards and to air their charges before juries, where they were presumably more likely to garner sympathy.

Of course, those provisions did nothing to alleviate the confusion over hostile environment sexual harassment. For employers, the issue of how to recognize and prevent conduct that created a hostile work environment remained a problem. Previous Supreme Court rulings on sexual harassment, the 1998 decisions in *Faragher v. City of Boca Raton* and *Burlington Industries v. Ellerth,* have not moved us much closer to an answer. The Court put employers on notice that, to avoid liability for hostile environment sexual harassment claims, they must exercise "reasonable care" to prevent sexual harassment in the workplace.[14] But specifics about what constitutes "reasonable care" remain elusive.

Feminist Legal Theory: Enamored of "Experience"

Understanding the difficulty in defining hostile environment sexual harassment requires a return to sexual harassment law's roots in feminist theory. In the 1970s feminist legal theorists such as Catharine MacKinnon argued that existing criminal and civil prohibitions failed to protect women from the problems they faced in the workplace. From their perspective, women's negative workplace experiences needed to be given a single label, "sexual harassment," and a heightened profile to ensure that the law could truly be an effective means of redress. The fact that the behaviors in question were already covered by existing criminal and civil prohibitions, including assault, battery, blackmail, lewdness, breach of contract, and intentional infliction of emotional distress, was insufficient, in part because the courts themselves were viewed as hostile, male-dominated domains.[15]

Accusations about the law's feebleness in punishing workplace discrimination against women had some validity. At the time MacKinnon and others were creating sexual harassment law, women constituted only about 36 percent of the labor force and were not yet well represented in most of the professions. Evidence of discrimination was easy to find, and feminist theorists believed that using the force of the law in a systematic way to end harassment was a necessary step for securing equal opportunity for women in the work force.

Today, things are different. Women are a major force in the working world; they surpass men in education and equal them in wages; they are chief executive officers, astronauts, physicians, and lawyers. The claim that women are victims of societywide discrimination no longer rings true. Nevertheless, as we have seen with debates over the wage gap and glass ceiling, contemporary feminism continues to take as its guiding principle the idea that women are victims of their social condition. Accordingly, feminist legal theorists have made that the basis for their approach to workplace harassment as well.

Indeed, feminist legal theorists frequently link other workplace issues—wages and occupational segregation, for example—to sexual harassment as proof of the intractability of male privilege. Building on MacKinnon's work, law professor Deborah Rhode has argued that to eradicate sexual harassment, a much broader social campaign is required. "We need to focus on job training, glass ceilings, affirmative action, pay equity, parental and childcare policies, and sex-role stereotypes," she said, since "harassing conduct is a symptom as well as a cause of broader patterns of gender inequality."[16] Other feminist theorists have claimed that sexual harassment is one of the main weapons men use to keep women segregated into lower-paying, lower-prestige jobs in the labor force.[17] In that rendering, sexual harassment is part of a larger campaign to keep women from more lucrative fields.[18]

The other idea that characterizes feminist legal theory on harassment and that flows from the wrongheaded assumption that women suffer from pervasive discrimination is an insistence that the law grant women's experiences primacy of place in sexual harassment cases. Since society, particularly our justice system, operates on principles crafted by men, the reasoning goes, the law cannot possibly respond to the needs of women. To ensure justice for women, then, feminists must transform the law.

That idea is a hallmark of feminist jurisprudence. As outlined ten years ago by one of its most forceful proponents, Professor Robin West, feminist legal theory is required to "reconstruct the reforms necessary to the safety and improvement of women's lives in direct language that is true to our own experience and our own subjective lives."[19] Feminists, in other words, need to rewrite law so that what women feel and experience—whether in the workplace or in the home—is understood as the truth in the eyes of the legal system. Unfortunately, the subjective, experiential standard West has advocated is not an innocuous one.

The danger of the experience-based standard pursued by feminists is that its logical conclusion is a legal system in which feelings trump facts. That is explicit in the work of feminist legal theorists and in the rhetoric of mainstream feminist organizations: "Just because an act may not meet the traditional common law definition of force," wrote law professor Toni Lester, "does not mean that the target of the harassment does not justifiably experience that act, *in her own mind,* as force" (emphasis added).[20]

A checklist developed by the Wellesley Center for Research on Women takes the experiential standard to its extreme:

Sexual Harassment	Flirting
feels bad	feels good
one-sided	reciprocal
feels unattractive	feels attractive
is degrading	is a compliment
feels powerless	in control
power-based	equality
negative touching	positive touching
unwanted	wanted
illegal	legal
invading	open
demeaning	flattering
sad/angry	happy
negative self-esteem	positive self-esteem

Nearly every phrase falling under the rubrics of sexual harassment and flirting is a matter of individual perception and feeling.[21]

The error of basing sexual harassment law on the subjective perceptions of women is well revealed by a study conducted by two University of Arizona psychologists. The researchers asked female college students to assess whether they felt harassed when given a series of fictional scenarios where they were approached by men of varying levels of attractiveness. The findings? As the attractiveness and availability of the man decreased, the women's experience of feeling harassed increased. Thus, only 2 percent of the women approached by a good-looking single man felt harassed, while a full 24 percent felt harassed when approached by an unattractive married man.[22]

Yet feminists disregard such evidence. Their effort to base sexual harassment law on women's experience includes a campaign to eliminate the "unwelcomeness" requirement in sexual harassment cases.[23]

The unwelcomeness standard protects against an entirely subjective approach to sexual harassment by asking, at the very least, whether the accused harasser might have been responding to signals sent by the purported victim. It provides a reasonable guidepost for assessing motives and an opportunity for defendants and plaintiffs to sort out potential misunderstandings, which is an especially important feature in sexual harassment cases involving romantic relationships that have soured. The requirement is not a defense for egregious misconduct.

Yet feminists view the unwelcomeness requirement as another vestige of patriarchy. The requirement is "one more indication of the legal supremacy of the male perspective," wrote one student of feminist legal theory. Professor Susan Estrich claimed that it is "personally humiliating for women" to have to prove that the behavior in question in sexual harassment cases was unwelcome.[24] Those feminists want to close what they see as a legal loophole for those accused of sexual harassment.

But eliminating the unwelcomeness requirement means disregarding intent in sexual harassment cases. That is a much desired development for feminists; after all, for those who understand sexual harassment as a broad conspiracy by men against women, no need exists to bother with details such as the motive or intent of the accused. But eliminating the unwelcomeness requirement also undermines our justice system's commitment to innocence until proven guilty. If the requirement is eliminated or even substantially eroded, then feminist legal theorists will have succeeded in installing a version of justice wherein any attempt to explore whether an alleged harasser intended to discriminate is itself taken as evidence of discrimination against women.

Feminists have employed another tactic in their ideological crusade against sexual harassment. By invoking simplistic stereotypes of men as predators and women as victims, feminists can link harassment to more serious acts of violence, a powerful rhetorical tool. Thus, Deborah Rhode wrote that "the dynamics of male entitlement, dominance, and control that foster harassment also contribute to more serious forms of abuse, such as domestic violence and rape."[25] That view is a mainstay of the organized feminist movement as well. The National Organization for Women has said that harassment is "a form of violence against women, used to keep women 'in their place,'" and the Feminist Majority Foundation has listed "leering, wolf whistles, sexual innuendoes," and "demanding 'Hey baby, give me a smile,'" next to sexual assault as equivalent experiences of sexual harassment.[26] The feminists' goal is to expand the scope of traditional common law to capture a range of behaviors—from offcolor jokes to suggestive remarks—and to place them on a continuum with more serious actions such as assault and rape, all of which can be traced, in their view, to men's oppression of women.

That campaign of hyperbole and overheated rhetoric does not help women. It is harmful because equating "leering" and "sexual innuendo" to rape succeeds only in trivializing the effects of both behaviors. It is a long way from recognizing that some men, acting on base prejudices, do, in fact, try to drive women from the workplace by means of harassment to arguing that such activities are systemic and evidence of a large-scale campaign of violence against women. Calling crude language a form of violence will not make it so. Feminists who cry wolf with regard to harassment and violence will eventually face a public skeptical of any of their claims about violence.

Finally, in their work, feminist theorists and activists assume that "women's experience" is, if not monolithic, then at least capable of generalization when it comes to how women understand sex in the workplace. But that is not the case. As the history of feminism itself reveals, reaching a consensus on what women need and want is nearly impossible. Defining what the reasonable woman considers sexual harassment is an equally frustrating exercise.[27] The feminist articulation of sexual harassment follows a rigid script, where women are always the victims and men the perpetrators. In that, feminists overlook the fact that some women, too, eagerly trade bawdy jokes and sexualized banter with male coworkers and that some women initiate sexual relationships with male colleagues.

Feminist-inspired sexual harassment law is fundamentally flawed. It relies on an outdated vision of women as victims of their social condition, trumpets subjective experience as the only standard of truth, and falsely equates harassment with violence. And those ideas have had real consequences. Feminist theorists are not toiling on the academic margins. Courts in landmark sexual harassment cases have cited their work. Kathryn Abrams was cited in the opinions for *Robinson v. Jacksonville Shipyards* and *Ellison v. Brady,* for example, and the Supreme Court cited Catharine MacKinnon's work in the *Meritor* case.[28] The reasoning of the Supreme Court in 1993 in *Harris v. Forklift Systems* embraced key elements of the idea that experience should be the ultimate arbiter in sexual harassment cases.[29]

Whether through inability or unwillingness, the courts and the federal government have failed to offer a detailed, coherent definition of hostile environment sexual harassment. Feminist theorists have been only too happy to fill that void. The real-world consequence for employers is that they feel a responsibility to modify workplace behavior—but only of their male employees. The underlying message of current sexual harassment law, based as it is on the notion that women suffer from pervasive sex discrimination in American society, is that only women can be real victims of harassment.[30] As we see below, that questionable claim has had a significant effect on the American workplace, as employers try to craft practical antiharassment proposals that conform to the misguided dictates of feminist theorists and the often confusing standards set by the law.

Sexual Harassment and the "Shadow of the Law"
Although the media have seized upon a few outrageous sexual harassment cases that have reached the nation's courts, such as the

1995 case where a jury awarded $50 million to a female Wal-Mart clerk who claimed to have been the victim of verbal harassment by supervisors—the award was later reduced to $350,000—excessive damage awards are not the norm in sexual harassment litigation.[31] Nevertheless, the attention granted high-profile harassment cases such as that of Paula Jones or the female employees at the Normal, Illinois, Mitsubishi plant have heightened employers' fears about their liability for sexual harassment lawsuits.[32] Whether those fears are legitimate, they have prompted employers to craft sexual harassment policies that try to conform to the standards set by the courts and the EEOC to limit their liability for potential lawsuits. Those policies have had a major effect on the American workplace. It is useful to explore what employers are doing voluntarily to comply with existing law—to see, in other words, how legal theories and court rulings about sexual harassment have translated in the real world. By exploring what is growing in "the shadow of the law," as legal commentators often call it, we gain a better understanding of the strengths and weaknesses of contemporary sexual harassment law.[33]

The vast majority of American businesses do not become embroiled in sexual harassment lawsuits. Most organizations have, however, written sexual harassment policies stating that sexual harassment is unlawful and prohibited and providing details for employees on how to report harassment.

If such preventive measures constituted the extent of employer activity with regard to sexual harassment, there would be little room for criticism. But that is not the case. The vagueness of sexual harassment law, particularly with regard to hostile environment claims, has created a built-in incentive for employers to err on the side of excessive monitoring of their employees' behavior. Refusing to pay a woman as much as a man for the same job is clearly wrong and illegal under the Equal Pay Act of 1963 and Title VII of the Civil Rights Act of 1964; the same principle holds true with regard to race discrimination. But the law does not so neatly categorize exchanging sexually charged remarks or even aggressively pursuing a relationship with a coworker. If the man or woman who is the object of such attention finds it flattering or desirable, the experience is called successful courtship. If not, it can be called harassment. How are employers to know where to draw the line?

The dilemma facing employers is perhaps best illustrated by the case of employee dating. Because of the vagaries of hostile environment sexual harassment law, employers today face two challenges when it comes to employee dating and sexual harassment. They face the possibility of lawsuits when relationships fizzle *and* they face potential lawsuits for favoritism filed by third-party employees who believe, for example, that an employee who is dating a supervisor might be receiving special benefits as a result of that relationship.

Some employers have attempted to craft policies that will protect them from liability for sexual harassment in cases of supervisor-subordinate dating, for example. Options include banning workplace relationships altogether; separating or transferring employees once they learn of a relationship; requiring or urging notification of dating situations so that reassignment can take place; or simply doing nothing. Motorola has prohibited relationships between supervisors and subordinates, for example, while Intel has explicitly and severely limited such office dating.[34]

Motorola and Intel occupy the more extreme end of that spectrum. General Motors merely encourages disclosure by noting that "managers are encouraged to report romantic involvements with subordinates," so that the subordinate is no longer reporting to the manager whom he or she is dating. Wal-Mart's policy is to transfer the subordinate if a subordinate and supervisor are dating; IBM moves the manager rather than the subordinate. And at ABC television, supervisors and subordinates involved in a relationship are "strongly encouraged" to report to management. ABC then helps the couple decide who will transfer, but if a transfer is not viable, one of the parties must resign, or the employees must agree to end the relationship.[35] In the few lawsuits that have been filed challenging those rules as invasions of employee privacy, the courts found in favor of employers by affirming that such dating regulations are a legitimate business interest.[36]

Corporations have also taken measures to prohibit conduct that could lead to claims of hostile environment sexual harassment. Hence, the Honeywell Corp. lists staring as an offense in its 1990 sexual harassment handbook, and Boeing Co. prohibits employees from telling jokes about blondes.[37]

From the perspective of the administrators and employers drafting those policies, the internal costs of monitoring and enforcing such rules are a small price to pay compared with potential sexual harassment lawsuits. But those policies have other costs. Legal commentators from both ends of the political spectrum have sounded alarm bells about the limits placed on free speech by sexual harassment policies and dating restrictions, for example. Law professor Eugene Volokh has noted that, with regard to hostile environment claims, "the risk of liability, combined with the law's vagueness, creates a huge incentive to overcensor." While employers do not have a duty to guarantee free speech, those intent on avoiding an EEOC investigation or a lawsuit feel some pressure to control their employees' office communications.[38]

But employers and free speech advocates face a formidable opponent in the battle for reasonable workplace regulations. In addition to the work of feminist interest groups and legal theorists, much of the effort to redefine workplace behavior is fueled by an expanding sector of workshop directors, consultants, and lawyers that University of Massachusetts, Amherst, women's studies professor Daphne Patai has aptly labeled the "Sexual Harassment Industry."[39] Playing on employers' liability fears, the sexual harassment industry has embraced the feminist view of harassment as pervasive and has encouraged employers to monitor employee behavior. Like feminist special interest groups, the sexual harassment industry has a financial stake in exaggerating the scope of the problem.[40] And as the above examples of corporate dating policies suggest, that industry is gaining a hearing among American businesses.

While businesses incur measurable costs for such policies, the more worrisome costs are those that are not quantifiable, such as the price paid in perceptions about women workers and in a chillier climate between male and female employees and their supervisors. Doubtless, most people would agree that all workers should behave appropriately in the workplace and maintain a modicum of good conduct and professional standards in their interactions with coworkers of either sex. Most workers do so. And most people want employers to punish workers who violate those standards. But when standards for what is and what is not harassment remain ambiguous, as they are with hostile environment harassment, employers have little choice but to rely on heavy-handed monitoring of the workplace to protect themselves. Relationships between men and women in the workplace inevitably suffer.[41]

Women's workplace advancement might also suffer. To protect themselves from potential lawsuits, reasonable men, particularly those in positions of authority, will limit their exposure to potentially ambiguous situations, such as social occasions and contact on business trips.[42] In today's litigious age, that is prudent; unfortunately, women workers who miss out on valuable time with mentors pay the price for such prudence. Ironically, that creates a situation in which employers, fearful of sexual harassment lawsuits, end up treating female employees differently—the very kind of behavior Title VII is intended to prohibit.

Feminists have thus far offered no reasonable response to that possibility; they claim instead that fears over potential sexual harassment lawsuits are overstated.[43] But theirs is a feeble defense that misses the point. Whatever the reality of the law in terms of cases filed, in the shadow of the law the fear of liability is a real one for employers—one on which they have acted.

Schools and Streets: The New Frontiers of Sexual Harassment Law

As we have seen, the evolution of sexual harassment law has brought us from an emphasis on egregious cases of quid pro quo harassment to more ambiguous claims of hostile work environment harassment. Contrary to available evidence, feminist hyperbole combined with an overzealous sexual harassment industry paints a picture of American workplaces rife with harassment. Although experience points to the need for greater precision in defining hostile environment sexual harassment and a more narrow scope for sexual harassment law in general, the most recent efforts by feminists on the front lines of sexual harassment law are having just the opposite effect. Feminists' attempts to broaden sexual harassment law should serve as a cautionary tale for American workers and employers.

Feminist ideologues have taken their sexual harassment campaign to the schools, with disturbing results. Waging war against "peer harassment," or harassment among students, feminists have used Title IX of the Educational Amendments of 1972 to expand sexual harassment law to children. In 1992, in *Franklin v. Gwinnett County Public Schools,* the U.S. Supreme Court found educational institutions liable for monetary damages to students who had been harassed by teachers.[44] That makes sense, given that teachers are the agents of the school district and are in positions of authority over students. But in 1999, in *Davis v. Monroe County Board of Education,* the Supreme Court ruled that schools that receive federal funds are liable for sexual harassment under Title IX if they show "deliberate indifference" to peer harassment. Aurelia Davis, mother of fifth-grader La Shonda Davis, filed the suit; she alleged that school officials in Forsyth, Georgia, ignored her requests to intervene and end the harassment her daughter allegedly suffered at the hands of a classmate.[45]

As in other Supreme Court sexual harassment cases, the majority in the *Davis* case provided no clear definition of peer harassment or of the parameters of deliberate indifference to student complaints. As Justice Anthony Kennedy noted in his dissent, given those vague standards and "arbitrary line-drawing" about conduct, the only certain outcome of the majority's decision was "that scarce resources will be diverted from educating our children and that many school districts, desperate to avoid Title IX peer harassment suits, will adopt whatever federal code of student conduct and discipline the Department of Education sees fit to impose upon them."[46] As employers do with hostile environment claims, school administrators have an incentive to punish even the most innocuous student conduct to protect themselves from liability.

Expanding sexual harassment law to incorporate the behavior of children has several problems. First, children are not adults. To call the behavior of adolescents and elementary school children sexual harassment makes a mockery of common sense and of the legislative intent of Title IX.[47] That reasoning also brings us such absurd situations as that of Jonathan Prevette, the six-year-old boy expelled for kissing a female first-grade classmate, and the policies of the Elm Road School in Indiana that forbid fourth graders from holding hands or chasing students of the opposite sex at recess.[48]

Second, applying sexual harassment standards to the schools, as the Supreme Court did in the *Davis* case, places the federal government in the position of overseeing discipline in local schools. In essence, that also undermines Title IX by transforming it into a "Federal Student Civility Code." The federal government should not be the arbiter of schoolyard behavior.[49] Students who engage in harassment should face punishment by local school officials, not by the federal government.

Finally, as Justice Kennedy suggested in his dissent in the *Davis* case, imposing standards meant to apply to adults in the workplace to children in schools places an unnecessary and costly burden on our nation's educational system. The majority's decision presents school administrators with a difficult choice. To comply with the Court's ruling, they will have to take aggressive steps to punish student harassers. Schools might decide, for example, that expulsion or suspension of a harasser is the best option to avoid a lawsuit. That exposes the schools to lawsuits from the punished harassers, however, who could credibly claim that expulsion or suspension violates their right to an education, which cannot be compromised without due process of law.[50] That legal Catch-22 comes with a potentially ruinous price tag, as school districts will find themselves spending millions of dollars in legal fees to defend themselves from such charges. That is money diverted from education to satisfy the dictates of an ideological crusade.

That crusade continues outside the schools as well. In their effort to expand sexual harassment law, feminist legal theorists have also set their sights on "street harassment." In a 1993 *Harvard Law Review* article, Northwestern University Law School professor Cynthia Bowman argued that "street harassment," defined as the unsolicited leers, whistles, or comments that women experience in public settings, is a form of sexual harassment that "accomplishes an informal ghettoization of women." A wink or crude comment on a street corner is in fact an implicit warning that women do not belong in public, Bowman argued, and such actions are equivalent to physical assaults.[51]

Bowman scornfully dismissed the notion that street harassment might be just one of the little indignities all citizens suffer in a society. Rather, in keeping with her feminist sisters on sexual harassment, she viewed street harassment as part of a larger conspiracy against women. Her remedy is the creation of state statutes and municipal ordinances prohibiting street harassment; violators would face a misdemeanor charge and a $250 fine.[52] Such proposals are not only unnecessary but also violate free speech.

Those proposals suggest a dangerous tendency among many feminist legal theorists to sacrifice fundamental freedoms on the altar of behavioral correctness, and indeed many feminists have noted their willingness to restrict freedoms of speech and expression in the cause of social engineering.[53] But the proposals also demonstrate the logical conclusion of the current trend in sexual harassment law. If the standards are ambiguous and experience is the arbiter, then excesses are bound to occur.

Expanding sexual harassment law to incorporate the behavior of children or comments made on the street ultimately weakens feminists' effort by sapping public patience for ending real harassment. If nearly any behavior, whether committed by children on a school playground or strangers on the street, can be seen as sexual harassment, then sexual harassment loses its meaning. It becomes, as it already has in some settings, fodder for jokes rather than serious concern.

A Reasonable Approach to Sexual Harassment

Any law that encourages employers to take excessive action in monitoring their work force or asks schools to impose adult standards of sexual conduct on children, as current sexual harassment law does, is clearly in need of reform. Our current, experience-based standards have bred employee confusion and employer overreaction. Today, most workers are aware that sexual harassment exists—and feminists deserve credit for raising awareness of the practice. But if recent sexual harassment lawsuits are any guide, then, as a society, we are becoming less able to discern between appropriate and inappropriate conduct in the workplace. The legacy of the experience-based standards first advocated by feminists in the 1970s is a working and educational environment where concerns over potential sexual harassment lawsuits infect even spontaneous social interaction.[54] Where should we go from here?

Many critics claim that the fundamental problem with sexual harassment law is that it is a bad fit to treat it as a form of sex discrimination under Title VII. As legal theorists such as Ellen Frankel Paul have correctly noted, in its current incarnation, sexual harassment law has at its core an ideological bias against men, who are seen as women's oppressors, and a misguided assumption that sexual harassers and sex discriminators act on the same motives. The solution proposed by those critics is to make sexual harassment a tort, resembling that of intentional infliction of emotional distress, for example. In that way, sexual harassment law would operate under an individual rights perspective—punishing the individuals who commit the acts—rather than under the group rights perspective embraced by feminists, which calls for strict liability for employers.[55]

We adopt a middle path between feminists' calls for strict liability in all sexual harassment cases and tort advocates' desire for no employer liability. A reasonable approach to sexual harassment understands the problem as the byproduct of a momentous social change: women's entrance into the work force. Seen in that context and separated from divisive feminist ideological agendas, the problem of sexual harassment is better understood. Eliminating sexual harassment does not require declaring war on men and employers, as feminists are eager to do. Neither does it free employers from the responsibility of preventing harassment when possible and from liability in cases of quid pro quo harassment.

Since the overwhelming problem with current sexual harassment law is its reliance on experiential standards of evidence, reasonable reform requires two steps. First, the EEOC should tighten the language of its guidelines to ensure that experience is weighed with motive in determining instances of harassment, especially hostile environment harassment. In particular, the section of the EEOC guidelines that describes conduct that has "the purpose or effect of unreasonably interfering with an individual's work performance or creating an intimidating, hostile, or offensive working environment" should be changed to apply to conduct that has "the purpose *and* effect" of imposing those burdens.[56]

Second, feminists should not be allowed to succeed in their battle to eliminate the "unwelcomeness" requirement. As we noted earlier, the question whether behavior was welcome or unwelcome provides a reasonable defense to sexual harassment charges. And unwelcomeness is not difficult to prove if a woman clearly refuses an overture. Further, an approach to sexual harassment that considers the intent of the alleged harasser squares with evidence gathered by psychologists and sociologists about the importance of context. Not all such interaction is harmful to women. In fact, on the basis of the actual behavior and experiences of men and women in the workplace, several social scientists have concluded that hostile environment sexual harassment law should be restructured to place greater emphasis on the intentions of the accused.[57]

Conclusion

If our goal is a society in which women can pursue fulfillment in the working world without falling victim to harassment, surely a reasonable goal, then current hostile environment clauses of sexual harassment law are sending the wrong message. It is difficult to reconcile the claim that women are capable of performing the jobs that men historically have held with the teachings of feminists who say that women need to be protected. Women cannot have it both ways.

Current sexual harassment law is flawed in another regard as well. Feminists' focus on sexual harassment as an abuse of male power assumes the existence of workplaces where men are always in charge and women are their subordinates. But that situation is becoming increasingly obsolete. As more women work their way into positions of authority—whether supervising other employees, in middle management, or in the CEO's office—more men will find themselves on the other end of the power differential. Feminists are operating from the misguided notion that the best force for changing the social norms that allow harassment is through litigation. But lawsuits are not the best means to change human behavior, and current sexual harassment law does not consider the different social context in which that behavior now occurs.[58]

The real question as we adjust to the revolution wrought by women's entrance into the workplace is how we ensure their continued freedom to participate in the economy without burdening businesses with restrictive regulations. After all, those regulatory costs will be passed down to all workers, male and female alike. Should the government strictly regulate male and female behavior by telling employers how to structure their workplaces, by encouraging them to monitor employee behavior, and by using the power of the courts and regulatory agencies to enforce those dictates? Or should we have a workplace with as little intrusive government activity as possible, a workplace where our existing antidiscrimination laws protect all workers and where employers who discriminate against women— whether by allowing sexual harassment or paying them lower wages—will soon find themselves liable, as well as cut off from half the talented labor pool? Although victims of discrimination will exist in either scenario, the costs to society are far greater and the potential for abuse more likely if we continue along the first path.

Perceptions are precarious things, and one person's good humor is another's insult. For feminists, the ultimate purpose of sexual harassment law is to reconfigure the relationships between men and women in the workplace. That is a task best accomplished through the gradual process of changing social norms, not by ideologically motivated government intrusion in the workplace. In their attempts to restructure relationships between males and females in the workplace, feminist ideologues have abandoned the reality of those relationships—how men and women interact not only as fellow workers, but also as friends and even as potential spouses—to see their agenda fulfilled.

As in other arenas where feminist ideologues claim that women need special protection, sexual harassment law has become another stage on which feminists play out their quest for their version of justice. But justice should be based on sound legal principles, not on slippery standards of experience and perception. Legal action should be based on facts, not feelings. With sexual harassment, as with other areas of employment discrimination law, there is no justice for women when ideology supplants reason.

7

Restructuring the Workplace: Mandatory Benefits and Optional Results

In addition to calling for government intervention in education and wages, feminists frequently propose that the government require employers to provide special benefits primarily or exclusively for women in the workplace. Examples of such benefits include paid maternity leave, time off with pay to deal with family issues, on-site day care for young children, telecommuting, and flexible or part-time hours. And feminists want all those benefits, of course, without sacrificing wages or promotion possibilities. Ironically, even after women have achieved equal opportunity in education and the professions—and even after women have reached positions comparable to men's—feminists argue that the workplace has to be further restructured to be tailored to women's specific needs. Success, it would seem, is not enough: women need even more help.

Modern feminists' call for additional preferences to accommodate family issues is reminiscent of the Americans with Disabilities Act, which holds that the employer must accommodate workers' disabilities.[1] Women are treating themselves as another type of disabled worker by asking employers to accommodate their special circumstances. Yet disabled workers have real handicaps; women do not.

When Equal Opportunity Is Not Good Enough: The Goal of a Kinder, Gentler Workplace

Supporters of special benefits for women claim that the choice of which costly benefits to provide should not be left to the allegedly faulty discretion of employers. The federal government should mandate certain benefits and require firms to offer a package to all employees. As is the case with sexual harassment laws, however, those proposed provisions could well have unintended consequences. In particular, mandated benefits primarily for women artificially raise the cost of employing them. It is illegal to pay equally qualified women less than men, even if they use more benefits. Hence, more mandated benefits for women artificially discourage employers from hiring women. Men as well as women are ultimately harmed, because as costs go up, firms hire fewer workers, and unemployment increases. The more costly the benefits, the more all workers, including women, suffer in terms of lost employment opportunities.

An examination of other countries shows little evidence that mandated benefits improve the economic status of women. On the contrary, in a globally competitive economy, higher mandated benefits are associated with lower rates of economic growth and higher rates of unemployment, which work against the interests of all—working men, working women, the unemployed, at-home moms, retirees, and children. One reason for women's economic progress in the United States has been the nation's ability to create new jobs. Although the United States has many regulations that discourage employment, other countries have even more punishing regulations. The higher the cost of employing individuals, the less willing are businesses to hire them, so raising the costs of employing workers through mandated maternity leave policies reduces the number of employees hired. But that does not sway many professional feminists, who continue to call for more government- and employer-provided benefits.

Betty Friedan, in her autobiography *Life So Far,* called for an expanded maternity leave:

> I think that we should have the option of a much longer leave for childbirth or any health emergency. . . . In many countries, Australia, Sweden, women can take up to a year, two years, even three years of parental leave, and are

guaranteed their original job or some kind of comparable work. I also think that family leave should be paid, so that people could afford to take it.[2]

Friedan took a similar view about child care; she called for then-president Clinton "to push for a national child care program and go beyond *saying* he's for national child care by using an executive order to *launch* it for any company or institution that has a government contract."[3] In a comparable vein, Rebecca Korzec, a contemporary feminist, advocated a "profound restructuring of the family and of the workplace in fundamental respects."[4] Sylvia Ann Hewlett, a fellow of Harvard's Center for the Study of Values in Public Life and chairman of the National Parenting Association, wrote in 2000, "The government and employers do such a poor job of supporting working mothers—providing little in the way of paid leave, flextime, or affordable child care—that women routinely become downwardly mobile in the labor market once they have children."[5] And Karen Kornbluh, former deputy chief of staff at the U.S. Department of the Treasury, called for mothers to "demand some of the policies that women in other industrialized countries take for granted."[6]

What, in sum, do women want from the workplace? In *Presumed Equal: What America's Top Women Lawyers Really Think about Their Firms,* a survey of women's experience in major law firms, authors Suzanne Nossel and Elizabeth Westfall claimed that despite women's educational gains in law schools, their demonstrated success in garnering jobs in good law firms, and the significant decline in workplace harassment, "systemic forces hold back women's progress and will continue to do so until institutional and societal changes are made."[7] While it was unclear from the respondents in their survey just what those mysterious "systemic forces" were, it was obvious to the authors what "societal changes" needed to be made: more benefits for female associates. The best-ranked firms, according to the authors, provided women with flexible hours, large amounts of paid maternity leave, and on-site child care. It was not just equal pay for equal work anymore, but equal pay plus more benefits for less work.

Nossel and Westfall admitted that women associates reported that their chances of promotion were equal to those of men as long as they were willing to put in the same effort. Hence, discrimination did not appear to be a major problem. They also reported that attrition rates for women associates were higher than for male associates and that the most frequently cited reason why women left law firms was that combining raising children with a career at a law firm was difficult. Even some men, they noted, were leaving law firms to have more time with their families. Overall, the women lawyers who responded to Nossel and Westfall's questions demonstrated "a keen awareness that the women who had achieved the greatest success in their firms did so at considerable personal cost."[8]

Nossel and Westfall's evidence, culled directly from female lawyers in law firms, demonstrates once more that the personal choices women make *outside* the workplace have significant consequences for their achievement *within* the workplace. Yet the authors did not recognize that reality. Their conclusion was that "offering women jobs and salaries commensurate with men's represents only the first tentative steps on the journey to making the legal profession an arena where women can thrive and contribute throughout the duration of their working lives."[9] The implication here is that equal pay and equal opportunity are not sufficient, and society must change the workplace to make it kinder and gentler for women.

Firms are in a lose-lose situation. In many companies women themselves have had the opportunity to craft workplace solutions to the many demands on their time, such as the creation of a "mommy-track" or "flex-time" work arrangements. Despite the creation of such programs by and for women, some feminists see discrimination. Companies that choose not to offer telecommuting and part-time hours are labeled as inhospitable to women, yet those that do are accused of downgrading women's status.

For example, Korzec, in her discussion of the "mommy-track" in law firms, concluded that "mommy-tracking reinforces undesirable stereotypes" and "forestalls the transformations, at home and at work, which could enable women to choose both motherhood and career." In her rendering she discussed motherhood only in terms of its career "costs" to women; indeed, Korzec argued that the idea that women might want to care for their children has "deprived women of the opportunities which are essential to achieving equality at work."[10]

Besides the disturbing way in which Korzec discussed motherhood in terms of costs, without any mention of the rewards, such characterizations imply that the choices women are making in their professional lives are not really choices at all, but delusions. Korzec asserted, "The career marginalization of women lawyers results neither from biology nor choice but from the family and workplace—institutions which have resulted from and now reinforce gender inequality."[11]

The recent trend of lower retirement ages and declining weekly hours of work for men challenges the idea that women are the only ones who make such choices. Men are also choosing more free time and less income, as Nossel and Westfall demonstrated. But men's decisions to sacrifice professional success for personal time are never linked to oppressive social forces. Why, then, are women's decisions in that regard treated with skepticism?

Professional feminists are not satisfied with existing antidiscrimination laws, laws that have—through court decisions, legislative revisions, and bureaucratic enforcement—already extended far beyond their initial stated purpose. Those feminists' statements offer further proof that their goal is not equality of opportunity, but special programs that will be used primarily by women. In that sense feminists are advocating a form of government-enforced social engineering, one that harks back to inefficient and unproductive socialist regimes.

What Is a Mandatory Benefit?

Employers provide different kinds of benefits to their workers, some required by federal and state governments and others optional. The Congressional Budget Office, the congressional agency in charge of calculating the costs of government programs, estimates that employers pay almost $800 billion in federal "mandatory benefits"—more than 10 percent of the $6 trillion wage economy.[12] But that huge figure is less than the real cost because it includes only direct cash benefits to workers, such as Social Security, health insurance, and retirement benefits.

The real cost of mandatory benefits includes not only those direct cash benefits, but also general programs that employers must make available to all employees. Many employees would never use those benefits, but it is still expensive to have them available. Two of the most visible federal programs are those created under the Americans with Disabilities Act and the Family and Medical Leave Act,[13] but countless other such programs exist at the federal, state, and local levels. Some are relatively benign, such as workers' compensation, a compulsory state insurance program for workers injured while on the job. But others have a more invasive and costly effect on the workplace.

The Family and Medical Leave Act, signed into law in 1993, allows workers to take up to twelve weeks unpaid leave a year for a serious illness experienced by the worker or a family member or for the birth or adoption of a child. It applies to public employers and private employers with more than fifty workers. To qualify for the leave, an employee must have worked for the employer for at least 1,250 hours the previous year. In 1999 Professor Jane Waldfogel noted that the act covered 46 percent of the private sector work force, much of which was covered by existing employer plans. Hence, the act did not result in a large increase in maternity leave coverage. It did, however, result in greater paternity leave coverage for men, although most are not taking advantage of that additional benefit.[14]

Although the Family and Medical Leave Act did not increase maternity leave coverage substantially, it can still raise costs for some smaller companies. Take the case of PermaTreat, a small Virginia company with seventy employees. In 1999 a female employee took time off under the act because of the imminent birth of her child. She said that she would return at the end of her permitted twelve-week period of unpaid leave. On the day that she was due to return, she called and said that she had decided to quit the job. PermaTreat was left with the expenditures for her health insurance premiums, which by law the firm must pay during the absence, and with the urgent need to find a replacement.[15] While large corporations may easily absorb such costs, they pose a serious expenditure for small firms.

George Daniels, president of Daniels Manufacturing, a Florida firm of 150 employees that makes tools for aerospace, encountered a different type of problem with the Family and Medical Leave Act. He found that rather than employees' not returning from maternity leave, many of his employees were taking intermittent amounts of time off for medical reasons. That was not only costly—he had to hire an additional personnel manager to deal with the time-keeping issues, and problems related to the act accounted for two-thirds of his legal bills—but also difficult for other employees, who had to cover for their absent colleagues. Under the Family and Medical Leave Act, Daniels calculated, an employee could miss just under two hours every day and still stay within the twelve-weeks-per-year limit. "It just drives you up the wall," he said in an interview.[16]

Dixie Dugan, the human resource coordinator of Cardinal Service Management, Inc., a private 175-person firm in New Castle, Indiana, echoed that sentiment. According to Dugan, the Department of Labor has changed and expanded the rules for dealing with the Family and Medical Leave Act since it was passed, and the act has now evolved into a national sick leave program, contrary to the law's original intent. One year the Department of Labor said that employees could not use the act's time allotment for colds, flu, strep throat, and nonmigraine headaches. The following year the department ruled that the act allowed time off for those illnesses. As a result, the firms face short-term, intermittent absences that are hard to plan for and are difficult for coworkers, who have to cover for their missing colleagues. As Dugan put it, "When employees request federally protected FMLA 'serious health condition' leave for minor illnesses such as headaches and strep throat, this type of misapplication has a direct impact on the morale of those expected to carry the work load in the employee's absence."[17]

Some mandatory benefits, such as Social Security taxes, raise the costs of employing all workers. While Social Security taxes may discourage employment generally, they do not change an employer's decision about whether to hire men or women, or the healthy or the disabled. In contrast, many other mandatory benefit programs have costs that vary substantially by workers' characteristics. In some instances, women are the primary "beneficiaries" of those programs, which means that the employer is discouraged from hiring them.

In 1999 President Clinton asked the Department of Labor to issue regulations allowing states to use their unemployment insurance funds to give paid parental leave to parents of new babies. That benefit is aimed primarily at women, since they take more time off than fathers when babies are born. The executive order extended the Family and Medical Leave Act by providing twelve weeks of paid, rather than unpaid, leave. Clinton said that "the current law meets just a fraction of the need, and the number one reason families give for not taking advantage of family and medical leave is that they simply can't afford to take time off without a paycheck."[18]

Such a program would have been expensive, and no state put it into practice. Although in 1999 the state unemployment insurance funds were at historically high levels because of a period of low unemployment, all workers' withdrawals from the funds had to be replaced with increased contributions from employers. The program is "experience-rated," meaning that as more unemployed workers draw from the fund, the rate at which employers pay unemployment insurance contributions rises. That gives employers an incentive not to lay off workers. Hence, using unemployment insurance contributions to fund paid maternity leave raises the cost of unemployment insurance to the employer, who would spread it among all workers.

Kimberley K. Hostetler, owner of Human Resources Management Services in Wallingford, Connecticut, testified before the Human Resources Subcommittee of the Ways and Means Committee in the U.S. House of Representatives about the disadvantages of the proposal.[19] In the early 1990s the Connecticut unemployment insurance system was in such financial trouble that the state had to issue a bond to keep the system from defaulting on its obligations. That bond was paid with a special employer assessment, with the extra payments ending in August 2000. Therefore, employers in Connecticut were naturally concerned about imposing any additional burden on state unemployment funds. Hostetler quoted one Connecticut Department of Labor director as saying that "whether paid leave is a good idea or not, state unemployment funds weren't set up to deal with this."[20]

Women as a group should be concerned about mandatory benefits programs for two reasons. First, many of the programs may make mandatory what many firms already voluntarily provide to their employees. Many firms today attract and retain employees, including women, with a compensation package that includes far more than wages; employees receive such benefits and services as health insurance, generous maternity and sick leave policies, and child care. Compensation packages are tailor-made to meet the needs of both employer and employees. Women, as well as men, can and do take advantage of those benefits packages.

Voluntary benefits packages allow businesses flexibility in developing and administering policies, often at relatively low costs. When the government makes certain benefits mandatory, however, the costs of doing business soar because businesses are required to provide the benefits even if employees do not want them and employers cannot afford them. Instead of remaining flexible, compensation packages become standardized—to the detriment of all concerned. Although everyone values flexibility in working conditions and compensation packages, working mothers are the most desirous of flexibility and are the group most harmed by its loss.

If a firm senses an unmet need for backup child care among its workers, perhaps because some of its workers are parents who have made many such requests on company surveys, it might institute the benefit in response to requests. The company would reap the rewards of worker satisfaction, such as greater work effort, fewer quits, and possibly less sick leave taken. That has happened with many companies, including Johnson & Johnson, based in New Brunswick, New Jersey.

In contrast, imagine for a moment that the government required firms to provide backup child care for all workers in case the regular child care provider was unavailable or the child was sick. Some employees with children might use that service, but other parents might prefer to make other arrangements. Childless workers would not use the benefit at all. Firms would have to spend the money for the potential availability of backup child care whether the employees benefited or not, and, if employees did not benefit, the money would be wasted. Many companies could conclude that the cost of child care would be excessive and thus would decide either to move offshore or to locate operations elsewhere. That would reduce employment opportunities for all women.

The second reason for women as a group to be concerned about mandatory benefits is that being a potential recipient of a mandatory benefit can be both a blessing and a curse. It is perhaps a blessing if a woman is actually employed and, as a result of the program, receives benefits at little or no personal cost. Of course, receiving those benefits might result in lower pay increases than would have been the case otherwise, as we discuss in greater detail below. And it could cause some resentment from other workers and from employers.

But being the potential recipient of a mandatory benefit might be a significant disadvantage to those who are not employed but who seek to be employed or to those who are employed and seek another job. Professors Ricardo J. Caballero and Mohamad L. Hammour extensively documented the costs of increased mandatory benefits in Europe, with a case study of France, over the past thirty years. Institutional pressures led to increased mandatory benefits for workers over the period 1968 to 1986. The French government increased unemployment benefits, raised the minimum wage, reduced weekly hours of work, and added a fifth compulsory week of vacation. Caballero and Hammour showed that the increasing cost of labor resulted in a change in firms' methods of production—away from labor and toward more machinery—and, as a result, unemployment rose from 2 percent in 1967 to 12 percent in the mid-1990s.[21]

Caballero and Hammour's work referred to the costs of employing all workers, but the same principles could be applied when a particular group was singled out as having higher labor costs. Costly mandatory benefits that accrue primarily to women make employers cautious about hiring an additional woman who might increase costs to a firm. A firm might consider whether it would be less costly to hire a new female employee with uncertain future costs or to contract out work with a more predictable cost structure. Ironically, mandatory benefits targeted at women reduce employers' willingness to employ women.

That is one of the great paradoxes of many mandatory benefits targeted at women: the programs may benefit some women, but only at great cost to others and to the economy at large.

Is There Any Benefit in a Mandatory Benefit?

All laws and regulations are designed with some benefits in mind. Advocates of a restructured workplace are quick to list desired benefits, as if listing them will make them much more certain. The sponsors of the Americans with Disabilities Act trumpeted access to the workplace for disabled Americans. The sponsors of the Family and Medical Leave Act emphasized the benefits to women in balancing work and family responsibilities. The sponsors of other mandatory benefit programs claimed significant advantages for their schemes as well.

But how much do those programs cost? Unlike Social Security and health insurance, the complete costs of many mandatory benefits programs cannot be gauged by the Congressional Budget Office or any other institution in terms of cash transfers. The cost is often more in terms of opportunities forgone—businesses that were never created, employees who were never hired and trained, investments that were never made, and products that were never developed.

As with preferential programs, everyone pays for mandatory benefits programs, but not everyone benefits from them. The costs are often spread across an entire firm or industry. Consequently, it is not surprising that the benefits are easily visible and advertised, while the costs often remain hidden. To get such programs accepted, the public has to be made to think that the value of those programs is great, sometimes even greater than the value actually is.

For example, no one has engaged in comprehensive or credible studies of the costs of major programs such as the Americans with Disabilities Act and the Family and Medical Leave Act. No government agency investigated the costs of those laws at the time of enactment or subsequently. In addition, no government agency has assessed the costs of any of the countless regulations issued subsequent to the passage of those laws. The failure by government agencies to consider, much less to measure, the costs of regulations is the norm rather than the exception.[22]

In the political calculus of modern-day America, measuring the direct costs and benefits of regulation—to businesses or consumers—is often not so important as projecting the proper image of a caring, compassionate government. The complete absence of any efforts to estimate the costs or benefits of such major government programs as the Americans with Disabilities Act and the Family and Medical Leave Act is telling. But politicians and government officials are quick to appear on television and extol the virtues of government programs as if the human emotions of caring are sufficient to outweigh the government's responsibility to put in place programs that are beneficial without being either wasteful or harmful.

Politicians continue to promote new benefits programs. In the 105th Congress, fifty-six bills providing for family leave, health, and child care benefits were introduced.[23] All included a list of purported benefits; none described possible costs.

Mandating Benefits: A Game the Whole World Can Play

Mandatory benefits are not a uniquely American phenomenon. Indeed, the United States appears to lag behind many other countries in a variety of areas of mandatory benefits, such as prenatal and postnatal maternity leave. Furthermore, other countries provide more government-subsidized benefits, such as child care and health care, than does the United States.

Maternity Benefits. In the United States specific maternity-related benefits are not mandated by government; businesses provide them voluntarily. But because Title VII of the Civil Rights Act prohibits discrimination on the basis of pregnancy, if an employer pays for workers' health care bills, then he must also pay for pregnancy-related health expenses. Similarly, if the employer allows either paid or unpaid leave for health reasons, he must also allow maternity leave for recovering from childbearing.

In addition to the Title VII provisions, businesses can vary their maternity benefits to meet the needs of the particular business and its employees. Some members of Congress, however, would like to make those maternity benefits mandatory. In the 105th Congress alone, eighteen bills were introduced to provide maternity benefits.[24]

The benefits of maternity-leave programs are used almost exclusively by women in their childbearing years. While paternity leave is also mandatory in some countries,[25] it is far less common and is used less frequently and for shorter durations than maternity leave. Many American employers voluntarily provide maternity leave. They find that such a benefit generates goodwill among employees and reduces the likelihood that valuable employees will leave their jobs after giving birth. Other firms, however, either cannot afford to provide maternity leave or find that the costs do not justify the benefits. Mandating that such firms provide maternity leave may benefit some women employees, but it is likely to also raise all labor costs and thus reduce employment opportunities for all men and women.

As with many other forms of mandatory benefits, mandatory maternity leave would weaken the flexibility of the compensation package that employers could offer workers. Firms could also decide that it is preferable to contract work out to independent firms, rather than to hire new employees, so that the company would not have to pay benefits. The employment of temporary workers rose from less than half a million in 1980 to more than 3 million in 1999.[26] The rising cost of benefits for regular employees is surely one reason for the trend.

Childbirth is not a one-time event that leaves a new parent with just as much time to spend at work as before childbirth. Raising children is a time-consuming responsibility, one for which flexibility—rather than government mandates—in the workplace provides the greatest opportunities. Yet the trend is inexorably toward more, not fewer, mandates.

A recent publication of the International Labor Organization lists the mandatory maternity benefits in more than 120 countries.[27] The duration of mandatory maternity leave, the extent of mandatory compensation during leave, the protection of job status during maternity leave, and other forms of regulation vary by country. The United States has none of those specific maternity-related mandated programs. The International Labor Organization sees those mandated programs as unambiguously good and vital to the progress of women in the workplace. Of course, the study mentions nothing about the possible costs.

Most European countries require employers to grant substantial amounts of maternity leave, and the mother's full salary is usually paid by the social security system from general revenues. Such countries include Hungary (twenty-four weeks leave); Norway and Denmark (eighteen weeks); France (sixteen to twenty-six weeks); and Spain (sixteen weeks). Italian mothers receive twenty-two weeks of maternity leave with 80 percent of their salary paid from the social security program. In Switzerland the employer must pay 100 percent of a mother's salary for eight weeks. Similarly, in Germany social security pays for benefits up to a wage ceiling, and the employer pays the rest, up to 100 percent of benefits, for fourteen weeks.

The social security system also funds maternity leave benefits in many Latin American countries. It is best to be a mother in Cuba or Venezuela, where maternity leave lasts for eighteen weeks at full salary. The Dominican Republic, Ecuador, Guatemala, and Trinidad Tobago provide mothers with twelve weeks of leave, with the costs divided between the employer and the social security program. Despite those benefits, the United States receives many immigration applications from those countries.

In Asia employers themselves are more commonly required to pay for maternity leave. China, India, Sri Lanka, and Pakistan all provide twelve weeks of employer-paid maternity leave. Mandatory time off without mandatory pay is the case in Australia (one year), New Zealand (fourteen weeks), and Papua New Guinea (six weeks). In Japan social security pays 60 percent of salary the women receive for fourteen weeks of maternity leave.

When the International Labor Organization's study came out, much was made of the comparison between Haiti and the United States. In Haiti, employers are required to provide twelve weeks of maternity leave, with six weeks paid at full salary by the firm. Newspapers marveled at how Haiti, one of the poorest countries in the world, could supposedly treat women so much better than the United States, one of the richest.[28] Yet one reason that Haiti is in such poor economic condition is that it swamps its citizens with regulations. Mandatory maternity benefits are just one example. After all, American women are not emigrating to Haiti to take advantage of the country's generous maternity benefits. To the contrary, women from Haiti and other countries are emigrating to the United States, where there are no federal maternity benefits. One of the most reliable indicators of the desirability of a country's economic system is how many people want to leave that country and how many want to enter. Despite its purportedly low level of mandatory benefits, the United States is the magnet for workers from around the world.

Child Care. Working mothers face two primary choices: leave the children at home with a relative or a hired child care provider or send the children to a commercial child care center outside the home. Each alternative has advantages and disadvantages that parents weigh in choosing between the two. In general, the parents (with some support from the government), rather than the employers, bear the burden of the cost of child care.[29]

But a third option, employer-sponsored child care centers, sometimes free or at reduced prices, is developing rapidly in larger firms. Unlike the other two options, businesses frequently cover a large share of the costs. As long as those centers are not required by the government, employers and employees view them as part of a flexible and negotiable compensation package. Employers use the centers and other services as part of a package to attract certain employees. With unemployment rates at historic lows, employers have to do everything that they can to attract and keep qualified workers.

For example, Eli Lilly not only has an on-site child care program, but also backup care resources to give parents other child care options. The firm has a summer science camp and provides activities for children on school vacation days.[30] Merck and MBNA America are other companies providing on-site day care.

Companies' decisions to provide child benefits to attract and keep workers are far different from some politicians' calls for mandatory employer-sponsored child care centers.[31] Such mandatory programs would discourage employment generally, reduce flexibility in the compensation package, and give employers a rational economic incentive to discriminate against young female employees.

In general, foreign countries provide far more government-subsidized child care than does the United States. Moreover, employers in other countries are required to provide more maternity leave than their American counterparts. Many Western countries, such as Sweden, Finland, France, the Netherlands, and Denmark, provide day care for children under three years of age. Children's participation in day care centers in those countries is not necessarily linked to parents' work status, because it is considered that preschool care provides benefits of socialization and child development. Hence, children attend child care programs even if their mothers do not work. Parents pay only 30 percent of operating costs of day care centers in Denmark, 18 percent in Italy, and 15 percent in France.[32]

Regulatory Consequences. Modern feminists cite the practices of other countries and assert that similar subsidized child care and mandatory maternity benefits in the United States would make it easier for women to participate in the work force.[33] Transferring the burden of child care responsibilities to the government leaves women free to concentrate on their careers, feminists argue, and makes men and women more equal in the workplace.

The experience of Western Europe does not bear out feminists' claims, however. If mandatory maternity leave and subsidized child care helped women enter and progress in the labor force, one would expect a higher percentage of European women to work for pay. But the reverse is true: the percentage of American women who work in the paid labor force is greater than in other major industrialized countries that boast mandatory maternity benefits and subsidized child care. In 1998 60 percent of American women were in the labor force, compared with fewer than half of women in Japan (49 percent), France (48 percent), Germany (49 percent), and Italy (35 percent). The United Kingdom, Sweden, and the Netherlands also had a lower percentage of working women than the United States.[34]

In addition to American women's having a higher percentage who work than women in countries with more mandatory benefits, American women face one of the lowest unemployment rates of any industrialized country. In 1998 the unemployment rate for American women was 4.6 percent. In contrast, unemployment rates for some European countries were two or three times as high. The unemployment rate for women in France was 13.9 percent; in Germany it was 10.3 percent; in Italy it was 16.3 percent; and in Sweden it was 8 percent.[35] Those numbers reinforce the argument that high labor costs discourage firms from hiring and make it harder for workers to find jobs.

Unemployment rates vary for all kinds of reasons that are internal to a country, and some may argue that it is unfair to compare unemployment rates for women in the United States with rates in other countries, because the United States might have a stronger labor market for reasons that have little to do with mandated benefits. But it is particularly noteworthy that the 1998 unemployment rate for American women (4.6 percent) was close to the rate for American men (4.4 percent), and in the United States the male and female unemployment rates have not differed by more than half a percentage point since 1980.[36] Hence, American employers are not rejecting women workers as potential hires.

But the same is not true in many other European countries. In 1998, when women in France faced an unemployment rate of 13.9 percent, the men faced a rate of 9.9 percent. When German women saw a 10.3 percent unemployment rate, the rate for men was 8.7. And at the time that Italian women, the ones with twenty-two weeks of maternity leave at 80 percent pay, faced a 16.3 percent unemployment rate, the rate for Italian men was 8.9 percent. Since 1986 Italian women have suffered double-digit unemployment rates, whereas the rate for men has been a single digit.[37] Although Sweden and the United Kingdom have higher male than female unemployment rates, in general women in Europe have higher unemployment rates than men. One reason for that is the higher cost of employing them.

Furthermore, the U.S. economy produces far more and has higher economic growth than other industrialized countries. The most common measure of economic product, gross domestic product per person, adjusted to reflect the purchasing power of the nation's currency, shows that no country exceeds the U.S. measure.

In 1998, with the United States at 100 on an index of levels of GDP per person, France and Italy came in at 69, Germany at 70, the Netherlands at 74, Sweden at 65, and the United Kingdom at 66.[38] The United States also had higher levels of real GDP growth per person than all those countries over the long-term period 1980 through 1998.[39]

Why Do Mandatory Benefits Have Optional Results?

Although economic rationality would lead to a contraction of mandated benefits, political forces are headed more toward expanding programs. That expansion is likely to harm women. Requiring firms to provide benefits to workers raises their costs of doing business. Someone has to pay those costs. In the short run, the increased costs could be paid for by some combination of the following: decreased profits, increased prices, delayed investments, reduced quality of product or service, minor adjustments downward in the number of hours worked, or other small adjustments in how the firm does business.

But later on, when the time comes to make major long-term decisions such as whether to hire more workers, to give raises, or to open a new facility, the firm's decisions will be different from what they would have been without the mandatory benefits. Rather than hire more workers, the firm could contract out extra work or invest in another kind of technology that does not require so much labor. Or the firm might hold down wage increases so that workers implicitly paid for the costs of the extra benefits.

Regulations raise the costs of doing business and cause inefficiency and misallocation of resources. In a world with cut-throat competition, it is unrealistic to assume that businesses can simply absorb all regulatory costs from their bottom line; investment capital will migrate to those firms that offer better profits. In general, regulatory costs are either passed on to consumers in the form of higher prices, lower quality of product and services, or both. Those costs also result in fewer jobs and lower wages. Sometimes, in the case of a mandatory program that benefits some workers, firms may generally hire fewer workers with smaller compensation packages. Firms may be particularly wary of hiring those workers who are likely to incur the greatest costs for the firm under the new mandatory benefits program.

Another rational solution for firms facing mandatory benefits is to set up plants in countries such as Mexico, Thailand, or China, where the cost of labor is far lower than in the United States. Although some of those countries may have some mandatory benefits, the prevailing wage is lower than in the United States, so the total wage bill is lower. George Daniels, president of Daniels Manufacturing, the firm described above that is plagued with frequent short employee absences, said, "[Y]ou wonder if you shouldn't become Nike and move overseas." One of his rivals moved production across the border to Mexico, he told us, and he doubts that the firm will ever come back to the United States: once a company transfers production offshore, it almost never returns that production to the United States, even if conditions here were to improve.[40]

For women in the workplace, the federal government is trying to do the impossible. Employers are told to give hiring preferences to women, to give promotion preferences to women, to give labor force reduction preferences to women, to pay women in a job classification the same as men, to provide preferential fringe benefits to women only, and to construct compensation structures that make it difficult to reward additional hours worked and intensive efforts and that do not punish absenteeism. Those mandates make women less desirable employees and raise the cost of employing everyone, including women. In the end, despite the best of intentions, such efforts hurt women most.

8

Playing Hardball: Title IX and Women's Athletics

Until now, we have analyzed how women's choices have played out in the arenas of education and the workplace. We have also examined the dilemma those choices present to feminists, who continue to claim that women's success is ephemeral and that women's rights are under siege. But the feminist campaign for equal numbers and special preferences for women has not been confined to academic and professional pursuits. It has also spread to college athletics. In this chapter we provide a glimpse of feminists' forays into the nation's locker rooms and the feminists' misguided campaign for equal percentages of men and women in college sports.

Introduction

In 1999 the U.S. women's soccer team won the women's World Cup championship in a final match against China. Filling the stands at the Rose Bowl in Pasadena, California, and setting a new attendance record for a women's sporting event were over 90,000 cheering fans, many of whom had closely followed the team's progress throughout the summer tournament. Millions more watched the final match on television. When the game, which had been tied at 0–0, ended with an impressive penalty kick by defender Brandi Chastain, cameras captured the entire stadium erupting in mass celebration. For weeks, newspapers and magazines carried photographs of the victorious team and waxed enthusiastic about the dawning of a new era in women's sports.[1]

The flood of publicity that accompanied the women's World Cup tournament was unprecedented. The media had touched on a definite shift in the public's mood about women's sports. That shift reflected an enthusiasm for female athletes that has spread not only to soccer but to women's tennis, women's basketball, women's track and field, and even women's professional boxing. Players on the U.S. women's soccer team became overnight role models for an entire generation of American girls.[2] Those new female fans, many of whom were themselves already active players in local soccer leagues, took it for granted that girls play soccer. That fact alone is testament to the broadening of our social expectations for girls and surely worth celebrating.

In the wake of the tournament, however, representatives from feminist organizations and the Clinton administration pointed to the U.S. team's victory as evidence of something else: victory in their own campaign to enforce Title IX of the Educational Amendments of 1972. "This victory, like many gains for women, comes from government action—Title IX," commentator Garry Wills said. Donna de Varona, head of the organizing committee for the women's World Cup, claimed that the team's victory "just wouldn't have happened without Title IX."[3]

But the victory to which those groups were laying claim was neither as clear-cut nor as inspiring as the one earned by the women's soccer team. Rather, it was an example of how feminist special interest groups and government bureaucrats have undermined the purpose of a well-intentioned piece of antidiscrimination legislation—and have done so through a process of administrative rulemaking and enforcement that has remained virtually invisible to the general public.

In the past decade those groups have succeeded in realizing their vision of equality in government and in the courts. Since that success has often been packaged as an inspiring story of women's athletic gains, it is difficult to criticize. But although the campaign has yielded new opportunities for girls in sports, we should not confuse opportunity with gender politics. While the intent of Title IX was the former, it is the latter that has triumphed. Expanded athletic opportunities for girls come at a hefty price. That price is the whole-sale elimination of many men's sports teams and the evisceration of the principle of equal opportunity. Feminists have extended their misguided campaign for absolute statistical parity to the soccer fields and basketball courts of our nation's schools, with predictably pernicious results.

Legislative Beginnings, Legislative Intent, and Bureaucratic Reinvention

The tale of Title IX and women's sports began in the early 1970s, a time when feminist activists, building on the achievements of the civil rights movement, were continuing to exert pressure on Congress to enact strong antidiscrimination legislation for women. After passage of the Equal Pay Act of 1963 and Title VII of the Civil Rights Act of 1964, many feminists set their sights on education. Female legislators in Congress responded with speeches, such as Democratic Representative Martha Griffiths's statement on discrim-ination against women in higher education in March of 1970, and hearings, notably Democratic Representative Edith Green's hearings on higher education in the summer of 1970, that challenged Congress to enact legislation guaranteeing women's equal rights to an education.[4]

As we note in chapter 3, those activities culminated in the pas-sage of Title IX of the Educational Amendments of 1972, which President Nixon signed into law. Modeled after Title VI of the Civil Rights Act of 1964, Title IX states, "No person in the United States shall, on the basis of sex, be excluded from participation in, be denied the benefits of, or be subjected to discrimination under any program or activity receiving Federal financial assistance."[5]

The phrase "any program or activity" included athletic programs on the campuses of any college or university that received federal funds, which nearly all do, in the form of grants, access to federally subsidized student loans, and other programs. Title IX's purpose seemed straightforward: ensuring that the law protected women's rights to pursue their educational interests, including their interest in sports.[6]

Before Congress passed a final version of Title IX, some policy-makers raised concerns about how the legislation might be interpreted. During hearings in the early 1970s, several observers presciently suggested that Title IX might be used to impose quotas on educational institutions. The reaction of legislators was unequivocal. Senator Birch Bayh of Indiana stated that gender quotas "were exactly what this amendment intends to prohibit. . . . The amendment does not contain, nor does the Senator from Indiana feel it should contain, a quota which says there has to be a 50–50 ratio to meet the test." In later debate, Senator Bayh repeated that sentiment. He said, "Let me emphasize again that we are not requiring quotas."[7]

Despite those assurances, Congress took the extra step of attaching an amendment, proposed by Representative Albert Quie, to the Title IX legislation specifying clearly that the act did not require quotas. The amendment noted:

> Nothing contained in subsection (a) shall be interpreted to require any educational institution to grant preferential or disparate treatment to the members of one sex on account of an imbalance which may exist with respect to the total number or percentage of persons of that sex participating in or receiving the benefits of any federally funded program or activity.[8]

By 1971, then, legislators in Congress felt that they had firmly settled the question of quotas and Title IX.

Congress named the Department of Health, Education, and Welfare (which later split to become the Department of Education and the Department of Health and Human Services) and its Office for Civil Rights as the agency responsible for drafting the initial regulations for Title IX. Unfortunately, the Office for Civil Rights was seriously lacking in technical expertise for interpreting and enforcing antidiscrimination laws in general and for college athletics in particular.[9] The resulting regulations, signed by President Gerald Ford in 1975, required that schools designate a Title IX compliance officer and grievance procedure but provided few details for school administrators on how fully to gauge their compliance with the law.

By the late 1970s, with little action taken by the Office for Civil Rights and considerable confusion remaining about the scope of the law, feminist groups began to organize to pursue their own Title IX agenda. With the creation in 1974 of the Women's Sports Foundation and a task force called the National Coalition for Women and Girls in Education—comprising the National Organization for Women, the Women's Equity Action League, and numerous other feminist groups—feminists finally had a strong lobbying presence in Washington on that issue.[10] They concentrated their efforts on influencing the Office for Civil Rights to draft an official policy interpretation for Title IX and to blunt the efforts of lobbyists for the National Collegiate Athletic Association, which opposed the feminists' agenda for college athletics.

The feminists were remarkably successful in that endeavor, as the resulting 1979 policy interpretation released by the Office for Civil Rights revealed.[11] As political scientists Joyce Gelb and Marian Palley documented, the feminists succeeded in thwarting the NCAA's attempts to exempt revenue-producing sports such as football and convinced the secretary of the Department of Education, Patricia Harris, to release the department's policy interpretation without submitting it to Congress for approval.[12] That measure meant that, as with many regulations, the substance of the policy interpretation, much of which was questionable in light of Congress's commitment to avoid quotas, was never subject to the oversight of the country's elected representatives. Once quotas were implemented, no one in Congress wanted to revisit the law or change it.

The Birth of the Proportionality Police

In its policy interpretation, the Office for Civil Rights developed a three-pronged test to determine whether colleges and universities were complying with Title IX in their athletic programs—whether they were, in other words, "fully and effectively accommodating" the interests of both sexes. In theory a school needed to meet the requirements of only one of the three prongs. The first prong was that the ratio of male and female athletes closely paralleled the ratio of male and female students in the student population. The second prong was that the college or university could demonstrate a history of expanding opportunities for athletes of the "underrepresented sex." The third prong was that, if the second prong could not be met, a college or university could show that the interests of the underrepresented sex had been "fully and effectively accommodated by the present program."[13]

The first prong of the three-part test raises concern, for it bears the mark of the prevalent but misguided feminist notion that equality exists only when the sexes have achieved statistical parity. As we have seen with feminist claims about women in education and in the working world, statistical proportionality is an illogical and destructive measure of equality. It denies the reality of individual choice. If the principle enshrined in the first prong of the Office for Civil Rights' proportionality test were taken to its logical conclusion in employment law, for example, women could lodge discrimination charges whenever fewer than 46 percent of their coworkers were female, since women represent 46 percent of the work force.[14] In theory, schools could avoid that restrictive mandate by meeting either of the other two prongs of the test.

With regard to athletics, the Office for Civil Rights' enforcement of Title IX effectively languished between its issuing of the policy interpretation in 1979 through the 1990s. The office did not produce its *Athletics Investigator's Manual*,[15] which outlines the office's procedures for addressing complaints, until April 1990, for example, and in the 1980s, it undertook only three formal Title IX reviews of college athletic programs.[16]

Soon, the courts were weighing in on Title IX. In 1984, in a case brought by a small Pennsylvania liberal arts college, *Grove City College v. Bell,* the U.S. Supreme Court ruled that only the program that actually received federal funds—and not the entire educational institution—need comply with Title IX. The six-to-three opinion effectively prevented the Office for Civil Rights from investigating a college athletic department for Title IX violations unless that department was the direct recipient of federal funds, which most were not.[17]

That was a clear setback for the feminists, and they quickly mobilized and began lobbying Congress for omnibus legislation that would effectively reverse the Supreme Court's decision in *Grove City.* They succeeded when Congress—overriding President Ronald Reagan's veto—passed the Civil Rights Restoration Act of 1987. The act stated that *all* programs at an educational institution were subject to Title IX compliance if *any* program received federal funds.[18] Title IX lawsuits and investigations by the Office for Civil Rights grew significantly after passage of the act, and feminist organizations, emboldened by their success in overturning *Grove City*, stepped up their campaign to make proportionality the defining test of Title IX compliance. Their favored weapon became the Title IX lawsuit.[19]

Proportionality and Women's Interest in Sports

Supporters of statistical proportionality in college sports have argued since the inception of Title IX that women's demonstrated interest in sports is not a true measure of equality because it fails to consider female athletic *potential*. Because society discriminated against women athletes for so long, the argument goes, generations of girls internalized the message that they did not belong on the soccer field or basketball court. The fact that women currently are not turning out for sports at rates as high as men is a legacy of that denial of opportunity. "Because of the historical discouragement of female participation," NCAA Gender Equity Task Force Cochair Phyllis L. Howlett noted, "an accurate measurement of interest in athletics among women can be difficult to achieve."[20]

That line of reasoning has truth. Culturally, the female athlete has been a role model only in recent years. Displays of female athleticism were rarely celebrated. Doubtless, many girls never ventured to challenge social norms that saw men, but not women, as athletes and lost out on athletic opportunities in the process. A similar set of cultural assumptions governed the labor market for generations. But once women have achieved formal equality of opportunity, as they did with the passage of Title IX, the question is whether the government's role is to enforce antidiscrimination legislation or to mandate a certain level of interest in athletics to achieve an equality of outcome. The intent of the legislation was clearly the former; feminists want the latter. What do the data tell us?

After all, although social norms about female athletes have changed significantly in a relatively short period of time, current facts about women's and men's interest in sports are critical if we are to reach reasonable conclusions about the effectiveness of Title IX. Such data are necessary despite the fact that many feminists are unwilling to admit the possibility that men and women might fundamentally differ when it comes to interest in athletics.

Numerous contemporary studies demonstrate that, more than twenty years after Title IX, on average, men and women still display different degrees of enthusiasm for sports. A recent study of Division I-A universities, for example, found that 70 percent of men, but only 45 percent of women, participated in intramural sports. Since intramurals are voluntary and open to all students, those sports are an excellent gauge of student preferences.[21] An analysis of responses to the student survey administered as part of the Scholastic Aptitude Test suggests a similar difference in preference for sports: nearly twice as many men as women wanted to play sports at the college level.[22]

As the SAT data suggested, an observed difference in interest in athletics begins earlier than college. According to the National Federation of State High School Associations' "High School Athletics Participation Survey," in 1992 girls made up 36 percent of sports participants at the high school level, compared with 64 percent for boys.[23] To proportionality wardens, that suggests discrimination at work. But the organization also conducted another survey: the gender breakdown of nonathletic interscholastic activities during the 1992–1993 school year. Girls made up 69 percent of participants in activities such as band, choir, debate teams, and drama clubs and dominated in journalism, speech, yearbook, student government, and service clubs. Boys dominated only in sports.[24] That is women's choice in action. Given a range of options, girls have gravitated toward some extracurricular activities over others, just as they have done, as chapter 3 shows, with respect to choices of academic pursuits.

Figures for Little League activity also confirm that observation, particularly since youth leagues are generally a matter of supply and demand; teams form depending on the number of interested players who register. Nationally, 2.4 million children, almost all of them boys, participated in Little League baseball in 1999. Little League softball, which has the same structure as Little League baseball, had only 384,000 players, almost all girls.[25]

The question of male and female interest in athletics points us to another important, but frequently overlooked, issue in the Title IX debate: comparable rates of injury to male and female sports enthusiasts. Since that point touches on the reality of biological differences between the sexes, it is a thoroughly taboo topic in today's feminist politics. But the facts are overwhelming: women are *five times more likely* to suffer serious knee injuries, particularly injuries to the anterior cruciate ligament, than men, for example. Every year, in high schools and colleges across the country, nearly 30,000 female soccer, volleyball, and basketball players sustain such injuries. A *Sports Illustrated* reporter found that those injuries were "virtually epidemic" in women's college basketball.[26]

That can be explained through simple biology. Sports physicians note that because women have wider hips, their bodies on average tend to slope in at the knee. Women also have looser joints and narrower femoral notches, through which the anterior cruciate ligament runs. Those factors can combine to spell greater risk of knee injuries for female athletes.[27] While such evidence should not be, and has not been, used to prevent women from playing sports, proportionality supporters would do well to consider physical differences between men and women when they contemplate the demonstrated difference in interest between men and women in athletics.

Testing Title IX—*Cohen v. Brown University* and Its Effects

In the spring of 1991, Brown University's athletic program, facing a financial crisis, downgraded four of its thirty-one teams from varsity to club status. That effectively eliminated university funding for men's golf and men's water polo and for women's gymnastics and women's volleyball. At the time, 63 percent of Brown's athletes were male, and 37 percent were female; Brown's student body was 52 percent male and 48 percent female. Soon thereafter, the female gymnasts and volleyball players whose teams had been downgraded filed a class-action lawsuit against the university in federal court; the suit alleged Title IX violations and sought the reinstatement of the two women's sports teams to varsity status. The U.S. District Court for Rhode Island granted the plaintiffs a preliminary injunction reinstating the teams, and Brown University appealed. The case, *Cohen v. Brown University,* reached the U.S. Court of Appeals for the First Circuit in 1993.[28]

In the *Cohen* case, the First Circuit "truly navigated uncharted waters," as one legal commentator aptly remarked. As noted above, in the twenty-one years that had elapsed since Title IX's passage, there had been little legal action—and nearly no case law—on Title IX and collegiate athletics. When cases did arise, such as *Haffer v. Temple University,* the litigants often resolved them in out-of-court settlements before the merits of the claims were tested in court, or, as in *Cook v. Colgate University,* the claims filed by plaintiffs were individual rather than class claims and thus became moot upon the graduation of the litigants.[29] With the *Cohen* case, however, the Title IX debate was poised to enter a new phase.

In *Cohen* the First Circuit ruled two to one for the plaintiff class. The court agreed with the contention that Brown University's decision to downgrade two women's sports teams was a violation of Title IX. In reaching that opinion, however, the court relied on several questionable assumptions—assumptions with significant repercussions for the debate over Title IX.

In rendering its decision, the court relied heavily on the Office for Civil Rights' 1979 policy interpretation in general and the proportionality test in particular. The court designated the proportionality test—the first prong of the office's three-pronged test—the "safe harbor" for schools' Title IX compliance. Maintaining a statistical balance of student athletes equal to the statistical balance of the sexes on the school campus at large was the best way for a college or university to avoid a lawsuit or an investigation by the Office for Civil Rights.[30] In practice, however, in a student body where boys nearly always express higher levels of interest in sports than girls and where male sports such as football have larger team rosters than women's sports such as volleyball, the proportionality test would become a brutal numbers game that colleges could not win without instituting quotas.

The court obliquely recognized that possibility in its *Cohen* decision when it noted that schools could achieve proportionality by "downsizing" men's teams, a process of "addition by subtraction." Though presented in a bureaucratically neutral way, the First Circuit effectively put schools on notice that to achieve that much desired safe harbor, they could eliminate men's sports teams with impunity.[31]

In its defense, Brown University argued that although it had not reached absolute proportionality in athletics, it had met the requirements of the other two prongs of the Office for Civil Rights' policy interpretation: showing a history of expanding opportunities for and "fully and effectively accommodating" the needs of the underrepresented sex. The First Circuit rejected both claims.[32]

As for the final prong, the court said that the existence of the *Cohen* lawsuit was proof that the university had failed to satisfy the Office for Civil Rights' test. Specifically, the complaints of disgruntled female athletes were evidence of Brown's failure to accommodate women's athletic interests fully and effectively. Unfortunately, the First Circuit's reasoning in that regard left unanswered a salient question: How can a school know whether it is accommodating its students without a lawsuit or complaint being filed? How can a school measure the athletic interests and abilities of its students? The First Circuit simply assumed that male and female students at Brown shared the same enthusiasm for collegiate athletic participation without establishing a procedure by which a school could prove or disprove that assumption.

In the wake of the First Circuit's *Cohen v. Brown* holding, supporters of the proportionality standard in college athletics correctly claimed a major victory. The casualties in the battle occurred in men's sports. By the time Brown University exhausted its appeals—in 1997 the U.S. Supreme Court refused to hear the case—it had been implementing the First Circuit's directives for four years. Given the budgetary constraints that had led to team downsizing—and the lawsuit—in the first place, Brown chose to pursue the path promoted by the First Circuit, that of statistical proportionality.

The results? In 1997 the seventeen women's sports teams at Brown all had room on their rosters for more athletes, while the sixteen men's teams all had long waiting lists. While coaches for women's teams scoured the student body for athletes, coaches for the men's teams had been turning away male athletes for four years; male students at Brown faced stiff competition merely to gain a position on a sports team.[33] Testifying before Congress in 1995, Vartan Gregorian, then president of Brown University, remarked on the absurdity and patent unfairness of the situation. Reaffirming his strong support for the antidiscrimination principle behind Title IX, he nevertheless noted that because of the misguided proportionality standard, Title IX enforcement had become "an assault on common sense."[34]

Title IX after *Brown*—The Elimination of Men's Sports Teams

The effect of the *Cohen v. Brown University* decision cannot be underestimated. After the Supreme Court's refusal in 1997 to consider Brown's appeal, the First Circuit's decision, with its strong endorsement of the proportionality test, became the compliance road map for schools across the country and for future lawsuits. The elevation of the proportionality standard, combined with the First Circuit's refusal to outline means for assessing student interest in athletics, reappeared in subsequent Title IX cases such as *Roberts v. Colorado State University* and *Favia v. Indiana University of Pennsylvania,* with similar results for male athletes at those schools.[35]

More alarmingly, athletic departments across the country began enforcing proportionality to protect themselves from lawsuits. The path of least resistance for most schools was the one traveled by Brown—downsizing or eliminating men's teams. The proportionality standard, that "safe harbor" endorsed by the First Circuit, has led to the widespread elimination of opportunities for male athletes.

In less than a decade, more than 80,000 slots for male athletes on intercollegiate teams have disappeared from American college campuses. Yet because those cutbacks have occurred over the course of several years at colleges and universities scattered across the country, the general public is relatively unaware of the trend. Between 1993 and 1999, as table 8-1 reveals, colleges and universities have terminated fifty-three men's golf teams, thirty-nine men's indoor

Table 8-1   Number of Men's Sports Teams Eliminated from 1993 through 1999

Sport	Division I	Division II	Division III
Baseball	9	2	5
Fencing	6	—	3
Football	4	7	2
Golf	6	19	28
Gymnastics	14	—	2
Ice Hockey	3	—	1
Lacrosse	5	2	3
Rifle	6	3	2
Skiing	—	1	2
Soccer	6	4	1
Swimming	13	3	7
Tennis	13	15	11
Track: Cross-Country	7	10	8
Track: Indoor	16	14	9
Track: Outdoor	8	12	7
Volleyball	2	2	3
Water Polo	3	1	1
Wrestling	18	7	18

Source: Kimberly Schuld, Independent Women's Forum, Arlington, Virginia.

track teams, forty-three wrestling teams, and sixteen baseball teams, among others. The men's swimming team at the University of California at Los Angeles, known for producing some of the country's finest Olympic athletes, is gone.[36]

In 1998 Providence College announced that it was dropping men's baseball, swimming, and golf. And in the spring of 1999, the board of trustees of Miami University in Ohio voted to eliminate men's tennis, soccer, and wrestling to meet Title IX's strict gender equity requirements.[37] The most recent men's teams to die by the Title IX proportionality sword were the men's crew, swimming, and diving teams at the University of Miami in Florida. Again, a training ground for future Olympics athletes is now closed; the Miami diving team had produced fifteen Olympic divers in its history, including four-time gold medalist Greg Louganis.[38]

Ironically, the sweeping reduction of male teams is not occurring to provide new opportunities for women athletes or to reallocate resources—most of the men cut are nonscholarship reserve players.[39] Colleges are making those cuts simply to make the numbers look appealing so that they can meet the proportionality requirement. Nationwide, for every four male athletes eliminated, only one female is added to an athletic roster.[40]

That was strikingly clear in the case of Princeton University. Forced to eliminate its men's wrestling program to comply with Title IX, Princeton administrators should have been overjoyed to hear that an alumni group organized and pledged to raise the more than $2 million necessary to restart the team. Not so. Because of the strict proportionality standard enforced by the Office for Civil Rights, Princeton administrators would have had to create new positions for female athletes to retain the athletic program's gender quota. They were not able to do so and thus could not accept the private money. Men's wrestling remains a memory at Princeton.[41]

A few male athletes have challenged the elimination of their sports. They have alleged violation of *their* Title IX protections, but they have met with little success. In 1994 in *Kelley v. Board of Trustees of the University of Illinois,* members of the men's swimming team, which had been eliminated because of Title IX compliance requirements and budget cuts, sued the school. Despite the fact that Title IX is gender-neutral, the court ruled that so long as the University of Illinois's athletic department was not proportional to the gender breakdown of the student population, only women could don the Title IX mantle. Individual male athletes at Illinois were sacrificed for the principle of proportionality.[42]

Current Enforcement of Title IX

While the publicity attending the First Circuit's endorsement of proportionality in *Cohen* in 1993 encouraged many schools to begin eliminating slots for male athletes, several universities have had to face the proportionality requirement after becoming targets of investigations by the Office for Civil Rights. A student or even a feminist advocacy group can file a complaint alleging Title IX violations at an institution; the office then launches an investigation.[43] The office, charged with enforcing Title IX, has used its regulatory and investigative powers to impose the proportionality standard— but with little accountability for its actions. The Office for Civil Rights' bureaucratic history does not inspire confidence in its ability to enforce the law fairly. As far back as 1987, the House

Committee on Government Operations convened hearings and issued a report citing fraud in the department, including allegations of backdating documents, and expressed concern about the office's sole use of statistical quotas and numerical goals in enforcing federal regulations.[44]

In its efforts to enforce Title IX, the Office for Civil Rights has employed questionable methods and has repeatedly revealed its incompetence as an investigative agency. In 1992, for example, the office began investigating Johns Hopkins University for Title IX violations. The school quickly found itself mired in a costly and lengthy investigation that at many points revealed the investigators' misunderstanding of the law and a fundamental ignorance of college athletics. During the investigation, the Office for Civil Rights investigators made three separate visits to the Johns Hopkins University campus. Coaches, administrators, and students had to respond to lengthy and often redundant questioning. Even worse, despite three written requests, the Office for Civil Rights refused to provide the university's Office of the General Counsel with a copy of the initial Title IX complaint. University officials ultimately managed to obtain the document under Freedom of Information Act guidelines.[45] Finally, the investigation clearly violated the guidelines set forth in the Office for Civil Rights' own *Title IX Athletics Investigator's Manual*. Despite a prohibition on such activity on page 29 of the manual, for example, investigators spent four and a half hours at Johns Hopkins counting jockstraps, sports bras, T-shirts, and socks in the men's and women's athletic departments to look for evidence of inequality.[46]

To satisfy the Office for Civil Rights, Johns Hopkins elevated women's lacrosse from a Division 3 to a Division 1 sport, which required approval of the NCAA. The university was then able to offer the same number of lacrosse scholarships to women as it did to men, even though men represented 60 percent of the student body. That satisfied the Office for Civil Rights, which continues to monitor the school's athletic program.[47]

But, as the investigation of Johns Hopkins suggests, the Office for Civil Rights has a questionable grasp of college athletics. Agents of a federal office charged with investigating college sports should at least be familiar with the fundamentals of the area they oversee. Proper enforcement of Title IX in college athletics requires regulators who, at the very least, understand that men's and women's athletic teams often require slightly different equipment, such as different size basketballs, or facilities.

Investigative incompetence such as that demonstrated by the Office for Civil Rights at Johns Hopkins also reveals the high cost of Title IX compliance. Schools must expend considerable time and resources complying with the agency's requests, and taxpayers foot the bills for those shoddy investigations. One questions whether such costs are worthwhile, particularly given the proportionality standard that the Office for Civil Rights is pursuing.[48]

Feminist Organizations and Title IX

While the courts and the Office for Civil Rights continue their enforcement of the proportionality principle, feminist groups have made their contribution in the form of overheated rhetoric, consent agreements, and lawsuits. In 1997 the National Coalition for Women and Girls in Education, that amalgam of early Title IX proportionality proponents, released a "report card" on girls in education that gave the country a C in athletics. "Females," the coalition claimed, "still have substantially fewer opportunities and incentives to participate in sports." Their solution? "The U.S. Department of Education's Office for Civil Rights should step up its enforcement in this area."[49]

Other groups such as the Women's Sports Foundation, the National Organization for Women, and the Feminist Majority Foundation have echoed those calls. In its publications the Feminist Majority has warned unsuspecting female students of the "pervasive discrimination against women and girls in sports." Like other feminist groups, the Feminist Majority has viewed the proportionality standard as the only viable means for Title IX compliance. "If you can prove that participation is not proportional . . . and/or that the funding is not proportional," they wrote in their *Strategies for Change* pamphlet, "your school is in violation of Title IX." Worse, the group has made unsubstantiated claims. It asserted, for example, that "male athletes in certain sports are taught to dehumanize and degrade women as part of their sports training" and that "by encouraging boys to become aggressive, violent athletes, and by encouraging girls to cheer for them, we perpetuate the cycle of male aggression and violence against women."[50] But the feminist proportionality campaign is not limited to rhetoric. Those groups have taken action as well by threatening universities with multimillion-dollar lawsuits if they refuse to enter into "consent agreements" with feminist organizations. Those agreements, of course, require strict proportionality in athletics.

In 1993 the California chapter of NOW filed a lawsuit on behalf of female athletes against San Jose State University—and later extended the complaint to all the California State University campuses. The suit alleged Title IX violations. To avoid protracted and costly litigation, the chancellor of the California State University system settled out of court and signed a consent decree with NOW. The consent decree contained several proportionality provisions, including that all athletic programs had to include a percentage of women that was within five percentage points of female enrollment in the general student population and that it would allocate scholarships and general athletic funds on the basis of that proportionality.[51]

Schools of the California State University system were justifiably concerned about that consent decree, and California State University at Northridge convened a Task Force on Intercollegiate Athletics to study its athletics program. To appease NOW, the university announced a policy of "community outreach to girls at the grade-school and middle-school level" designed "to encourage the development of athletic skills and interest in young girls" as well as a "communication and public relations program" that would "increase awareness of athletics opportunities for girls and women."[52]

The task force's efforts raised a number of questions. Did the university intend to provide similar outreach programs for boys to increase the number of men in dance, drama, or nursing programs, where they were underrepresented? The report also raised an important criticism. "The Task Force," the report stated, "has strong concerns for the requirement of proportionality in participation."

From the perspective of the university's administrators, the school had two options for meeting the standards imposed by the consent agreement: it could eliminate male athletic opportunities or add substantially new opportunities for female athletes. The university was determined to avoid the former. But the task force quickly found itself confronting a harsh reality. Adding opportunities for women without eliminating athletic slots for men was "not as simple as it [might] appear." Indeed, the authors of the report stated, "Even though women are a majority of the student body, the pool of potential athletes is not as large." Women at the university simply were not as interested in athletics as were men.

The university's head softball coach, Janet Sherman, provided an enlightening anecdote to demonstrate that dilemma. Increasing the rosters for female sports such as softball would not work, she said, "because when women realize that they will not be able to play in games, most tend to quit the team." Sherman and other college coaches at the university testified to a "clear difference in sports culture between men and women" on campus. Male athletes were willing to invest more time and energy in sports, even if they did not get a lot of playing time, while female athletes were not.[53] The differences in preferences between the sexes at the university were, in practice, extremely hard to overcome.

Yet those facts had little bearing on what ultimately occurred at California State University at Northridge. By 1997 the men's Division I baseball team, men's soccer, men's volleyball, and men's swimming teams were all eliminated to satisfy the terms of the settlement with NOW. Forty-one men's athletic scholarships were eliminated. Mark Fitzpatrick, then a sophomore at the university, lost his scholarship just before the start of the soccer season. "I don't know if I'm going to be able to get into another school," he said, "and if I did, there wouldn't be any scholarship money left" at the new school by the time he transferred.

Paul Bubb, athletic director at the university, noted that before the agreement men's and women's teams were treated equally:

> When the women's basketball team traveled, did they stay in the same type of hotel or did they have the same type of meal money that the men's basketball team did? Did they travel by the same mode of transportation? Yes.

> We were doing those things. It wasn't like the women were traveling in vans and the men were flying in first class.[54]

Nevertheless, Fitzpatrick and his fellow male athletes had to pay for proportionality with the elimination of their teams.

Even when a university has solid evidence of men's and women's different preferences for athletics, it often ends up settling lawsuits rather than standing up for principles. The University of Texas at Austin is one such example. In 1993 it was the target of a Title IX lawsuit filed by seven female students seeking the creation of four new female varsity sports: soccer, softball, gymnastics, and crew. The evidence that the university marshaled from student surveys and participation rates in intramural sports revealed that "women at Texas simply displayed less interest in sports than their male counterparts."[55] Despite such strong evidence, the University of Texas settled the case before it came to trial to avoid a long and potentially costly court battle. The university agreed to raise female participation rates in sports from from 23 percent to 44 percent and created a women's softball team and a women's soccer team. The university also agreed to increase the percentage of athletic scholarships awarded to women. Robert M. Berdahl, the university president, estimated the cost to the university for those new teams and scholarships at $1 million.[56] Settlements are many schools' best option, since the odds are not in colleges' favor in the courts. As Donna Lopiano of the Women's Sports Foundation gleefully noted, of the estimated forty-five cases brought against colleges and universities, "everybody who has sued has won."[57]

The U.S. Supreme Court has yet to rule on the merits of the proportionality standard. In June 2000 the Court refused to hear the appeal of a group of male wrestlers and soccer players from Illinois State University who were suing under Title IX after their teams were cut. In 1993 Illinois State's Gender Equity Committee decided that the school's athletic department was not in compliance with Title IX since student enrollment stood at 45 percent male and 55 percent female, but student athletic participation was 66 percent male and 34 percent female. After cutting men's wrestling and men's soccer and adding women's soccer, the school was closer to achieving proportionality, with 48 percent male athletes and 52 percent female athletes, but the male athletes argued that in eliminating their teams, the university had violated their Title IX protections. The Seventh Circuit Court of Appeals upheld the university's action.[58]

The Supreme Court might still have a chance to hear a Title IX case involving male athletes. The elimination of men's sports teams that occurred in the wake of the consent agreement between NOW and the California State University system spawned *Neal v. California State University, Bakersfield.* Athletic directors at California State University at Bakersfield, facing dilemmas similar to those at California State University at Northridge in their attempts to institute strict gender proportionality, decided to cut seven male wrestlers from the team to come into compliance. Several members of the team, including Stephen Neal, the leading plaintiff, sued the university in federal court.[59]

In February 1999 district court Judge Robert E. Coyle issued a preliminary injunction preventing the university from cutting the wrestlers from their team. His reasoning provides a small glimmer of hope that the courts might be starting to notice the profoundly misguided reasoning behind current Title IX enforcement. In his ruling Judge Coyle noted that "relying on proportionality to cap the men's athletic teams at CSUB in order to comply with the Consent Decree constitutes implementation of a quota based on gender in violation of Title IX."[60] A three-judge panel of the U.S. Court of Appeals for the Ninth Circuit refused to uphold the injunction in December 1999.[61]

Feminists are also pushing their proportionality campaign by filing complaints with the Office for Civil Rights. In June 1997 the National Women's Law Center, based in Washington, D.C., filed Title IX complaints against twenty-five colleges and universities, including Duke University, Vanderbilt University, Wake Forest University, Boston College, and Brigham Young University. The complaints claimed that women's athletic participation and scholarship allocations were not proportionate to the total student body.[62]

The law center's complaints were less an attempt to remedy discrimination than a publicity stunt for the organization. The center purposely chose twenty-five schools to highlight the twenty-five years of Title IX's existence, and the center's president, Marcia D. Greenberger, put other schools on notice that they too would face investigations by the Office for Civil Rights if they did not reach proportionality.[63] Reaction to the center's stunt was swift and critical. Boston University noted that the complaint was "inconsistent with the facts," while Michael Schoengeld, vice chancellor at Vanderbilt University, suggested that "the simple and, we would argue, misleading way it is presented doesn't advance the issue" of equal opportunity for female athletes.[64]

In accordance with its procedure, the Office for Civil Rights immediately began investigating the twenty-five schools listed in the National Women's Law Center complaint, and in August 1998 Mary Frances O'Shea, national coordinator for the office's Title IX athletics enforcement, sent the schools a clarification of the office's policy. While denying that the office imposes quotas in its Title IX enforcement, O'Shea's letter dictated an even narrower quota for athletic scholarships. Shea noted that "there will be a strong presumption that an unexplained disparity [in the scholarship budget for athletes of either gender] of more than 1 percent is in violation of the 'substantially proportionate' requirements." In other words, if women are 50 percent of the athletes in a given department, they must receive 49 to 51 percent of the scholarship budget. Besides the imposition of a new, narrower quota, O'Shea's "clarification" violated standard administrative procedure by ignoring the requirement that new guidelines be published in the *Federal Register* and open to public comment.[65]

Yet even the highhandedness of the office's bureaucrats sympathetic to the gender equity wardens' cause could not overcome the facts. After further investigation—and with little fanfare or publicity—the Department of Education cleared eight of the institutions named in the center's complaint of any violations and formally dismissed the center's groundless claims.

Who Is to Blame? Football and Fairness

When pressed, some commentators who support such a de facto quota system will admit that Title IX, a law intended to guarantee equal opportunity, has become a tool for achieving a form of athletics socialism—a redistributive weapon whose wielders argue that its use is justified because of a history of discrimination against women. Title IX proportionality standards are viewed as reparations for earlier eras' discrimination against women. "It's unfair," says Public Broadcasting System television host Bonnie Erbe, "but so is life sometimes. And the overall goal of promoting women's participation in college and later professional sports is important enough that perhaps we can be unfair temporarily."[66] One wonders how Erbe and other like-minded proportionality supporters justify that principle legally. The U.S. Constitution, after all, guarantees *equal protection* of the laws, not *temporary unfairness* in their enforcement.

Other proportionality proponents are less forthcoming than Erbe. They blame football, not the proportionality test, for the elimination of men's teams. Testifying on behalf of the Women's Sports Foundation before the Subcommittee on Commerce, Consumer Protection, and Competitiveness of the 103d Congress in 1993, Lopiano claimed that "men's sports participation has not suffered at the expense of providing participation opportunities for women." Instead, she said, the decimation of men's teams could be blamed on schools that were too concerned with making "football fanatics" (whom she later described as "a flying flock of golden geese with beer bellies wearing football helmets") happy. Her solution? "The standard of living of many football programs will have to be reduced in order to redistribute funds for the cause of gender equity."[67]

Critics of current Title IX enforcement standards have suggested that sports such as men's baseball and football, which carry large numbers of players, should be given special consideration in the Title IX equation. In addition to the revenues generated by the large number of football fans buying tickets to games or watching them on television, there are "hidden" revenues such as the money alumni give to a school because of their interest in the football team.

Those arguments arose early in the Title IX debate as well. Although Congress rejected the Tower Amendment, which would have exempted all revenue-producing sports from Title IX, it did pass the Javits Amendment to Title IX, which required the Office for Civil Rights to consider "the nature of the particular sports" when assessing Title IX compliance. Such factors as football players' much higher risk of injury, and hence the sport's greater need for more players to replace the injured, apply there. In addition, men's sports in general, and football in particular, generate more revenue for athletic departments than women's sports.[68] In 1997 Meritt Norvell, Michigan State University's athletic director, noted in testimony before Congress that 80 to 85 percent of his entire athletic program's revenues came from three sports: men's basketball, men's ice hockey, and football.[69] At Division I colleges and universities, for example, women's sports generate only 5 percent of athletic revenues, while men's teams bring in 67 percent of revenues.[70]

Moreover, the fallacy that football rather than the proportionality standard is fueling the elimination of men's teams is revealed by a key fact: if the Office for Civil Rights and the country's courts excluded football altogether when they measured compliance, 55 percent of Division I institutions—those with the most well-funded football teams—would still not meet the proportionality standard.[71] Proportionality wardens such as Lopiano ignore those uncomfortable facts; they find it easier to blame male prejudice than to confront the logical conclusion of their illiberal proportionality principle. Of the male coaches and athletes who see their opportunities for athletic participation dwindling, Lopiano told Congress that "we are hearing the arguments of boys or men who think that sports is their protected domain and values like sharing and equal opportunity do not apply to them."[72]

Proportionality supporters fail to recognize that in the market for college athletics—and it is a market—football simply occupies a different realm from most women's sports. As the Independent Women's Forum's Title IX policy expert Kimberly Schuld told us, "If football really is the villain that the Women's Sports Foundation and other groups claim it is, then we wouldn't be seeing so many schools that don't even have football teams still having to eliminate men's teams in order to come into compliance."[73]

In fact, for the past decade, athletic directors and college administrators have struggled mightily to meet the proportionality test endorsed by the First Circuit in *Cohen v. Brown* without eliminating opportunities for male athletes. They have not been successful.

During the same House subcommittee hearings at which Lopiano testified, Thomas K. Hearn, Jr., president of Wake Forest University, noted that eliminating football would likely have a negative effect on revenues—revenues that provided opportunities for male and female athletes at the school. Grant G. Teaff, athletics director at Baylor University in Waco, Texas, agreed. "Shrinking financial resources and increasing operating costs, not some effort to maintain intercollegiate athletics as an entrenched boys' club, constitute the greatest single obstacle to achieving gender equity." Poor sports, indeed.[74]

Conclusion

Title IX has traveled a long way from its original intent. Given the current Title IX enforcement strategy, Senator Bayh's insistence that the statute was not about quotas appears quaint. The quotas he hoped to prevent are now entrenched in collegiate athletic programs, and advocates of larger quotas flout the careful concern of the law's creators. For example, during a legislative markup in the House Subcommittee on the Constitution in 1997, a debate erupted over the legislative intent of Title IX. Representative Maxine Waters claimed that the purpose of Title IX was to institute gender quotas.

Representative Charles Canady disagreed; he cited the language of the Quie amendment, which clearly condemned the use of quotas. Representative Waters insisted, however, that Title IX "is the biggest quota you've ever seen. It is 50/50. It is a quota—a big, round, quota."[75] While laughter greeted her remarks in the hearing room, the principle Representative Waters and others espoused is no laughing matter. It demonstrates how thoroughly the ideal of equal opportunity has been corrupted.

Title IX proportionality police justify their aggressive action by claiming that they are merely removing another unfair barrier to women's equality. Just as women once lacked equal opportunity at the ballot box, they say, so they now lack equal opportunity on the basketball court. While chairing the subcommittee hearings on Title IX in the House in 1993, Representative Cardiss Collins compared gender discrimination with discrimination based on race. "When I hear suggestions that gender equity or equal treatment for women collegiate athletes will harm opportunities for men," she said, "I am reminded of the arguments 30 years ago by opponents of civil rights that equal employment opportunities for minorities would mean fewer jobs for white men."[76]

In a similar vein, President Clinton linked Title IX to equal opportunity when he proclaimed August 26, 1997, "Women's Equality Day." In his proclamation Clinton claimed that Title IX was built "on the spirit of the Nineteenth Amendment."[77] That is a serious misunderstanding. The Nineteenth Amendment to the Constitution ended discriminatory *legal* barriers that prevented women from voting. There are *no legal barriers* for women who want to participate in college athletic programs. Those who wish to participate can do so.

Women's interest in athletics is likely to grow in the next several decades, and universities will probably find themselves with an ever enlarging pool of female athletes. Yet what the proportionality police fail to understand is that changes in social attitudes toward female athletes and women's own interest in athletic participation should never be imposed by the government. As we have seen, attempts by the government and feminist groups to mandate certain levels of participation by women lead to misguided standards of proportionality and the denial of opportunity to male athletes. By assuming that all women have the same degree of interest in sports as all men, without bothering to consider whether that is, in fact, true, proportionality proponents reveal their real purpose: social engineering. Proportionality is not equality.

Those proponents' efforts also reject the reality of women's choices. Feminists would do well to remember that their proportionality standard could turn out to be a double-edged sword. In *Cohen v. Brown University,* the school provided the court with statistics revealing that gender ratios in other university programs were also skewed: students enthusiastic about dance, music, and drama were 91 percent, 66 percent, and 56 percent women, respectively.[78] Thus far, courts have not been sympathetic to male athletes' claims of reverse discrimination. But it is useful to remember that there is a logical conclusion to the proportionality standard: quotas in every classroom, including those in which women currently are overrepresented, to ensure proportionality.

The Title IX debate has no simple solutions; athletic directors, administrators, and students will continue to quibble over who should get what. But there is hope for finding better answers. With a recognition by courts, policymakers, and bureaucrats that Title IX guarantees women equal opportunity in education, including athletics, but not necessarily equal outcomes, we can return to the original intent of Title IX. Young women should have every opportunity to pursue sports. We should be enforcing equal opportunities—not ideology and quotas. The story of the gradual perversion of Title IX's intent as yet does not concern a majority of the American public. But it should. The proportionality principle behind that and other feminist campaigns is destructive to free choice and to relations between the sexes, is debasing to women, and is wasteful of our nation's limited educational resources.

9

Preference Programs for Women

Our earlier chapters show how and why equal opportunities are not leading to equal outcomes for men and women in education, the workplace, and even the athletic field. Whereas the law can ensure that similar opportunities exist, it is far more difficult to guarantee similarity of outcomes. Women's careers suffer when they are given the chance in college to major in business and instead choose literature. Their earnings are lower than men's when, given the cultural freedom to work long hours in male-dominated professions and make it to the top, they choose to scale back work hours to balance family and career. In response, feminists, who once railed against discrimination against women, have become advocates of preferential programs for women—and of discrimination against men. For example, DePaul University College of Law professor Mary Becker wrote, "Affirmative action for women and people of color is the only effective remedy for patriarchal biases favoring white men and deeply (subtly) embedded in cultural values and measures of merit, whether subjective or objective."[1]

This chapter presents examples of preference programs for women in government, private industry, and academia. It briefly reports on how cumbersome and costly those programs are.

Implementing Federal Preference Programs for Women

Most private companies and institutions keep their employment and membership records private. But federal government agencies are required to make their hiring, promotion, compensation, and

155

contract information public. Each agency compiles detailed employee records and changes in status by occupation and sex.

To hear some feminists speak, America is filled with women-hating bosses who undervalue women by paying them less than their due and by preventing them from career advancement. The one exception in that rhetoric is the bastion of enlightenment—the federal government. Surely, then, one would expect women to do better in the federal government than elsewhere. Indeed, one might expect the federal government, devoid of discrimination, to have no need for preference programs.

Yet federal agencies implement preference programs for women with a vengeance and with an uncharacteristic passion for program efficiency. In addition to laws such as the Civil Rights Act and the Equal Pay Act that govern how private employers treat female workers, the federal government has several ways to regulate the hiring of women. First, it has laws and regulations governing federal agencies' employment decisions that favor women in recruitment and hiring, promotion, compensation, and leadership. Second, the federal government controls contracting with companies that produce its goods and deliver its services.

Current and Planned Composition of Federal Government Employees. The federal government, the largest employer in the United States, with approximately 2.5 million civilian workers in 1999, has a detailed system for keeping track of demographic characteristics, including the race and gender of the employees of its agencies. That system derives originally from section 717 of the Equal Employment Opportunity Act of 1972, which requires each federal agency to establish an affirmative employment program. Originally, the Civil Service Commission was given the authority to ensure that federal government hiring was free of discrimination and "affirmatively oriented towards equal employment opportunity."[2] In 1978 President Jimmy Carter moved that function from the Civil Service Commission to the Equal Employment Opportunity Commission.

In 1987 the EEOC issued Management Directive 714 (EEO-MD-714), which requires each federal agency to prepare reports detailing by race and sex the numbers of workers employed, together with proposals to increase hiring in those areas where minorities and women fall below the proportion found in the civilian labor force. The directive was renewed in 1992 and will remain in force until it is canceled. Those reports, known as Affirmative Employment Program Accomplishment Reports, are filed with the EEOC on an annual basis.

The reports reveal that the federal government employs large numbers of women. In 1999 women made up 42 percent of the federal work force, compared with 46 percent of the labor force as a whole. That ranges from a high of 71 percent for the Social Security Administration to a low of 21 percent for the Tennessee Valley Authority. Some large agencies have relatively few women, such as the U.S. Postal Service, whose approximately 800,000 employees are only 37 percent female. Other large agencies have more, such as Veterans Affairs, 57 percent of whose 200,000 workers are women.[3]

The reports of the different agencies vary in their detail, but they all lay out in tabular format the number and percentage of workers that are male and female, as well as the standard federal agency categories of white, African American, Hispanic, Asian American/Pacific Islander, and American Indian/Alaska Native. The workers are cross-classified by occupational category and compared with their percentages in the civilian labor force, with the object of matching workers' representation at the agencies with their percentages in the civilian labor force.

The clear original purpose of those tables was to reveal under-representation of women and minorities in different job classifications. From such tables it is possible to learn that in 1998, for example, 2.47 percent of the Department of Transportation's paralegal specialists were Asian American/Pacific Islander females or that in 1997 .28 percent of the Department of the Treasury's management analysts (GS-343) were American Indian males. Such micro-analysis carries social engineering to an infinitesimal—and absurd—degree. With such finely calibrated goals, if not quotas, what happens to merit hiring, especially in smaller labor markets?

Table 9-1 is one typical summary table. The table is taken from the 1998 Affirmative Employment Program Accomplishment

Table 9-1 EEO Group Representation by Employment Category for HHS Professionals (numbers and percentages)

EEO Group	FY 1995		FY 1996		FY 1997		Civilian Labor Force Comparison
African Americans	1,445	8.5%	1,450	8.4%	1,492	8.5%	5.6%
Males	561	3.3%	543	3.2%	551	3.1%	2.4%
Females	884	5.2%	907	5.3%	941	5.3%	3.2%
Hispanics	540	3.2%	539	3.1%	585	3.3%	3.5%
Males	284	1.7%	279	1.6%	298	1.7%	2.1%
Females	256	1.5%	260	1.5%	287	1.6%	1.4%
Asian Americans/ Pacific Islanders	1,094	6.4%	1,139	6.6%	1,212	6.9%	5.4%
Males	577	3.4%	594	3.5%	628	3.6%	3.5%
Females	517	3.0%	545	3.2%	584	3.3%	1.9%
American Indians/ Alaska Natives	1,401	8.2%	1,419	8.3%	1,477	8.4%	.4%
Males	245	1.4%	248	1.4%	260	1.5%	.02%
Females	1,156	6.8%	1,171	6.8%	1,217	6.9%	.02%
Nonminority Females	6,310	36.9%	6,354	37.0%	6,451	36.5%	30.3%
NonMinority Males	6,307	36.9%	6,251	36.4%	6,410	36.3%	54.7%
Total	17,115		17,174		17,652		

Source: Department of Health and Human Services, *Affirmative Employment Program and FY 1998 Update for the Department of Health and Human Services, Work Force Analysis*, p. 5.

158

Report of the Department of Health and Human Services. It shows all the professional employees of the agency divided into sex and race groupings in number and percentage terms. The last column compares the agency's percentage with the percentage of each category in the civilian labor force. A companion table, not reproduced here, gives similar data for administrative positions.[4]

An interesting aspect of the table—one that the department plays down—is that the white women and all the minority groups with the exception of Hispanic males are *overrepresented* at HHS in terms of their percentages in the civilian labor force. For example, professional Asian American/Pacific Islander females represent 1.9 percent of the general labor force, yet 3.3 percent of the professional labor force at HHS. Similarly, African American females represent 3.2 percent of the general labor force, yet 5.3 percent of the HHS professional work force.

In contrast, however, the table shows that white males—labeled in the table as "nonminority males"—were *underrepresented* at HHS in 1997. They accounted for 54.7 percent of the labor force, yet only 36.3 percent of the professional HHS work force, a difference of eighteen percentage points. Similarly, in the table for administrative HHS employees, white males constituted 27.9 percent, yet 42.1 percent of the civilian labor force.

In addition to the composition of the current federal work force, the report shows which workers the agency sought to hire in 1997. A section in the HHS report entitled "Standard Deviation Report" describes by race and sex the new employees that would be required to bring the HHS work force into a statistical mirror of the civilian labor force. Tables for men and women for the standard deviation report are reproduced in tables 9-2 and 9-3. They show how many men and women of different races need to be hired for the agency to have the same percentage of sex and race groups as those that exist in the entire U.S. labor force.[5]

According to tables 9-2 and 9-3, for most race and sex categories no additional hires are needed for an equitable work force. The glaring deficiencies, however, are white men and women. Specifically, the agency reported that it needed to hire 3,130 white women and 7,437 white men but only 18 black females and 14 black males; 313

Table 9-2 Department of Health and Human Services Work Force Inventory Profile System, Permanent Career/Career Conditional Employees, Standard Deviation Report, Males

Grade	Total Count	Total Males	Black Males Current on Board	Black Males Lowest Expected Value	Black Males Gain Needed	Hispanic Males Current on Board	Hispanic Males Lowest Expected Value	Hispanic Males Gain Needed	Asian/Pacific Island Males Current on Board	Asian/Pacific Island Males Lowest Expected Value	Asian/Pacific Island Males Gain Needed	American Indian Males Current on Board	American Indian Males Lowest Expected Value	American Indian Males Gain Needed	Nonminority Males Current on Board	Nonminority Males Lowest Expected Value	Nonminority Males Gain Needed
Professional																	
1–4	8	1	0	0	0	1	0	0	0	0	0	0	0	0	0	2	2
5–8	419	126	11	4	0	11	3	0	15	7	0	23	0	0	66	209	143
9–12	8,098	2,514	220	166	0	117	144	27	152	249	97	179	8	0	1,846	4,340	2,494
13–15	9,127	5,506	320	189	0	169	164	0	461	283	0	58	10	0	4,498	4,896	398
Administrative																	
5–8	433	121	24	8	0	7	5	0	10	2	0	25	0	0	55	162	107
9–12	7,409	2,079	424	235	0	68	165	97	65	84	19	226	12	0	1,296	3,035	1,739
13–15	7,387	3,580	375	234	0	90	164	74	54	83	29	161	12	0	2,900	3,026	126
Technical																	
1–4	802	63	5	19	14	2	16	14	0	7	7	52	0	0	4	26	258
5–8	5,512	986	291	170	0	40	150	110	25	85	60	242	12	0	388	1,918	1,530
9–12	1,174	542	115	30	0	14	26	12	10	12	2	109	1	0	294	392	98
13–15	30	11	3	0	0	0	0	0	1	0	0	0	0	0	7	5	0
Clerical																	
1–4	858	127	41	14	0	2	7	5	3	1	0	31	0	0	50	100	50
5–8	4,231	312	114	96	0	8	56	48	12	22	10	65	0	0	113	546	433
9–12	254	4	3	1	0	0	0	0	0	0	0	0	0	0	1	24	23
Other																	
1–4	49	31	5	1	0	0	0	0	3	0	0	16	0	0	7	27	20
5–8	87	60	13	2	0	3	0	0	3	0	0	2	0	0	39	51	12
9–12	23	12	4	0	0	0	0	0	0	0	0	0	0	0	8	12	4
Administrative																	
ES	489	325	27	10	0	8	5	0	2	1	0	8	0	0	280	184	0
RS	1	1	0	0	0	0	0	0	0	0	0	0	0	0	1	0	0
Professional																	
RS	91	72	0	0	0	0	0	0	6	0	0	1	0	0	65	40	0
Total Gains Needed					14			387			224			0			7,437

Note: ES=executive service; RS=research service.

Source: Department of Health and Human Services, *Affirmative Employment Program and FY 1998 Update for the Department of Health and Human Services, Supporting Data, Standard Deviation Report,* p. 54.

Table 9-3 Department of Health and Human Services Work Force Inventory Profile System, Permanent Career/Career Conditional Employees, Standard Deviation Report, Females

Grade	Total Count	Total Females	Black Females — Current on Board	Lowest Expected Value	Gain Needed	Hispanic Females — Current on Board	Lowest Expected Value	Gain Needed	Asian/Pac. Island Females — Current on Board	Lowest Expected Value	Gain Needed	American Indian Females — Current on Board	Lowest Expected Value	Gain Needed	Nonminority Females — Current on Board	Lowest Expected Value	Gain Needed
Professional																	
1-4	8	7	0	0	0	0	0	0	0	0	0	7	0	0	0	0	0
5-8	419	293	25	5	0	10	2	0	24	2	0	112	0	0	122	109	0
9-12	8,098	5,576	494	227	0	189	91	0	302	130	0	1,035	8	0	3,556	2,372	0
13-15	9,127	3,604	422	258	0	88	106	18	258	147	0	63	10	0	2,773	2,677	0
Administrative																	
5-8	433	312	84	13	0	14	5	0	10	2	0	72	0	0	132	155	23
9-12	7,409	5,325	1,519	355	0	152	165	13	150	84	0	513	12	0	2,991	2,909	0
13-15	7,387	3,805	697	354	0	86	164	78	86	83	0	135	12	0	2,801	2,900	99
Technical																	
1-4	802	738	21	39	18	4	17	13	1	5	4	699	0	0	13	316	303
5-8	5,512	4,524	1,294	328	0	104	161	57	98	70	0	1,602	12	0	1,426	2,291	865
9-12	1,174	632	188	59	0	18	28	10	17	11	0	127	1	0	282	470	188
13-15	30	19	1	0	0	1	0	0	0	0	0	4	0	0	13	7	0
Clerical																	
1-4	858	731	64	64	0	9	31	22	5	8	3	567	0	0	86	516	430
5-8	4,231	3,917	1,245	368	0	92	192	100	64	62	0	1,062	11	0	1,454	2,620	1,166
9-12	254	250	61	14	0	3	5	2	2	1	0	8	0	0	176	145	0
Other																	
1-4	49	18	11	0	0	2	0	0	2	0	0	0	0	0	3	1	0
5-8	87	27	12	0	0	1	0	0	1	0	0	0	0	0	13	4	0
9-12	23	11	5	0	0	0	0	0	0	0	0	0	0	0	6	0	0
Administrative																	
ES	489	163	25	16	0	6	5	0	5	1	0	5	0	0	122	176	54
RS	1	0	0	0	0	0	0	0	0	0	0	0	0	0	0	0	0
Professional																	
RS	91	19	0	0	0	0	0	0	1	0	0	0	0	0	18	20	2
Total Gains Needed					18			313			7			0			3,130

Note: ES=executive service; RS=research service.

Source: Department of Health and Human Services, *Affirmative Employment Program and FY 1998 Update for the Department of Health and Human Services, Supporting Data, Standard Deviation Report*, p. 53.

161

Hispanic females and 387 Hispanic males; 7 Asian American/Pacific Islander females and 224 such males; and no Native American/Alaskan Native men or women.[6]

That distribution is ironic in light of the report's transmission letter from then-Secretary Donna Shalala, a noted champion of "political correctness." She focused on the "employment areas for which representation of minorities and women could be enhanced,"[7] without mentioning the largest category of underrepresentation, white males. It would be repugnant for HHS or any government agency to favor recruitment of white males for any reason, even if an analysis showed that white males were underrepresented. It is odd that HHS does not regard it as equally repugnant to focus recruiting on other groups or on any group.

Managers are rewarded in part on the basis of fulfilling their diversity goals. For example, in the HHS's Indian Health Service, a truly bureaucratic and Orwellian sentence reads: "Recognition is recommended for all individuals who provide outstanding contributions to EEO [Equal Employment Opportunities], conversely, appropriate administrative action is recommended for individuals who fail to satisfactorily demonstrate support for EEO objectives."[8]

One can also observe such behavior in other agencies. For example, if an individual wanted to join the Department of Housing and Urban Development in 1998 as a "criminal investigator, administrative,"—a GS-1811 to be precise—it would be useful to be a female, because all the planned hires were female. But the individual should not just have been any female—she should have been a white female, for the department planned to hire five of those, or an Asian American/Pacific Islander or an American Indian/Alaskan Native, for the agency planned to hire one each of those. If the individual were a male, even a member of a minority, or a black or Hispanic female, it is likely that he or she would have been out of luck, because he or she was not a planned hire for that category.[9]

Or if an individual wanted to be a "housing management assistant, technical"—a GS-1101—at HUD and he was a minority male, he would be in luck, because HUD planned to hire seven males for that position: three blacks, two Hispanics, one Asian American/Pacific Islander, and one American Indian/Alaskan Native. The department also planned to hire nine females: one American Indian/Alaskan Native and eight whites. If the individual were a black or Hispanic female, there would have been little point in applying to be a housing management assistant in 1998.

Just as at HHS, managers at the Department of the Interior are given bonuses if they comply with the planned targets. The Affirmative Employment Report reads:

> Bureaus shall establish, as one relevant factor, a clear link between the presentation of bonuses, awards, and promotions of managers/supervisors with the successful achievement of their diversity performance standard.
>
> SES [Senior Executive Service] performance bonuses are linked to success in meeting diversity performance standards. During FY 1999, a tool will be developed to allow [sic] the current tracking of cash and time-off awards.[10] (Emphasis added.)

As inappropriate as that situation is, it prevails among the federal agencies and makes a mockery of merit-based hiring. That such efforts are made to catalog different groups of individuals and match their percentages to their proportions in the civilian labor force is worrisome. Such an approach to hiring knowingly advances some groups at the expense of others.

The EEOC's Management Directive 714, which requires agencies to submit data on the composition of their work forces, has outlived its usefulness with regard to data collection on women. The federal government has no need to keep track of women versus men. A logical step would be to get rid of the cataloging of positions by male and female: that would significantly diminish the costs associated with hiring and halve the number of pages of the report.

Preferences for Women in Government Contracting. Besides giving women preferences as direct hires, the federal government gives them preferences in contracting. The Federal Acquisition Streamlining Act of 1994 established a target that 5 percent of all federal contracts and subcontracts be given to women-owned small businesses. That initiative is under the auspices of the Small Business Administration, which in 1998 put out a plan to increase the share of federal contracts going to such businesses.

The SBA's plan, outlined in a press release from Administrator Aida Alvarez, contained the following elements. First, each agency was asked to commit to specific strategies to increase the share of its contracts performed by women-owned firms and to put those strategies in writing in a memorandum of understanding. Second, the SBA ruled that agencies were required to solicit bids from a specific number of women-owned small businesses when awarding contracts. For contracts between $2,500 and $100,000, agencies were required to get bids from at least five small companies, at least one of which had to be woman-owned. Third, Alvarez announced a greater effort to get more women-owned firms listed on an SBA database of such firms, so that, according to Alvarez, contracting officers could be sure to find a qualified such business.[11]

As part of the effort, the SBA asked each agency to appoint a women-owned business *advocate* (the SBA's term) to act as a liaison between that agency and SBA.[12] The list of advocates is available from the SBA and consists almost exclusively of women (HUD and the National Aeronautics and Space Administration are exceptions).

The memorandums of understanding from the individual agencies describe the efforts made to award contracts to women-owned businesses. The efforts include policy statements by the secretary of the agency, women business enterprise days, special newsletters aimed at women-owned businesses, and joint efforts with women's groups such as the National Women's Business Council. In its memorandum of understanding, the Department of Transportation offers special loan programs for women, including a "Short-Term Lending Program" and a "Bonding Assistance Program." Those programs are also open to minorities but not to white men. According to Pat Hodge, the advocate for women-owned businesses at the Department of Transportation, white men do not need such programs.[13]

Significantly, the memorandums of several agencies describe plans for rewarding managers on the basis of how many contracts are awarded to women, just as managers in the Department of the Interior and the HHS are rewarded for hiring more women employees. For example, the General Services Administration's memorandum states that the agency "will develop an awards program to reward the buying activities that are the most successful in promoting and awarding contracts to WOSB [women-owned small businesses]." Section 5 of the Department of Defense memorandum asserts:

> The DoD Office of Small and Disadvantaged Business Utilization (OSADBU) will develop an awards program to recognize those buying activities that have been most successful in promoting and awarding WOSB contracts and to recognize DoD prime contractors that have been the most successful in promoting and awarding WOSB subcontracts.[14]

Preference Programs for Women in the Private Sector

Preference programs for women are not limited to federal and state government. Through the EEOC and the Office of Federal Contract Compliance Programs of the Department of Labor, the government provides incentives for private firms and universities to have programs similar to those in the federal government for the recruitment, hiring, promotion, and compensation of women.

Firms and Corporations. Ask any midlevel manager at any major private-sector company in America about whether business plans are being met. Many may not know with certainty whether financial, technological, or business objectives will be met. But with near certainty, most know whether numerical hiring and promotion targets for women or minorities in a division or section are being met. Today, in many corporations, meeting hiring and promotion targets is rewarded in executive compensation, and the results are easily monitored.

The federal government requires private firms with more than fifteen employees to keep records on the numbers of workers by job category and by sex and race (black, white, Hispanic, Asian American/Pacific Islander, and American Indian/Alaskan Native). In addition, three categories of firms have to report that information on the EEOC's Standard Form 100 (see table 9-3): all employers with more than 100 workers, all employers with more than 50 workers who have contracts of more than $50,000 with the federal government, and all employers who are owned by another firm. Approximately 200,000 firms do business with the federal government. They have about 26 million workers, just under a quarter of the work force. For 1999 the EEOC received fewer than 40,000 forms. Thus, noncompliance with the regulation is substantial.[15]

That requirement comes from Title VII of the Civil Rights Act of 1964, as amended by the Equal Employment Opportunity Act of 1972. Employers are instructed by the EEOC and the Office of Federal Contract Compliance Programs to look at workers, make judgments about their race and sex, and keep track of that information separately from other personnel records. Specifically, employers are asked to "acquire the race/ethnic information necessary for this report either by visual surveys of the work force or from postemployment records as to the identity of the employees. Eliciting information on the race/identity of an employee by direct inquiry is not encouraged."[16]

Identifying workers by sex is easy, but it is harder to do visual surveys of race with the increasing rate of intermarriage in the population. An employer of the famous golfer Tiger Woods, who identifies himself as "Cablasian"—Caucasian, black, and Asian—would have a difficult time pigeonholing him into one of those categories. Fortunately, Tiger Woods is self-employed, but millions of others of mixed ancestry are not.

The burden on employers, not just of annually filling out the forms, but also of ensuring that their work force meets the desired criteria, is enormous. The estimate of the EEOC and the Office of Management and Budget that, including data collection, it takes only 3.7 hours to complete Standard Form 100 ("including the time for reviewing instructions, searching existing data sources, gathering and maintaining the data needed, and completing and reviewing the collection of information")[17] is absurd. And it takes even more time and effort for an employer to determine, for each position open, how the hiring of a particular individual will affect the tally on the official form that has to be submitted to the EEOC and whether the numbers will open the firm to possible lawsuits.

The required division of job categories in the EEOC's Standard Form 100—namely officials and managers; professionals; technicians; sales workers; office and clerical; craft workers; operatives; laborers; and service workers—puts pressure on firms to promote women to higher job categories. As shown in chapter 5, firms as large as Sears and as small as Joe's Stone Crab have been found guilty by the EEOC of not having enough women in higher-skill categories. That can be a nightmare for corporate managers, since they may feel compelled to promote women to positions for which not enough qualified candidates exist.

Karen Jones-Budd of Oakton, Virginia, gave us examples of that circumstance.[18] She was a math major who completed graduate work in civil structural engineering and spent her career working for Control Data Corporation and Digital Equipment, both members, during their time, of the Fortune 100. Both were manufacturers of large-scale computer equipment and software. Control Data was the preeminent designer and assembler of large-scale computers. The defense weapons complex and the national laboratories frequently bought the firm's computer systems. Digital Equipment had a consistent and solid reputation in those same scientific and technical markets as well as in many others. The target markets for both companies' high-powered machines included the nuclear industry, the defense weapons complex, and the National Aeronautics and Space Administration.

Before Jones-Budd was thirty years old, she was the only woman managing a $40 million hardware and software branch focused on infrastructure for nuclear and fossil-fuel utilities. She described those corporations' struggles to promote women, both to meet EEOC requirements and to "do the right thing." She also described how she was always encouraged to endeavor to hire women and minorities. Both firms had expectations and compelling reasons for Jones-Budd to have certain percentages of women and minorities in professional positions on her staff. Digital Equipment brought large numbers of secretaries into the sales ranks to position them for greater upward mobility. Control Data continually flew women to headquarters for briefings to make special attempts and plans to accelerate their careers.

Their efforts, however, did not succeed in producing enough top women managers, because, in Jones-Budd's view, many women chose not to pursue top corporate positions once they had children because of the demanding hours and travel. Qualified women with children either chose jobs with family-friendly hours and thus ruled out certain types of corporate positions or, as their husbands' salaries rose, abandoned the work force entirely, as Jones-Budd did a few years ago.

Jones-Budd also noted that she observed several women such as herself parleying their early successes and achievements into flexibility for family in lieu of power and position. She commented that she, as well as others with solid records whom the companies wanted to retain, took several years' worth of leaves of absence to be with their children. She noted that at Digital Equipment, where she worked for ten years, most of the top women were either unmarried or childless. She, herself, repeatedly refused promotional overtures and turned down opportunities to interview for more powerful positions so as to have more family time.

Employment quotas for women can be a nightmare for rank-and-file employees. Consider personnel data on the relative compensation of male and female scientists at a large federal research center operated by the state of California. The data clearly show that, by any measure, women scientists were paid as well as if not better than men at that facility in the late 1990s. Yet women at the research center received special treatment and better opportunities for advancement. A male scientist from whom the authors obtained the data contacted an employee at the EEOC to complain, "but it was difficult to convince her that men could be discriminated against in pay and salary actions."[19] Ultimately, the scientist did not pursue the case with the EEOC or elsewhere for fear of bad publicity and loss of promotion opportunities for himself and for his boss and for concern about the embarrassment to his division.

Colleges and Universities. In 1993 the U.S. Department of Education took over the oversight of college and university employment from the EEOC. Colleges and universities eligible for Title IV funds and employing more than fifteen staffers must complete the Department of Education's Integrated Postsecondary Education Data System Fall Staff Survey every other year. The form for the survey is far more complex than the EEOC's Standard Form 100. Not only does the survey divide all employees into race and sex categories (male, female, black non-Hispanic, white non-Hispanic, Hispanic, American Indian/Alaskan Native, Asian/Pacific Islander, nonresident alien), but it also separates employees into different types of teaching, administrative, and support positions.[20]

In the survey universities must complete race and sex data for full-time faculty with nine- or ten-month and eleven- or twelve-month contracts in Part A. In Part B they complete the data for all other full-time employees, divided into executive, administrative, and managerial; other professionals; technical and paraprofessionals; clerical and secretarial; skilled crafts; and service and maintenance. Part C asks for information on university executives with academic rank and tenure and staff paid from outside sources. Part D requests data on part-time employees, including executives, faculty, research assistants, and other categories of skills from Part B. In Part E the Department of Education asks for information on contracted and donated services to the university (unlike in the other parts, that information is not requested by race and sex). In Part F the university provides the length of service of all faculty, tenured and nontenured, by race and sex. Part G asks for the race and sex of all new hires in the university, including all faculty, support staff, and other workers.[21] It is astounding that the form was estimated by President Clinton's Office of Management and Budget (the federal office that estimates the length of time to fill in all government forms) to take only from one to ten hours to complete—including data collection—with an average of five hours. It does not appear physically possible that the form could be completed in one hour, and it would be difficult to complete in ten hours.[22]

As with private firms and the EEOC antidiscrimination laws, the survey form places universities under great pressure to hire and promote women faculty. The tenure system makes that even harder for institutions of higher education than for private firms, because tenure reduces job turnover and leaves fewer slots for younger professors. Many current professors were hired in the 1960s and 1970s, a time when women were just beginning to enter the professorial ranks in significant numbers.

Furthermore, the output of professors, namely research, is harder to evaluate than that of professionals in other fields and involves complex measurement issues. With sales or account executives, productivity or value to the firm can be measured through dollar amounts of business generated. With electricians or hair stylists the value can be measured through numbers of clients served per day. With professors, however, the value is in the number or the quality of articles and the number of citations, and those are far harder to measure than business generated or clients per day. Hence, it is harder for universities to defend themselves against accusations that they are discriminating against certain groups.

It is well-known that the average number of publications for female professors is lower than that for male professors.[23] Yet female professors sometimes argue that the higher quality of their research makes up for the smaller quantity and that male professors place a lower value on publications in certain areas, such as women's studies.

In 1998 the U.S. Department of Labor brought a suit against Stanford University that alleged discrimination against women. At this writing that suit is unresolved.[24] Perhaps the government's action may have led to the production of studies alleging discrimination against women in academia. In 1999 officials at the Massachusetts Institute of Technology asserted that female professors in the School of Science suffered from pervasive—yet unintentional—discrimination.[25] Newspapers and magazines all over the country summarized the study uncritically. A few months later, the University of Illinois at Urbana-Champaign produced a similar report.[26] Other academic institutions, such as the California Institute of Technology, Case Western Reserve University, Harvard Medical School, and the University of Arizona, are working on similar studies.

One indicator that MIT produced the report to stave off potential lawsuits is that MIT Professor Nancy Hopkins, the chair of the committee that produced the report, admitted that MIT convened the committee after she contacted a lawyer.[27] Further, the study is so flawed that no reputable statistician would lay claim to it. The reports were not data-driven at all, and the stated conclusions did not follow from the information provided. Indeed, the conclusions were based more on feelings and perceptions than on verifiable quantitative evidence. There were no details of qualified female professors being turned down for tenure on the basis of their sex. There were no documentation of salaries, publications data, estimates of quality of research, and data on teaching ability and administrative skills. Rigorous analysis of such data is commonplace in discrimination cases.[28]

In the MIT report, the only quantitative evidence of discrimination was the so-called leaky pipeline, with data on numbers of male and female undergraduates, graduate students, postdoctoral fellows, and faculty members from 1985 through 1994. The data showed a sharp decline from the percentage of females who were undergraduates to those who were faculty, both for 1994 and for the ten-year period 1985 through 1994. Those data, however, while striking the usual call for proportionality that is common in athletics, did not prove discrimination.[29] Moreover, studies of females who leave science majors do not support assertions that they do so because of discrimination.[30]

First, the 1994 data represented a stock of individuals in different positions in the same year. Just because female biologists, to use one example, represented 147 undergraduates, 101 graduate students, 27 postdoctoral fellows, and 7 faculty members did not mean that discrimination existed, since those numbers ignored the qualified pool—candidates available to be on the MIT faculty in 1994. The undergraduates, graduate students, and postdoctoral fellows were not qualified to be hired as professors in that year. Furthermore, no reason existed for MIT's choice of female faculty to be dominated by MIT graduates. Some schools make a point of not hiring their own students immediately after graduation. Second, the time-series data should have extended further back than 1985, since many professors hired in the 1990s would have received their undergraduate degrees before 1985.

The University of Illinois report cited data on average salaries of women compared with men in a variety of academic departments. Those averages were meant to support the claim that women were underpaid at the University of Illinois, but no precise instances or proofs were given.[31] As with the MIT report, the Illinois report did not list female professors whose accomplishments were greater than those of their male colleagues who had been passed over for promotion.

Although the data could have been consistent with better-qualified women's being denied tenure or other opportunities at the two universities, other plausible explanations exist for smaller numbers of female professors and female professors' earning lower salaries. Women could have been leaving to take academic positions elsewhere, to take positions outside academia, or to spend more time with their families. Women could have earned lower salaries or not have been hired because they were not as productive as their male counterparts. The lack of mention of any of those explanations is yet another indication of the studies' weaknesses. It is remarkable that universities all over the country are imitating those studies when they would not be accepted as evidence by a court, much less as articles by a peer-reviewed journal.

Discrimination against women at universities is being described as a problem of the unconscious, "a pattern of powerful but unrecognized assumptions and attitudes that work systematically against women faculty even in the light of obvious good will."[32] Such a problem can be solved only through quotas and proportionality, the feminists' favorite solution. Hence, the authors of the MIT report piously stated that half of the best available talent was female, and so more women had to be hired. Is it therefore discriminatory that only 5 percent of the Faculty of the Committee on Degrees in Women's Studies at Harvard is male? The answer depends on who chooses to major in a particular field at a particular time. One clue: according to the MIT report, 37 percent of all graduate students in the School of Science were female in the mid-1990s, far fewer than 50 percent.

Conclusion

In today's world, with its talk of male oppression and its labyrinth of preference progams, it is easy for women to lose sight of individual responsibility. If they fail, they are led to believe that they do so because of their sex, not because of individual performance. Their attainment is diluted, because neither women nor outside observers know whether success is due to their achievements or their sex.

Preference programs for women of the type enforced today would not exist if the government and businesses believed that individuals were more important than groups. Individuals may need public support because of wrongs they have suffered as individuals. They do not need support because of their association with one demographic group or another. It is patronizing to assume that every member of a single demographic group, such as women, has shared identical experiences that require the same government intervention in the form of preference programs.

Furthermore, preference programs hurt all businesses. They interfere with firms' efficiency and fair market practices. An efficient business is one that discovers the best practices at the lowest costs to satisfy its customers and finds employees that can implement those practices. Outside groups or even governments do not have enough information to dictate business practices or the class of employees to be hired.

A fundamental principle of fairness is treating similarly situated individuals the same. If an individual man and an individual woman are equally qualified in every respect for a job, a fair firm would treat them in the same way. Another fundamental principle of fairness is rewarding a better match over a less good fit. If one job candidate is clearly superior to another, the better candidate should receive an offer before the weaker candidate.

In contrast, preferential programs instruct businesses to hire employees to meet certain preordained, government-planned outcomes that often do not account for differences in choices between men and women. Advocates of special preferences for women must keep alive the notion that women are weaker and should be treated as a protected class. If women and men were ever to be treated equally and if individual identity mattered more than group identity, the entire concept of affirmative action for women would vanish.

Preferential programs obliterate principles of fairness. Under such programs, female job candidates and employees often do not compete directly with male candidates and employees. In contrast to the original feminists' rhetoric—with which we agree—about women's being able to stand up for themselves, job candidates and employees are treated separately by sex. That is neither efficient nor fair, and it is eerily reminiscent of the bad old days when group identity was more important than individual merit.

10

Recognizing Success

Over the past fifty years the United States has moved from a society that limited opportunities for women by both law and custom to a nation where inflexible standards of numerical parity are often the measure of equality. Half a century ago, being among the best and brightest sometimes meant less if one was a woman. Many educational institutions and professions excluded women, and it was common for businesses to advertise jobs at one salary for men and another for women. Now, discrimination against women is illegal, and women are succeeding educationally and professionally in a historically unprecedented fashion. The evidence is clear: given equality of opportunity, American women have triumphed.

Yet a host of social institutions, including our nation's schools, the media, federal and state government agencies, and even many corporations have not fully acknowledged those accomplishments. The perception persists that women need protection by the federal government and that their success is a fragile and potentially fleeting thing.

In large part, that perception is fueled by the rhetoric and activities of mainstream feminist organizations, which continue to claim that women are victims—an ironic message for a movement whose original, animating impulse was that women were as intelligent and capable as men and thus should be given equal opportunity to participate in civic life. Success has bred a new dilemma for modern feminists, for acknowledging women's progress would require a radical redefinition of their movement. Instead of reorienting themselves, they have chosen to snatch defeat from the jaws of victory by continuing to claim that women are victims.

A Level Playing Field and Fair Results

Our earlier chapters document the triumph of women in education, in the labor market, and in a range of other vocations and avocations. What accounts for feminists' unwillingness to acknowledge that triumph? In part, their willful blindness to women's success is a necessary strategy, given their reliance on federal funds. As we have shown, feminists' claims about women have garnered a particularly strong hearing throughout the federal government bureaucracy, and feminist organizations are beneficiaries of federal largesse. Since bureaucracies are naturally averse to change and notoriously incapable of reasonable self-assessment, many ill-conceived feminist projects, such as the Women's Educational Equity Act programs at the Department of Education, appear to have established permanent homes in our institutions of government.

Feminists have also successfully continued to draw on the political capital of their movement's history. In the 1960s feminists' claims about wage gaps and unequal treatment had the weight of fact and immediate experience behind them. In such an environment, calls for preferential treatment for women were understandable. Today, the facts no longer justify such rhetoric; they certainly do not justify feminists' claims that a careful reassessment of preferential programs for women spells the end of equality.

A careful reassessment is necessary, since many of those federal programs have outlived their usefulness or, worse, have evolved over the years into systems in which gender often trumps merit.

Today, federal and state governments carefully monitor the number of female employees in the labor market, and the federal Equal Employment Opportunity Commission requires private institutions with over ten workers to do the same. To comply with EEOC regulations, universities, governments, and private corporations are required to show that they have the "right" mix of men and women—not that they have the best-qualified students, faculty, or employees.

Few, if any, private or public employers in America would dream of keeping detailed records of employees that are based on religion, height, weight, baldness, skin condition, or left-handedness, even if clear evidence existed of past discrimination on the basis or one or more of those characteristics. People with different personal characteristics compete freely in job markets, and employers do not keep track of those characteristics. The same principle should apply to women. In today's environment of equal opportunity for women, gender is just as meaningless as height in determining whether a person should get special preference for a job.

Opportunity or Outcomes?

Today, mainstream feminism is characterized by a very different vision of equality from the one that originally inspired the movement. Today's feminists emphasize equality of outcomes and statistical parity between men and women rather than equality of opportunity. They pursue a numbers game that sees discrimination against women in any area in which they constitute less than 50 percent of participants. That standard is insidious, for it cannot be achieved without substantial social engineering. It also rejects individual choice and freedom, which bring with them unpredictability.

One could argue, for example, that preferences for African Americans are a worthy social objective, given the legacy of slavery, Jim Crow laws, and historical patterns of systematic discrimination, whose effects may persist today. Economic and cultural indicators reveal that blacks are still at a disadvantage to whites; paying heed to race conceivably could enable policymakers to better assess and engage such problems. Those issues are complex, and the subject of many other books.[1] The logic behind preferential programs for minorities does not hold when applied to women. As the evidence clearly demonstrates, women are a better-educated, longer-living majority of the population.[2] No consistent, fact-based argument exists for giving women preferential treatment in such circumstances.

Feminists' emphasis on equality of outcomes has also undermined existing antidiscrimination legislation. The earliest laws passed to combat discrimination against women in the workplace—the Equal Pay Act of 1963, the Civil Rights Act of 1964, and Title IX of the Educational Amendments of 1972—protected women from overt cases of unfair treatment, such as jobs that paid one salary for men and a lower salary for women, or educational programs that barred entry to women.

Some legal scholars, most notably Richard A. Epstein of the University of Chicago, have suggested that the antidiscrimination provisions contained in Title VII of the Civil Rights Act were ill-advised and should be repealed.[3] By prohibiting discrimination on the grounds of gender, race, and national origin, the argument goes, employers lost a vital freedom of contract, namely, freedom of choice over whom to employ. Epstein argued that although the goal of the drafters of the Civil Rights Act was to increase opportunities for individual employment and make hiring a more rational process, it has ended up by having the reverse effect. Hiring was made more costly, and employers created fewer jobs. Further, the main test of antidiscrimination laws has become a near match between the percentage of men, women, and minorities in a business and their representation in the labor force as a whole. Employers who fail to meet that narrow standard often find themselves accused of discrimination. Although we do not advocate the repeal of the Civil Rights Act, Epstein is correct to identify its dangers.

In recent years, Congress has considered numerous proposals to expand the reach of existing antidiscrimination law. In 1999 then-President Clinton suggested expanding antidiscrimination provisions to make parents a protected workplace class.[4] Others have proposed expanding Title VII to cover sexual orientation. As we have seen, however, the regulations drafted to enforce the law are already unnecessarily complex and in many cases actually contrary to the clearest reading of the intent of the law. Reforming—rather than expanding—them should be a priority.

Women Need Good Government, Not Apologists for Failed Programs

Mainstream feminist organizations claim to speak on behalf of all women. Yet, time and again, feminist groups have proven just the opposite. A case in point is Proposition 209, a ballot initiative in California in 1996. Proposition 209 outlawed the use of preferences, including preferences for women, in most state programs. Claiming that it would harm women, feminists groups ardently opposed it. Yet most Californians, and most women, voted for Proposition 209.

In attacking Proposition 209, feminists contended that, without special programs, women could do nothing in California. The feminists threatened politicians with the certain loss of support from women. In turn, most government officials opposed the proposition. So, too, did many large corporations and media outlets. Although large institutions opposed the proposition, the majority of voters, including women, supported the proposition.

Intelligent and honest politicians have nothing to fear from scrapping affirmative action programs. In fact, women enjoyed great success in California both before and after Proposition 209. By many measures, women have done even better with the elimination of preferences. For example, the percentage of women in the freshman class of the University of California at Berkeley and in many other universities across California actually *increased* after passage of Proposition 209.

Feminist organizations may succeed in coopting some parts of government, the media, and corporations, but they have not succeeded in coopting all American women. Like individual men, individual women want success. Personal success comes from individual efforts, not government programs.

Politicians cannot legislate success. Removing special government programs liberates women from the shadow of dependence that the feminist movement originally intended to eliminate. Throughout this book, we have sought to remind readers of the incredible accomplishments of American women, for theirs is a success story that bears telling. The equality of opportunity that the law guarantees has dramatically expanded the range of choices available to women. In the twenty-first century, American women are the freest and most successful women on earth. The feminist movement of the 1960s deserves a great deal of credit for that; we must also credit an economy that allows for flexibility and entrepreneurship.

Above all, however, credit goes to the women themselves—women who are investing in an education, entering the workplace in record numbers, and venturing into the world of cyberspace; women who are physicians, lawyers, educators, chief executive officers, soccer players, and astronauts; and women who are raising children, volunteering, running for office, and running small businesses—the fastest-growing segment of the American economy.

It is in that context that the message of the contemporary feminist movement is implausible, for it is so clearly at odds with fact. Radical feminists' emphasis on women as victims—and, to a lesser degree, their assumption that the government must guarantee women's successes by enacting further protections for them—is not only misguided, but, as we have seen in some cases, harmful as well. Today, the "woman question" is no longer a debate over what women are capable of doing. Women have proven themselves capable of doing anything they set their minds to do. Rather, the debate today is over how we define equality and success and how we understand individual choice.

Contemporary feminism defines success not as equality of opportunity, but as equal outcomes for women and men in educational and workplace fields. By that definition, women will have achieved success only when they are half of all math majors, half of all corporate CEOs, or half of all college athletes. But that is a misguided standard of success, for it fails to account for the heterogeneity of the female population and the powerful force of individual choice. We are not denying the need for legal protection for women. The Equal Pay Act of 1963, Title VII of the Civil Rights Act of 1964, and Title IX of the Educational Amendments of 1972 ensure legal equality of opportunity for all Americans, and our government and legal institutions continue to enforce them.

What we do not need, however, are the misguided mandates and policy interpretations whose ill effects we have documented in these pages. We should do away with the proportionality principle in all its various incarnations, whether it be the EEOC's acceptance of disparate impact theory in its enforcement of Title VII in workplace discrimination claims or in the Department of Education's Office for Civil Rights' use of the proportionality test for enforcing Title IX in college athletics. We should reject proportionality as the measure of equality when feminists claim that our educational system short-changes girls or when they loudly protest that there are not enough women CEOs. The assumption that, without discrimination, women would make up half of all truck drivers or half of all soccer players is one based on ideology and ignores the available evidence on women's preferences. And it is an assumption that is demeaning to women, for it suggests that we are incapable of making choices for ourselves.

We should also reject the underlying victim myth that informs contemporary sexual harassment law, particularly hostile environ-ment sexual harassment claims, and the related drive to restructure the workplace so that it will be more "family-friendly." In both cases the feminist message that women need protections clashes with fact. In addition, as we have seen, overly broad definitions of sexual harassment and sweeping programs for working parents often end up harming the people they are meant to help. Such policies raise the costs of hiring and heighten employers' wariness about the risks a woman employee might pose with regard to discrimination law-suits and the like.

Feminists today are a special interest group, and like any special interest group, they pursue an agenda that will increase their influ-ence and ensure their own organizational existence. Unfortunately, they achieve their agenda through bureaucratic stealth by using the regulatory power of the federal government to transform work-places and classrooms to conform to their vision of equality. And because of the tactics employed, the public is not always aware that those changes are occurring.

In noting how the feminists' definition of equality is misguided, we have also demonstrated how it rejects one of the hallmarks of a free society: the ability to choose one's own path. Ultimately, that is the feminists' dilemma. If they acknowledge the validity of women's choices, whether those choices be to pursue a college degree in nursing, command a space shuttle, or raise children, then they must also finally realize that their goal—equal numbers of men and women in all areas of society—is not one that most women or men in this country share.

For radical feminists, individual success is not enough. Yet a recognition of women's freedom and choices is precisely what feminism is supposed to be about. It is that original feminist vision that we pursue. Perhaps one day the movement that was borne of that vision and that claims to speak for all women will acknowledge that success. That success proves that true equality for women is not a matter of equal outcomes, but of equal opportunities.

Notes

Chapter 1: Setting the Stage

1. Betty Friedan, *The Feminine Mystique* (New York: Dell Publishing Co., 1963).
2. Simone de Beauvoir and Betty Friedan, "Sex, Society, and the Female Dilemma: A Dialogue between Simone de Beauvoir and Betty Friedan," *Saturday Review,* June 14, 1975, 14–20, 56.

Chapter 2: Feigning Discrimination

1. William J. Clinton and Hillary R. Clinton, Remarks of the President and First Lady at Roundtable on Equal Pay, Office of the Press Secretary, White House, April 7, 1999.
2. Women in help-wanted classified advertisements were often referred to as "girls" or "gals," and terms such as *good-looking* were sometimes published requirements. See, for example, issues of the *Los Angeles Times* from 1961.
3. Irving Kristol, "Life without Father," *Wall Street Journal,* November 3, 1994.
4. Heidi Hartmann and Martha Burk, "The Unfinished Agenda: Why Women Must Continue to Organize as Feminists," paper presented at "Beyond Identity Politics: The Changing Role of Gender," American Enterprise Institute, Washington, D.C., April 24, 1997.
5. Feminist Majority Foundation, "Women's Groups Unite to Fight for Affirmative Action," press release, Arlington, Va., March 15, 1995, http://www.feminist.org/news/pr/pr031595.html, accessed June 10, 1999.
6. Hartmann and Burk, "The Unfinished Agenda," 7.
7. Patricia Ireland, National Organization for Women fundraising letter, 1998.
8. Virginia Valian, *Why So Slow? The Advancement of Women* (Cambridge: MIT Press, 1997), 288.
9. Ibid., 290.

10. National Organization for Women, "Affirmative Action," issue report, October 1998, http://www.now.org/issues/affirm/affirmre/html, accessed June 10, 1999.

11. Deborah Rhode, *Speaking of Sex: The Denial of Gender Inequality* (Cambridge: Harvard University Press, 1997), 249.

12. Hartmann and Burk, "The Unfinished Agenda," 10–11.

13. For "stealth discrimination," see National Organization for Women, "Affirmative Action," issue report, http://www.now.org, accessed November 13, 1997. For "hidden curricula," see, for example, Barbara Anne Murphy, "Education: An Illusion for Women," *Southern California Review of Law and Women's Studies* 3 (fall 1993): 40.

14. Richard A. Epstein, personal communication with the authors, spring 2000.

15. E. Christi Cunningham, "Preserving Normal Heterosexual Male Fantasy: The 'Severe or Pervasive' Missed Interpretation of Sexual Harassment in the Absence of a Tangible Job Consequence," *University of Chicago Legal Forum* 21 (1999): 199–275.

16. National Organization for Women, "Who Needs an Equal Rights Amendment? You Do!" http://www.now.org/issues/economic/cea/who.html, accessed June 10, 1999.

17. Eleanor Smeal, "From Gender Gap to Gender Gulf: Abortion, Affirmative Action, and the Radical Right," speech delivered at the National Press Club, February 13, 1997, http://www.feminist.org/news/pr/pr021397.html, accessed June 9, 1999.

18. See S. 74, 106th Cong., 1st sess., January 19, 1999; S. 702, 106th Cong., 1st sess., March 24, 1999; and White House, Office of the Press Secretary, "The President Announces Equal Pay Initiative and Urges Passage of Paycheck Fairness Act," January 30, 1999.

19. William J. Clinton, Executive Order 13152, "Further Amendment to Order 11478, Equal Employment Opportunity in Federal Government," White House, Office of the Press Secretary, May 2, 2000. See also David E. Rosenbaum, "Work Rules: Going Easy on Parents Isn't So Easy," *New York Times,* May 7, 2000.

20. William J. Clinton, "Radio Address by the President to the Nation," White House, Office of the Press Secretary, February 12, 2000. See also White House, Office of the Press Secretary, "President Clinton Announces New Funds Enabling States to Provide Paid Leave to America's Working Parents," February 12, 2000; White House, Office of the Press Secretary, "President Clinton: Helping Parents Meet Their Responsibilities at Home and at Work," May 24, 1999; William J. Clinton, "Memorandum for the Heads of Executive Departments and Agencies; Subject: New Tools to Help Parents Balance Work and Family," White House, Office of the Press Secretary, May 24, 1999; William J. Clinton, "Remarks by the President on Parental Leave," White House, Office of the Press Secretary, November 30, 1999; White House, Office of the Press Secretary, "President Clinton

Announces New Funds Enabling States to Provide Paid Leave to America's Working Parents," February 12, 2000; and William J. Clinton, "Radio Address by the President to the Nation," White House, Office of the Press Secretary, February 12, 2000.

21. *Paycheck Fairness Act,* 106th Cong., 1st sess., S. 74; and *Fair Pay Act of 1999,* 106th Cong., 1st sess., S. 702.

22. *Equal Employment Opportunity Commission v. Joe's Stone Crab, Inc.,* 15 F. Supp. 2d 1364, August 12, 1998, decretal provisions.

23. Ibid.

24. *Equal Employment Opportunity Commission v. Joe's Stone Crab, Inc.,* 220 F.3d 1263, August 4, 2000.

25. See, for example, *Equal Employment Opportunity Commission v. Sedita,* 755 F. Supp. 808 (N.D. Ill. 1991); and *Equal Employment Opportunity Commission v. Sedita,* 816 F. Supp. 1291 (N.D. Ill. 1993).

26. Mary Ellen Podmolik, "Women's Workout World Agrees to Hire Male Workers," *Chicago Sun Times,* June 15, 1994.

27. J. M. Lawrence, "Law Lets Women Sweat Where the Boys Aren't," *Boston Herald,* February 7, 1998.

28. Edward W. Lempinen and Pamela Burdman, "Measure to Cut Back Affirmative Action Wins," *San Francisco Chronicle,* November 6, 1996; and Tom Brune, "Poll: I-200 Passage Was Call for Reform," *Seattle Times,* November 4, 1998.

29. Richard A. Epstein, *Forbidden Grounds: The Case against Employment Discrimination Laws* (Cambridge: Harvard University Press, 1992).

30. Nadine Strossen, "Women's Rights under Siege," *North Dakota Law Review* 73 (1997): 207–30.

31. *Muller v. Oregon,* 208 U.S. 412 (1908). See also Nancy Woloch, "Introduction," *Muller v. Oregon: A Brief History with Documents* (New York: Bedford Books of St. Martin's Press, 1996).

32. *Family and Medical Leave Act of 1993,* Public Law 103-3, February 5, 1993.

Chapter 3: Learning a Lesson: How Women Have Surpassed Men in Education

1. Edward Clarke, *Sex in Education; or, A Fair Chance for Girls* (Boston: Osgood and Company, 1873), 127. On Clarke, see Rosalind Rosenberg, *Beyond Separate Spheres: Intellectual Roots of Modern Feminism* (New Haven: Yale University Press, 1982), chap. 1, "In the Shadow of Dr. Clarke."

2. On women and education, see Mabel Newcomer, *A Century of Higher Education for Women* (New York: Harper, 1959), and Jill Conway, "Perspectives on the History of Women's Education in the United States," *History of Education Quarterly* 14 (spring 1974): 1–12.

3. Gabrielle Lange, "The Gender Bias Debate," *AAUW Outlook,* spring 1997, 16.

4. Ibid.

5. Warren W. Willingham and Nancy S. Cole, eds., *Gender and Fair Assessment* (Mahwah, N.J.: Lawrence Erlbaum Associates, 1997), 57.

6. Ibid., 61.

7. Ibid. On claims of gender bias in standardized testing, see the 1989 report by the Center for Women Policy Studies and Equality in Testing, "The SAT Gender Gap: Identifying the Causes." For the legal implications, see Katherine Connor and Ellen J. Vargyas, "The Legal Implications of Gender Bias in Standardized Testing," *Berkeley Women's Law Journal* 7 (1992): 13–89.

8. Peter Applebombe, "Pupils Know but Cannot Apply Scientific Facts, New Test Finds," *New York Times,* May 4, 1997.

9. Carol A. Dwyer and Linda M. Johnson, "Grades, Accomplishments, and Correlates," in Willingham and Cole, eds., *Gender and Fair Assessment,* 150–51.

10. *AP National Summary Report* (New York: College Board, 1985, 2000).

11. Christina Hoff Sommers, *The War against Boys* (New York: Simon and Schuster, 2000).

12. Yupin Bae, Susan Choy, Claire Geddes, Jennifer Sable, and Thomas Snyder, U.S. Department of Education, National Center for Education Statistics, *Educational Equity for Girls and Women,* NCES 2000-030 (Washington, D.C.: Government Printing Office, 2000).

13. David Lubinski and Camilla Persson Benbow, "Gender Differences in Abilities and Preferences among the Gifted: Implications for the Math-Science Pipeline," *Current Directions in Psychological Science* 1, no. 2 (April 1992): 61–65.

14. Ibid.

15. "Test-Makers to Revise Nat. Merit Exam to Address Gender Bias," *FairTest Examiner* (fall 1996), http://www.fairtest.org/examarts/fall96/natmerit.htm, accessed June 5, 2000. See also Jennifer C. Braceras, "Affirmative Action, Gender Equity," *Independent Women's Forum Issue Analysis: The Gender Quota Mega-Reg* (Arlington, Va., 1999).

16. Thomas G. Mortenson, "Where Are the Boys? The Growing Gender Gap in Higher Education," *College Board Review,* no. 108, August 1999, 8–17.

17. See Sarah Glazer, "Boys' Emotional Needs: Is Growing Up Tougher for Boys Than for Girls?" *Congressional Quarterly Researcher,* June 18, 1999, 521; Tamar Lewin, "U.S. Colleges Begin to Ask: 'Where Have the Men Gone?'" *New York Times,* December 6, 1998; Tamar Lewin, "How Boys Lost Out to Girl Power," *New York Times,* December 12, 1998; and Brendan I. Koerner, "Where the Boys Aren't," *U.S. News & World Report,* February 8, 1999, 46.

18. U.S. Department of Education, National Center for Education Statistics, *Digest of Education Statistics, 2000* (Washington, D.C.: Government Printing Office, 2001), table 101.

19. Dwyer and Johnson, "Grades, Accomplishments, and Correlates," 155; and Sommers, *The War against Boys.*

20. U.S. Department of Education, National Center for Education Statistics, Integrated Postsecondary Education Data System, "Completions" surveys.

21. Marvin H. Kosters, *Wage Levels and Inequality* (Washington, D.C.: AEI Press, 1998), 35.

22. Lewin, "U.S. Colleges Begin to Ask: 'Where Have the Men Gone?'"

23. Ibid. See also Koerner, "Where the Boys Aren't." On the University of Georgia's gender balancing, see "Editorial: Big Woman on Campus," *Savannah Morning News,* December 16, 1998. See also Barry Klein, "Men Slowly Disappearing from Florida Campuses," *St. Petersburg Times,* February 15, 1999.

24. David Graves, Admissions Office, University of Georgia, Athens, personal communication with the authors, May 4, 2000.

25. U.S. Department of Education, National Center for Education Statistics, "Degrees and Other Formal Awards Conferred" surveys, and Integrated Postsecondary Education Data System, "Completions" surveys.

26. Allen R. Sanderson, Bernard Dugoni, Thomas Hoffer, and Lance Selfa, *Doctorate Recipients from United States Universities: Summary Report 1998* (Chicago: National Opinion Research Center, 1999). The center's report gives the results of data collected in the "Survey of Earned Doctorates," conducted for the National Science Foundation, the National Institutes for Health, the National Endowment for the Humanities, the U.S. Department of Education, and the U.S. Department of Agriculture.

27. Shulamit Kahn, "Women in the Economics Profession," *Journal of Economic Perspectives* 9 (fall 1995): 199–200.

28. Sarah E. Turner and William G. Bowen, "Choice of Major: The Changing Unchanging Gender Gap," *Industrial and Labor Relations Review* 2, no. 2 (January 1, 1999): 289.

29. National Women's Law Center, "Discrimination against Women and Girls in Education: Why Affirmative Action in Education Remains Essential," *NWLC Information Sheet* (Washington, D.C.: National Women's Law Center, July 1997), 6.

30. Ibid., 5, 2.

31. Lange, "The Gender Bias Debate," 15.

32. National Women's Law Center, "Discrimination against Women and Girls in Education," 5.

33. Ibid.

34. Charles Brown and Mary Corcoran, "Sex-Based Differences in School Content and the Male–Female Wage Gap," *Journal of Labor Economics* 15 (1997): 431–32.

35. Ibid. and authors' calculations.

36. Brown and Corcoran, "Sex-Based Differences in School Content," 460.

37. Victoria Benning, "Gender Gap in Fairfax Computer Classes," *Washington Post,* July 14, 1998.

38. Ibid. The AAUW report recommended that counties review their classroom computer software for "gender content, appeal, and acceptance" and that

guidance counselors and teachers receive "special training in breaking down sex segregation."

39. We discuss the effect of Title IX on women's collegiate athletic programs in chapter 8.

40. See U.S. Code, vol. 20, sec. 1681 (b).

41. National Coalition for Women and Girls in Education, "Executive Summary, Title IX: Report Card on Gender Equity," June 23, 1997, 25.

42. Ibid.

43. Ibid. and National Women's Law Center, "Discrimination against Women and Girls in Education," 7.

44. William J. Clinton, "Nondiscrimination on the Basis of Race, Sex, Color, National Origin, Disability, Religion, Age, Sexual Orientation, and Status as a Parent in Federally Conducted Education and Training Programs," Executive Order 13160, June 23, 2000, *Federal Register* 65, no. 1245 (June 27, 2000): 39775–78.

45. *Federal Register* 64, no. 209, pt. 3 (October 29, 1999): 58568–606.

46. At this writing, three agencies have published their individual final rules: the Department of Justice, the Department of Energy, and the Nuclear Regulatory Commission. Kimberly Schuld, Independent Women's Forum, Arlington, Va., personal communication with the authors, February 20, 2001.

47. See John Leg, "Gender Police: Pull Over," *U.S. News & World Report,* March 23, 1998.

48. Flora Davis, *Moving the Mountain: The Women's Movement in America since 1960* (New York: Simon and Schuster, 1991): 211–12.

49. Andrew Fishel and Janice Pottker, *National Politics and Sex Discrimination in Education* (Lexington, Mass.: Lexington Books, 1977): 67, 90. In 1988 Congress amended the Women's Educational Equity Act by eliminating the National Advisory Council on Women's Education Programs and by appropriating less money for implementation of programs. See Sharon L. Sims, "Women's History and the Public Schools," *Women's Rights Law Reporter* 14 (winter 1992), 9.

50. Ibid.

51. http://www.edc.org/WomensEquity/weeainfo/, accessed June 6, 2000; Christina Hoff Sommers, *The War against Boys: How Misguided Feminism Is Harming Our Young Men* (New York: Simon & Schuster, 2000); and Independent Women's Forum, "WEEA Fact Sheet," 1999.

52. In 1999 the center's attorneys represented Aurelia Davis in the sexual harassment lawsuit she filed on behalf of her daughter against the Board of Education of Monroe County, Georgia.

53. Barbara Anne Murphy, "Education: An Illusion for Women," *Southern California Review of Law and Women's Studies* 3 (fall 1993): 25.

54. Ibid., 30, 36, 39–40. See also Christina Hoff Sommers, *The War against Boys,* and Judith Kleinfeld, "The Surprising Ease of Changing the Belief That Schools Shortchange Girls," in Rita J. Simon, ed., *From Data to Public Policy*

(New York: Women's Freedom Network and University Press of America, 1996).

55. For "stealth discrimination," see National Organization for Women, "Affirmative Action," *Issue Report,* http://www.now.org, accessed November 13, 1997. For "hidden curricula," see, for example, Murphy, "Education: An Illusion for Women."

56. Murphy, "Education: An Illusion for Women," 48, 58.

57. Sims, "Women's History and the Public Schools," 10, 19.

58. Ibid., p. 23. In a footnote Sims said that "by feminist, I mean a perspective which encompasses the views of women as a group." But her arguments gave her away. She suggested, for example, that Catharine MacKinnon's work "would adapt well to history or social studies courses." See Sims's footnotes 150 and 135.

59. Ibid., footnote 110.

60. New England Council of Land-Grant University Women, "Vision 2000," University of Maine, February 1997, www.ume.maine.edu/~pcw/vision2.htm, accessed June 6, 2000. Ann Ferguson, director of Women's Studies at the University of Massachusetts at Amherst, attempted to defend Vision 2000 in a 1998 opinion piece. Ann Ferguson, "Gender Equity on the College Campus," *Boston Globe,* February 23, 1998.

61. Daphne Patai, "Why Not a Feminist Overhaul of Higher Education?" *Chronicle of Higher Education,* January 23, 1998.

62. Ibid. See also John Leo, "No Takeovers, Please," *U.S. News & World Report,* January 19, 1998, 13.

63. Pamela Ferdinand, "Feminist Teacher Prefers All-Woman Class," *Washington Post,* February 26, 1999; and Robin Estrich, Associated Press, "Radical Feminist BC Prof Told She Must Teach Men," February 25, 1999. For examples of feminists praising Daly's actions, see Maria Karagianis, "Mary, Mary, Quite Contrary," *Ms.,* June/July 1999.

64. National Women's Law Center, "Discrimination against Women and Girls in Education," 8.

Chapter 4: Choosing a Job: From the Kitchen to the Boardroom

1. "Jennifer Simon" (pseudonym), interview with the authors, spring 1999.

2. Raju Chellam, "Fiorina's Fun Formula for Success," *Business Times* (Singapore), October 29, 1999; and Patricia Sellers, "The 50 Most Powerful Women in American Business," *Fortune,* October 12, 1998, 76. For the 1999 rankings, see Patricia Sellers, "Powerful Women: These Women Rule," *Fortune,* October 25, 1999, 94. For the 2000 list, see David Grainger, Christopher Tkaczyk, and Alynda Wheat, "The Power 50," *Fortune,* October 16, 2000, 139.

3. See the *Los Angeles Times,* various issues, 1961.

4. Laura Ingalls Wilder, *These Happy Golden Years* (New York: HarperCollins, 1971); and Laura Ingalls Wilder, *The First Four Years* (New York: HarperCollins, 1972).

5. Laura Ingalls Wilder, *Little Town on the Prairie* (New York: HarperCollins, 1971).

6. Wilder, *These Happy Golden Years.*

7. U.S. Department of Commerce, Bureau of the Census, *Historical Statistics* 1, Series D, 49-62; *Statistical Abstract of the United States: 1999,* no. 658; and *Statistical Abstract of the United States: 1981,* no. 652.

8. Bureau of the Census, *Current Population Reports,* Series P20-514, "Marital Status and Living Arrangements: March 1998 (Update)," and earlier reports, http://www.census.gov/population/socdemo/ms-la/tabms-2.txt, accessed January 7, 1999.

9. U.S. Department of Labor, *Employment and Earnings* 48, no. 1 (January 2001): 167–68; and *Historical Statistics* 1, Series D, 29-41, 1975, 131–32.

10. *Employment and Earnings* 48, no. 1 (January 2001): 168; Bureau of Labor Statistics, "Civilian Labor Force Participation Rates of Men by Age, Annual Averages, 1948–98," facsimile, March 10, 1999; and *Historical Statistics* 1, Series D, 29-41, 132.

11. U.S. Department of Labor, *Handbook of Labor Statistics, 1967* (Washington, D.C.: Government Printing Office, 1967), table 8.

12. *Statistical Abstract of the United States: 1999,* 413, table 653, "Civilian Labor Force and Participation Rates by Educational Attainment, Sex, Race, and Hispanic Origin, 1992–1998."

13. Bureau of the Census, "Marital Status and Living Arrangements: March 1998 (Update)," *Current Population Reports,* Series P20-514, and earlier reports, http://www.census.gov/population/socdemo/ms-la/tabms-2.txt, January 7, 1999, accessed June 26, 2000.

14. Claudia Goldin, "Career and Family: College Women Look to the Past," in Francine D. Blau and Ronald G. Ehrenberg, eds., *Gender and Family Issues in the Workplace* (New York: Russell Sage Foundation, 1997).

15. *Statistical Abstract of the United States: 1999,* table 659, "Employment Status of Women by Marital Status and Presence of Children, 1960–1998."

16. Bureau of Labor Statistics, Division of Labor Force Statistics, unpublished table, "Employment Status of the Civilian Noninstitutional Population by Sex, Age, Presence, and Age of Youngest Child, Marital Status, Race, and Hispanic Origin, March 1999 ADF," facsimile, August 8, 2000.

17. Bureau of the Census, *Current Population Survey;* and U.S. Department of Labor, *Employment and Earnings.*

18. Bureau of Labor Statistics, Division of Labor Force Statistics, unpublished table, "Employment Status of the Civilian Noninstitutional Population by Sex, Age, Presence, and Age of Youngest Child, Marital Status, Race, and Hispanic Origin, March 1999 ADF."

19. *Current Population Reports,* Series P20-482 (1995).

20. Bureau of Labor Statistics, Division of Labor Force Statistics, unpublished table, "Employment Status of the Civilian Noninstitutional Population by Sex, Age, Presence, and Age of Youngest Child, Marital Status, Race, and Hispanic Origin, March 1999 ADF."

21. John Pencavel, "The Market Work Behavior and Wages of Women: 1975–94," *Journal of Human Resources* 33, no. 4 (fall 1998): 771–804.

22. Chinhui Juhn and Kevin M. Murphy, "Wage Inequality and Family Labor Supply," *Journal of Labor Economics* 15, no. 1 (1997): 75.

23. Arlie Russell Hochschild, *The Time Bind: When Work Becomes Home and Home Becomes Work* (New York: Henry Holt & Company, 1997), 105, 263.

24. "Preference for Employment Compared with Staying at Home," question 24, *Voices of Women: The Virginia Slims Opinion Poll, Year 2000* (New York: Philip Morris Inc., 1999), 44.

25. Patricia Sellers, "The 50 Most Powerful Women in American Business," *Fortune,* October 12, 1998, 76; Stuart Elliot, "An Anomaly on Madison Avenue: Why Is Ogilvy's Boss One of the Few Women at the Top?" *New York Times,* February 19, 1997; Caroline Marshall, "The Queen of Madison Avenue," interview, *ASAP Haymarket Publications Ltd. (UK) Campaign,* January 29, 1999, 24. See also Patricia Sellers, "Powerful Women: These Women Rule," *Fortune,* October 25, 1999, 94, where Lazarus was ranked as the fourth most powerful woman.

26. Adrian Michaels, "Heidi Miller Quits Dot-Coms for Insurance," *Financial Times* (London), January 11, 2001; Donna Rosato, "Priceline's Thrills Lure Executive Miller—Quits Citigroup to Help Upstart Grow," *USA Today,* March 29, 2000; Bloomberg News, "Priceline.com Attracts Another Key Exec," *Los Angeles Times,* February 24, 2000; and Patricia Sellers, "The 50 Most Powerful Women in American Business," *Fortune,* October 12, 1998, 76. For *Fortune's* 1999 rankings where Miller was ranked second, see Sellers, "Powerful Women."

27. Del Jones, "Avon Names Asian-American Woman as CEO," *USA Today,* November 5, 1999; Del Jones, "Avon Takes Breast Cancer Fight Personally," *USA Today,* March 7, 2000; and Sarah Rose, "Remaking the Avon Lady; Andrea Jung Must Show U.S. Women That Her Brand Hasn't Gone out of Style," interview, *Money* 29, no. 2 (February 2000): 46. See also Sellers, "The 50 Most Powerful Women in American Business," and for *Fortune's* 1999 ranking where she was ranked fourteenth, see Sellers, "Powerful Women: These Women Rule."

28. Jan Hoffman, "Executive Sets Her Own Price and Style," *New York Times,* March 9, 2000.

29. Heidi Miller, "Using Mergers as Career Stepping Stone; Interview with Travelers Group Senior VP and CFO Heidi Miller," interview by Patti Verbanas, *Corporate Cashflow Magazine* 16, no. 12 (December 1995): 48.

30. Betsy Morris, "Tales of the Trailblazers," *Fortune,* October 12, 1998, 114.

31. Anne Faircloth, "The Class of '83," *Fortune,* October 12, 1998, 127.

32. National Foundation for Women Business Owners, "Key Facts," 2000, http://www.nfwbo.org/key.html, accessed July 5, 2000; National Foundation for Women Business Owners, "Home-Based Women-Owned Businesses Number and Employ Millions," November 16, 1995, http://www.nfwbo.org/LocLink/BIZC/RESEARCH/LinkTo/11-16-1995/11-16-1995.htm, accessed July 5, 2000; and Bureau of the Census, "Characteristics of Business Owners," report number CBO92-1 (1992), 11, 22.

33. Catalyst, National Foundation for Women Business Owners, and Committee of 200, *Paths to Entrepreneurship: New Directions for Women in Business* (New York: Catalyst, National Foundation for Women Business Owners, and Committee of 200, 1998).

34. Marla Dickerson, "Small Business Strategies: For 'Mamapreneurs' Industry Begins at Home," *Los Angeles Times,* September 15, 1999.

35. Faircloth, "The Class of '83," 127.

36. *Adarand Constructors, Inc. v. Pena,* 515 U.S. 200 (1995).

37. Small Business Administration, "Women-Owned Small Business Procurement Program," http://www.sba.gov/GC/wbpprgm.html, accessed June 23, 2000.

38. Small Business Administration, "Memorandum of Understanding between the U.S. Department of Transportation and the U.S. Small Business Administration," December 1998, http://www.sba.gov/GC/dot-mou.pdf, accessed June 23, 2000.

39. Small Business Administration, "Memorandum of Understanding between the U.S. Department of State and the U.S. Small Business Administration," March 15, 1999, http://www.sba.gov/GC/dos-mou.pdf, accessed June 23, 2000.

40. Susan Estrich, *Sex and Power* (New York: Riverhead Books, 2000): 71–72.

41. Heather Hodson, "Doing It All with Martha: Martha Stewart Has Made a Business Empire out of Home-Making," *Daily Telegraph,* October 10, 1997.

42. Online with Oprah, "The Fact Sheet—1999/2000 Season," September 2, 1999, http://www.oprah.com/about/press/about_press_owsfaq.html, accessed July 5, 2000.

43. Angie K. Young, "Assessing the Family and Medical Leave Act in Terms of Gender Equality, Work/Family Balance, and the Needs of Children," *Michigan Journal of Gender and Law* 5 (1998): 113–62. In the article Young draws a distinction between "real" and "forced" choices for working women. See also Nancy E. Dowd, "Maternity Leave: Taking Sex Differences into Account," *Fordham Law Review* 54 (April 1986): 720–21.

44. Historian Julia Kirk Blackwelder traces the origins of the term *pink collar* to the 1960s, when it was used to "separate low-level white-collar positions from better-paying service jobs. While nonmanual and typically used in office environments, the skills demanded for pink-collar jobs do not require collegiate educational training, and the positions hold little opportunity for advancement." Julia Kirk Blackwelder, *Now Hiring: The*

Feminization of Work in the United States, 1900–1990 (College Station: Texas A&M University Press, 1997), 178–79.

45. Deborah Rhode, *Speaking of Sex: The Denial of Gender Inequality* (Cambridge: Harvard University Press, 1997), 142. See also Glass Ceiling Commission, *Good for Business: Making Full Use of the Nation's Capital* (Washington, D.C.: Government Printing Office, March 1995), 12.

46. Beth Dollinger, personal communication with the authors, summer 2000.

47. See Nancy Gabin, "Women and Work," *Encyclopedia of American Social History*, vol. 2 (New York: Charles Scribner's Sons, 1993): 1551.

48. Glass Ceiling Commission, *Good for Business,* 16.

49. Mary E. Becker, "Barriers Facing Women in the Wage-Labor Market and the Need for Additional Remedies: A Reply to Fischel and Lazear," *University of Chicago Law Review* 53 (1986): 934–49; and Margaret Oppenheimer, speech before the Chicago Lawyers Chapter of the Federalist Society, Chicago, July 22, 1997.

50. U.S. Department of Labor, Women's Bureau, "Department of Labor Awards $1.5 million to Assist Women in Nontraditional Training and Job Placement in Six States," press release, July 29, 1996, http://www.dol.gov/opa/public/media/press/wb/wb96301.htm, accessed July 5, 2000.

51. U.S. Department of Labor, Women's Bureau, "Department of Labor Awards $1 million to Promote Women in Apprenticeship and Nontraditional Occupations," press release, September 30, 1998, http://www.dol.gov/opa/public/media/press/wb/wb98405.htm, accessed July 5, 2000.

52. American Medical Association, *Physician Characteristics and Distribution in the U.S.* (Chicago: American Medical Association, 2000), 17, table 1.2, "Total Physicians by Age and Specialty, 1998."

53. Catherine E. Shanelaris and Henrietta Walsh Luneau, with Ellen S. Cohn and Kathleen Bauman, "Ten-Year Gender Survey," *New Hampshire Bar Journal* 39 (March 1998): 56–78.

Chapter 5: Mythical Problems and Solutions: Wage Gaps, Glass Ceilings, and Incomparable Worth

1. Strossen's remarks in that regard are worth repeating in full: "To a large extent, attacks on affirmative action reflect the ongoing racial stereotyping and injustice that continue to plague this country. But they also reflect gender stereotyping and injustice, given that white women have been the major beneficiaries of affirmative action in employment and education. . . . Even with affirmative action, there is still rampant gender discrimination at work, so I shudder to think how much worse it would get without affirmative action." Nadine Strossen, "Women's Rights under Siege," *North Dakota Law Review* 73 (1997): 207–30.

2. Mary K. O'Melveny, "Playing the 'Gender' Card: Affirmative Action and Working Women," *Kentucky Law Journal* 84 (1995–1996): 898.

3. U.S. Department of Labor, *Employment and Earnings* 47, no. 1 (January 2000): 198, table 22, "Persons at Work in Nonagricultural Industries by Age, Sex, Race, Marital Status, and Usual Full- or Part-Time Status."

4. Susan Bianchi-Sand, personal communication with Diana Furchtgott-Roth, Pay Equity Day, April 3, 1998.

5. Sara M. Evans and Barbara J. Nelson, *Wage Justice: Comparable Worth and the Paradox of Technocratic Reform* (Chicago: University of Chicago Press, 1989), 18. See also William H. Chafe, *Women and Equality: Changing Patterns in American Culture* (Oxford: Oxford University Press, 1977), 31–33.

6. See, for example, Kimberly Bayard, Judith Hellerstein, David Neumark, and Kenneth Troske, "Why Are Racial and Ethnic Wage Gaps Larger for Men Than for Women? Exploring the Role of Segregation Using the New Worker-Establishment Characteristics Database," National Bureau of Economic Research Working Paper 6997, March 1999; Francine D. Blau and Lawrence M. Kahn, "Swimming Upstream: Trends in the Gender Wage Differential in the 1980s," *Journal of Labor Economics* 15, no. 1 (1997): 1–42; and Charles Brown and Mary Corcoran, "Sex-Based Differences in School Content and the Male/Female Wage Gap," *Journal of Labor Economics* 15, no. 3, pt. 1 (July 1997): 431–65. Wage gap calculations are by Randolph Stempski, research associate, American Enterprise Institute.

7. Yupin Bae, Susan Choy, Claire Geddes, Jennifer Sable, and Thomas Snyder, U.S. Department of Education, National Center for Education Statistics, *Educational Equity for Girls and Women*, NCES 2000-030 (Washington D.C.: Government Printing Office, 2000).

8. U.S. Department of Education, National Center for Education Statistics, Integrated Postsecondary Data System, "Completions" survey.

9. Bureau of the Census, *Current Population Reports*, Series P-70, no. 10 (1987).

10. See, for example, Francine D. Blau and Andrea H. Beller, "Trends in Earnings Differentials by Gender, 1971–1981," *Industrial and Labor Relations Review* 41 (July 1988): 513–29; Blau and Kahn, "Swimming Upstream"; Stephen G. Bronars and Melissa Famulari, "Wage, Tenure, and Wage Growth Variation within and across Establishments," *Journal of Labor Economics* 15 (1997): 285–317; David A. Macpherson and Barry T. Hirsch, "Wages and Gender Composition: Why Do Women's Jobs Pay Less?" *Journal of Labor Economics* 13 (1995): 426–71; and Robert G. Wood, Mary E. Corcoran, and Paul N. Courant, "Pay Differences among the Highly Paid: The Male–Female Earnings Gap in Lawyers' Salaries," *Journal of Labor Economics* 11 (1993): 417–41.

11. June O'Neill, "The Shrinking Pay Gap," *Wall Street Journal,* October 7, 1994. See also June O'Neill, "Discrimination and Income Differences," in *Race and Gender in the American Economy,* edited by Susan Feiner (Englewood Cliffs, N.J.: Prentice Hall, 1994); and June O'Neill and

Solomon Polachek, "Why the Gender Gap in Wages Narrowed in the 1980s," *Journal of Labor Economics* 11 (1993): 205–29.

12. Jane Waldfogel, "Working Mothers Then and Now: A Cross-Cohort Analysis of the Effects of Maternity Leave on Women's Pay," in *Gender and Family Issues in the Workplace,* edited by Francine D. Blau and Ronald G. Ehrenberg (New York: Russell Sage Foundation, 1997).

13. Kimberly Bayard, Judith Hellerstein, David Neumark, and Kenneth Troske, "New Evidence on Sex Segregation and Sex Differences in Wages from Matched Employee-Employer Data," NBER Working Paper No. W7003, March 1999; and Francine D. Blau, "Trends in the Well-Being of American Women, 1970–1995," *Journal of Economic Literature* 36 (1998): 112–65.

14. Kimberly Bayard, Judith Hellerstein, David Neumark, and Kenneth Troske, "New Evidence on Sex Segregation and Sex Differences in Wages from Matched Employee-Employer Data," April 2000.

15. Jane Waldfogel, "Working Mothers Then and Now: A Cross-Cohort Analysis of the Effects of Maternity Leave on Women's Pay"; Claudia Goldin, "Career and Family: College Women Look to the Past," in *Gender and Family Issues in the Workplace;* and David Neumark and Sanders Korenman, "Sources of Bias in Women's Wage Equations: Results Using Sibling Data," *Journal of Human Resources* 29 (1994): 379–405.

16. William J. Clinton, "Further Amendment to Executive Order 11478, Equal Employment Opportunity in Federal Government," Executive Order 13152, White House, Office of the Press Secretary, May 2, 2000, http://www.pub.whitehouse.gov/uri-res/I2R?urn:pdi://oma.eop.gov.us/2000/5/3/11.text.2.

17. See Claudia Goldin and Solomon Polachek, "Residual Differences by Sex: Perspectives on the Gender Gap in Earnings," *American Economic Review* 77 (May 1987): 143–51.

18. Victor R. Fuchs, *Women's Quest for Economic Equality* (Cambridge: Harvard University Press, 1988), 54.

19. Goldin and Polachek, "Residual Differences by Sex," 150. Goldin and Polachek were careful to point out that their findings were not meant to suggest that women did not sometimes face discrimination in the workplace.

20. National Committee on Pay Equity, "Equal Pay Day Organizing Kit," October 1998.

21. Statement of Congresswoman Rosa DeLauro, "Wage Gap versus Republican Reality Gap," April 22, 1999.

22. National Committee on Pay Equity, "Questions and Answers about Equal Pay Day," http://feminist.com/fairpay/epdqa.htm, accessed September 12, 2000.

23. Heidi I. Hartmann, Katherine R. Allen, and Christine Owens, *Equal Pay for Working Families: National and State Data on the Pay Gap and Its Costs* (Washington, D.C.: AFL-CIO and the Institute for Women's Policy Research, 1999).

24. Catalyst, *1998 Census of Women Corporate Officers and Top Earners* (New York: Catalyst, 1998).

25. Judith H. Dobrzynski, "Study Finds Few Women in 5 Highest Company Jobs," *New York Times,* October 18, 1996. See also David D. Kirkpatrick, "Women Occupy Few Top Jobs, A Study Shows," *Wall Street Journal,* October 18, 1996.

26. Kingsley R. Browne, "Sex and Temperament in Modern Society: A Darwinian View of the Glass Ceiling and the Gender Gap," *Arizona Law Review* 37, no. 4 (1995): 1069. The study was conducted by Hoffman Research Associates, and the Fortune 500 company was listed only as "the XYZ Company." See Browne, p. 1069, footnote 669.

27. Bureau of Labor Statistics, Division of Labor Force Statistics, unpublished table 25B, "Persons at Work by Actual Hours of Work at All Jobs during the Reference Week, Age, Sex, Race, and Hispanic Origin, Annual Average 1998," facsimile, June 2, 2000.

28. The Civil Rights Act of 1991 created the Glass Ceiling Commission to report on diversity in the workplace. See Federal Glass Ceiling Commission, *Good for Business: Making Full Use of the Nation's Human Capital* (Washington D.C.: Government Printing Office, March 1995).

29. Glass Ceiling Commission, *Good for Business,* 28.

30. O'Melveny, "Playing the 'Gender' Card," 867.

31. *Equal Employment Opportunity Commission v. Joe's Stone Crab, Inc.,* 969 F. Supp. 727, July 3, 1997, 738 B, challenged employment practice.

32. For a complete discussion of disparate impact in theory and in practice, see Richard A. Epstein, *Forbidden Grounds: The Case against Employment Discrimination Laws* (Cambridge: Harvard University Press, 1992): 182–241 and 367–92. See also Richard A. Epstein, "Gender Is for Nouns," *DePaul Law Review* 41, no. 2 (summer 1992): 981–1005; and Richard A. Epstein, "Liberty, Patriarchy, and Feminism," *University of Chicago Legal Forum* 21 (1999): 89–114.

33. Walter Olson, *The Excuse Factory* (New York: Free Press, 1997).

34. *Watson v. Fort Worth Bank & Trust,* 487 U.S. 977, 990–92 (1988), 108 S. Ct. 2786–87.

35. *Equal Employment Opportunity Commission v. Joe's Stone Crab, Inc.,* 15 F. Supp. 2d 1364, August 12, 1998, decretal provisions.

36. *Equal Employment Opportunity Commission v. Joe's Stone Crab, Inc.,* 220 F.3d 1263, August 4, 2000; and Joanne Bass, owner of Joe's Stone Crab, personal communication with the authors, February 21, 2001.

37. Peter Brimelow and Leslie Spencer, "When Quotas Replace Merit, Everybody Suffers," *Forbes,* February 15, 1993, 80.

38. Epstein, *Forbidden Grounds,* 385–92.

39. *American Federation of State, County, and Municipal Employees v. Washington,* 578 F. Supp. 846 (W.D. Wash. 1983).

40. Ellen Frankel Paul, *Equity and Gender: The Comparable Worth Debate* (New Brunswick, N.J.: Transaction Publishers, 1989).

41. U.S. Department of Labor, Bureau of Labor Statistics, *National Census of Fatal Occupational Injuries, 1998,* table 4, "Fatal Occupational Injuries and

Employment by Selected Worker Characteristics, 1998," August 4, 1999, http://www.stats.bls.gov:80/news.release/cfoi.toc.htm, accessed April 6, 2000.

42. William J. Clinton, "Remarks by the President in Statement on Equal Pay," White House, Office of the Press Secretary, January 24, 2000.

43. *Paycheck Fairness Act,* 106th Cong., 1st sess., S. 74, January 19, 1999, 11.

44. Ibid., 12.

45. National Organization for Women, "Action Alert: Support Strong Pay Equity Bill," February 28, 2000, http://www.now.org/issues/economic/alerts/03-03-00.html, accessed July 24, 2000.

46. Ibid.

47. Susan E. Gardner and Christopher Daniel, "Implementing Comparable Worth/Pay Equity: Experiences of Cutting-Edge States," *Public Personnel Management* 27, no. 4 (winter 1998): 475–90.

48. Faith Zwemke, Minnesota Department of Employee Relations, personal communication with the authors, November 2, 1999.

49. For additional information, see Steven E. Rhoads, *Incomparable Worth: Pay Equity Meets the Market* (Cambridge, U.K.: Cambridge University Press, 1993).

50. Ibid.

51. *Hayward v. Cammell Laird Shipbuilders Ltd.*, House of Lords (U.K.), [1988] 1 AC 894, May 5, 1988; and Steven E. Rhoads, "Pay Equity Won't Go Away," *Across the Board,* July/August 1993, 39.

52. Equal Opportunities Commission (United Kingdom), "EOC's Code of Practice on Equal Pay Comes into Effect," press release, March 21, 1997.

53. Naomi Caine, "Girls Catch Up in Fair Pay Race," *Sunday Times* (London), April 5, 1998.

54. Letter, *Ottawa Citizen,* May 5, 2000.

55. Kathryn May, "Another Pay-Equity Battle Looms," *Ottawa Citizen,* June 4, 2000.

56. "Native Health-Care Workers Win $45M Pay-Equity Settlement," *Ottawa Citizen,* June 30, 2000.

57. May, "Another Pay-Equity Battle Looms."

58. Ibid.

59. See Karyn Standen, "Bell Turns over Operator Service to Arizona Firm," *Ottawa Citizen,* January 12, 1999; Dave Rutherford, "Poppycock Pay Equity Costs Women Their Jobs: Faced with Absurd Wage Burden, Bell Rightly Chose to Bail Out," *Calgary Sun,* January 15, 1999; Alison Macgregor, "Jobs to Stay Here, Bell Says: But Union Remains Skeptical," *Gazette* (Montreal), January 13, 1999; Grant Buckler, "Supreme Court Won't Hear Bell Canada Appeal on Pay Equity," *Newsbytes,* July 9, 1999; Vanessa Lu, "Bell Offers Pay Equity Deal Just as Operators Lose Jobs," *Toronto Star,* October 1, 1999; "Top Court Won't Hear Old Pay-Equity Case," *Vancouver Sun,* July 9, 1999; James Daw, "Bell Operators Dealt Pay Equity Blow," *Toronto Star,* November 9, 2000; and Valerie Lawton, "Pay Equity Impasse," *Toronto Star,* February 15, 2001.

60. See Standen, "Bell Turns over Operator Service"; Rutherford, "Poppycock Pay Equity"; Macgregor, "Jobs to Stay Here"; Buckler, "Supreme Court Won't Hear Bell Canada Appeal"; and Lu, "Bell Offers Pay Equity Deal."

61. Paul cogently explored those questions and others in *Equity and Gender,* 50–57.

62. Ibid., 65.

63. Dorothy L. Sayers, *Are Women Human?* (Grand Rapids, Mich.: Eerdmans Publishing, 1971), 26, 34.

64. *Muller v. Oregon,* 208 U.S. 412 (1908).

65. "More Women Taking Executive Positions; Figures Show Income Gap Remains Sizeable," *Dallas Morning News,* April 25, 2000.

66. Nancy F. Gabin, "Women and Work," *Encyclopedia of American History*, vol. 2 (New York: Charles Scribner's Sons, 1993), 1549.

Chapter 6: No Laughing Matter: Sexual Harassment

1. Equal Employment Opportunity Commission, "Sexual Harassment Charges: EEOC and FEPAs Combined, FY 1992–FY 1999," http://www.eeoc.gov/stats/harass.html, accessed June 19, 2000; and authors' calculations from Bureau of Labor Statistics data.

2. Ibid.

3. Equal Employment Opportunity Commission, "Sexual Harassment Statistics, EEOC and FEPAs Combined: FY 1991–FY 1997," received from EEOC Office of Communications and Legislative Affairs, December 30, 1997. For 1999 data, see EEOC, "Sexual Harassment Charges, EEOC and FEPAs Combined: FY 1992–FY 1999," http://www.eeoc.gov/stats/harass.html, accessed January 6, 2000. The EEOC defines "merit resolutions" as "charges with outcomes favorable to the charging parties and/or charges with meritorious allegations," including negotiated settlements, withdrawals from benefits, successful conciliations, and unsuccessful conciliations. After "no reasonable cause," the second highest percentage of EEOC cases in 1999 (32.7 percent) were deemed "administrative closures," meaning that the cases were closed for administrative reasons such as "failure to locate charging party."

4. *Barnes v. Train,* No. 1828-73 (D.D.C. 1974); and *Barnes v. Costle,* 183 U.S. App. D.C. 90 (D.C. Cir. 1977).

5. Catharine A. MacKinnon, *Sexual Harassment of Working Women* (New Haven: Yale University Press, 1979), 65–68. In addition, see Catharine A. MacKinnon, "Symposium: Fidelity in Constitutional Theory: Does the Constitution Deserve Our Fidelity? 'Freedom from Unreal Loyalties': On Fidelity in Constitutional Interpretation," *Fordham Law Review* 65 (March 1997): 1703–38; and Catharine A. MacKinnon, "Pornography as Defamation and Discrimination," *Boston University Law Review* 71 (November 1991): 793–815.

6. MacKinnon, *Sexual Harassment of Working Women,* 215, 217–18.

7. Equal Employment Opportunity Commission Guidelines on Discrimination Because of Sex, 29 CFR 1604.11 (July 1, 1996). See also Equal Employment Opportunity Commission, *Sex Discrimination Issues* (Washington, D.C.: EEOC Technical Assistance Program, April 1996); and Equal Employment Opportunity Commission, "Facts about Sexual Harassment," http://www.eeoc.gov/facts/fs-sex.html, accessed May 19, 1999.

8. Michael Verespej, "New Age Sexual Harassment," *Industry Week,* May 15, 1995, 64.

9. *Meritor Savings Bank v. Vinson,* 477 U.S. 57 (1986).

10. The first cases where federal courts recognized sexual harassment as a form of sex discrimination were *City of Milwaukee v. Saxbe,* 546 F.2d 693 (1976), and *Alexander v. Yale University,* 631 F.2d 178 (2d Cir. 1980), although in both cases sexual harassment was found to be a violation of Title IX rather than Title VII of the Civil Rights Act of 1964.

11. *Rabidue v. Osceola Refining Co.,* 805 F.2d 611 (6th Cir. 1986).

12. In 1991, in *Robinson v. Jacksonville Shipyards,* for example, the District Court for the Middle District of Florida took a far less lenient approach to hostile environment harassment than the *Rabidue* court had. In *Robinson* the court held that displays of pornographic pictures of women were enough to constitute a hostile work environment. *Robinson v. Jacksonville Shipyards,* 760 F. Supp. 1486 (M.D. Fla. 1991).

13. *Civil Rights Act of 1991,* Public Law 102-166, November 21, 1991. The provisions of the 1991 Civil Rights Act are as follows: for each complaining party, the amount of compensatory and punitive damages may not exceed $50,000 for employers with more than 14 and fewer than 101 employees; $100,000 for employers with more than 100 and fewer than 201 employees; $200,000 for employers with more than 200 and fewer than 501 employees; and $300,000 for employers with more than 500 employees. See Marian C. Haney, "Litigation of a Sexual Harassment Case after the Civil Rights Act of 1991," *Notre Dame Law Review* 68 (1993): 1044, 1055–56. Many feminist legal commentators have urged Congress to eliminate those damage award caps in sexual harassment cases. See, for example, Susan Estrich, "Sex at Work," *Stanford Law Review* 43 (April 1991): 813–61; and Toni Lester, "Efficient but Not Equitable: The Problem with Using the Law and Economics Paradigm to Interpret Sexual Harassment in the Workplace," *Vermont Law Review* 22 (spring 1998): 519–57. See also Peter Brimelow, "Is Sexual Harassment Getting Worse?" *Forbes,* April 19, 1999, 92.

14. *Faragher v. City of Boca Raton,* 524 U.S. 775 (1998); and *Burlington Industries, Inc. v. Ellerth,* 524 U.S. 742 (1998). The Court also allowed employers to use in their defense evidence that the plaintiff failed to take advantage of existing preventive measures by the employer.

15. Richard A. Epstein, *Forbidden Grounds: The Case against Employment Discrimination Laws* (Cambridge: Harvard University Press, 1992): 352–53.

16. Deborah Rhode, *Speaking of Sex: The Denial of Gender Inequality* (Cambridge: Harvard University Press, 1997), 107.

17. Feminist economist Barbara Bergmann wrote, for example, that "sexual harassment of women in the workplace plays an important part in keeping males and females segregated . . . and helps to maintain occupational segregation and can have seriously negative results for women's careers." Barbara Bergmann, *The Economic Emergence of Women* (New York: Basic Books, 1986), 104, 106.

18. Deborah Rhode wrote, for example, that "for women *as a group,* harassment perpetuates sexist stereotypes and discourages gender integration of male-dominated workplaces." Rhode, *Speaking of Sex,* 101. For similar sentiments, see also Toni Lester, who claimed that one of the reasons harassment occurs is that "many men want to reinforce their feelings of male superiority by trying to subordinate women in the workplace." Lester, "Efficient but Not Equitable," 521.

19. Robin West, "Jurisprudence and Gender," *University of Chicago Law Review* 55 (1988): 70. Toni Lester wrote, "Feminists see the legal system as just one of many places where men have traditionally tried to justify their domination of women." Lester, "Efficient but Not Equitable," 537.

20. Lester argued later that "the broader definition of force that has been advocated by feminist scholars, however, addresses the fact that harassment, whether it is physical or verbal, can be tantamount to force in the eyes of the victim. And it is her experience, and the experience of women in general, that needs to be more appropriately acknowledged." Lester, "Efficient but Not Equitable," 545, 548.

21. Feminist Majority Foundation, "What to Do If You or Someone You Know Is Sexually Harassed," www.feminist.org, accessed December 30, 1999.

22. Virgil L. Sheets and Sanford L. Braver, "Perceptions of Sexual Harassment: Effects of a Harasser's Attractiveness," paper presented at the Seventy-third Annual Convention of the Western Psychological Association, Phoenix, Ariz., April 22–25, 1993. The findings of the study were discussed in Cathy Young, "Sexual Harassment: Is There a Better Way?" in *From Data to Public Policy: Affirmative Action, Sexual Harassment, Domestic Violence, and Social Welfare,* edited by Rita J. Simon (Lanham, Md.: Women's Freedom Network and University Press of America, 1996), 38. In addition, the study found that 11 percent of the women felt harassed when the man was good-looking but married, and 14 percent experienced the advance as harassment when the man was single but not particularly good-looking. On feminists' insistence on experience as the standard for sexual harassment lawsuits, see chapter 7, "The Authority of Experience," in Daphne Patai, *Heterophobia: Sexual Harassment and the Future of Feminism* (Lanham, Md.: Rowman & Littlefield, 1998).

23. The U.S. Supreme Court first engaged the issue of unwelcomeness in the *Meritor* case and agreed with the EEOC's assessment that because sexual advances are ambiguous and dependent on context, a showing of unwel-

comeness by the plaintiff is necessary to establish a claim of sexual harassment. As the EEOC noted in its amicus curiae brief in *Meritor,* sexual remarks or propositions "may be intended by the initiator, and perceived by the recipient, as denigrating or complimentary, as threatening or welcome, as malevolent or innocuous." Charles Fried, William Bradford Reynolds, Richard K. Willard, Carolyn B. Kuhl, Albert G. Lauber, Jr., John F. Cordes, John F. Daly, and Johnny J. Butler, brief for the United States and the Equal Employment Opportunity Commission as Amici Curiae on Writ of Certiorari to the United States Court of Appeals for the District of Columbia Circuit, No. 84-1979 (D.C. Cir. December 11, 1985).

24. Niloofar Nejat-Bina, "Employers as Vigilant Chaperones Armed with Dating Waivers: The Intersection of Unwelcomeness and Employer Liability in Hostile Work Environment Sexual Harassment Law," *Berkeley Journal of Employment and Labor Law* 20 (1999): 351; and Estrich, "Sex at Work," 859.

25. Rhode, *Speaking of Sex,* 107.

26. National Organization for Women, "Sexual Harassment," National Organization for Women Issue Report, March 1997, http://www.now.org, accessed July 29, 1999; and Feminist Majority Foundation, "What to Do If You or Someone You Know Is Sexually Harassed," http://www.feminist.org, accessed December 30, 1999. One of the editors of a special issue of the *National Women's Studies Association Journal* devoted to sexual harassment began her introduction by describing the violent, brutal mugging of a man she met; he was stabbed twice and left for dead on a sidewalk. She then noted the "obvious analogy—the experience of being sexually harassed feels very much like that of being mugged." See Patrocinio P. Schweickart, "Introduction," *National Women's Studies Association Journal* 9 (summer 1997): 152.

27. As Elizabeth Fox-Genovese noted, "[S]exual harassment policies depend upon some agreement about who constitutes the reasonable woman, and contemporary experience confirms that few concepts provoke more intense disagreement." Elizabeth Fox-Genovese, "Rethinking Sexual Harassment," in *Rethinking Sexual Harassment,* edited by Cathy Young (Washington, D.C.: Women's Freedom Network, 1998), 46.

28. See *Robinson v. Jacksonville Shipyards; Ellison v. Brady,* 924 F.2d 872, 879 (9th Cir. 1991); and *Meritor Savings Bank v. Vinson.* See also Young, "Sexual Harassment."

29. *Harris v. Forklift Systems, Inc.,* 510 U.S. 17, 22 (1993).

30. As Elizabeth Fox-Genovese noted, "It is unacceptable to say that the presence of women in a specific workplace—say, a construction site, a fire truck, or a police beat—may make men uncomfortable, but positively noble to say that the presence of men intimidates women." Fox-Genovese, "Rethinking Sexual Harassment," 47.

31. In *Kimzey v. Wal-Mart, Inc.,* 907 F. Supp. 1309, 664 (1995), the district court judge found the jury-assessed punitive damages of $50 million to be "improper" and reduced the award to $5 million. Later, in *Kimzey v. Wal-Mart, Inc.,* 107 F.3d 568 (8th Cir. 1997), the appeals court further reduced

the punitive damages award to $350,000 but allowed for the compensatory damages and back pay of $35,001 to remain and thus left a total of $385,001 for the plaintiff. See also Young, "Sexual Harassment," 35.

32. *Jones v. Clinton,* 161 F.3d 528 (1998); and *EEOC v. Mitsubishi Motor Manufacturing of America,* 102 F.3d 869 (1996).

33. Young used the "shadow of the law" phrase in "Sexual Harassment," 36.

34. Nejat-Bina, "Employers as Vigilant Chaperones Armed with Dating Waivers," 341–42.

35. Ibid., 342–43.

36. *Rogers v. International Business Machines Corp.,* 500 F. Supp. 867 (W.D. Pa. 1980); and *Wright v. MetroHealth Medical Center,* 516 U.S. 1158, 116 S. Ct. 1041 (1996).

37. Cathy Young, "Sexual Harassment in the '90s: The Legal and Cultural Landscape," in *Rethinking Sexual Harassment,* 36; and Elizabeth Rhodes, "The Work World's Next Frontier," *Seattle Times,* October 16, 1992.

38. Eugene Volokh, "What Speech Does 'Hostile Work Environment' Harassment Law Restrict?" *Georgetown Law Journal* 85 (February 1997): 647.

39. Patai, *Heterophobia.*

40. Vendors for the sexual harassment industry encourage subjective interpretations of harassment; one producer of sexual harassment training videos said that "if you feel like you're being sexually harassed, then you are. You are the judge." Lawyers in the industry encourage businesses to have their employees sign dating waivers and "love contracts" to limit liability. See Gary Meyers, "Sexual Harassment Can Take Many Forms," *State Journal-Register* (Springfield, Ill.), January 5, 1997. For examples of "love contracts," see Tom Kuntz, "For Water Cooler Paramours, the Ties That (Legally) Bind," *New York Times,* February 22, 1998. For estimates of annual revenue of the sexual harassment industry (in the billions), see Stuart Silverstein, "Fear of Lawsuits Spurs the Birth of a New Industry," *Los Angeles Times,* June 29, 1998.

41. See, for example, Joan Kennedy Taylor, "America's Overprotective Sexual Harassment Law," *Cato Commentary,* January 7, 2000. Taylor noted that "men and women are not natural enemies, but they are being told that they are. Men are warned that if they offend female coworkers, they may be disciplined or even fired. Women are being instructed that offensive speech, if heard from men in the workplace, is probably illegal. And to top it off, the Supreme Court is requiring businesses to give those warnings."

42. Judge Alex Kozinski noted that "the personal networks that are so important in building a career may exclude women, as men fear getting too chummy with female coworkers and subordinates. To the extent that sexual harassment litigation raises the level of suspicion between men and women, it may ultimately hamper efforts at gender integration." Alex Kozinski, "The False Protection of a Gilded Cage," *American Lawyer Media, L.P. The Recorder,* May 27, 1992.

43. For example, Deborah Rhode claimed that the argument is misleading and assumes that everyone shares her perspective on the fear of a sexual harassment lawsuit: "[G]iven the financial and psychological costs of bringing such lawsuits and the limited remedies available, it is doubtful that unfounded claims will be more prevalent in this context than in any other." Rhode, *Speaking of Sex,* 235.

44. *Franklin v. Gwinnett County Public Schools,* 503 U.S. 60 (1992).

45. *Davis v. Monroe County Board of Education,* 526 U.S. 629, 119 U.S. 1661 (1999).

46. Dissent of Justice Anthony M. Kennedy (joined by Chief Justice William H. Renquist, Justice Antonin Scalia, and Justice Clarence Thomas), *Davis v. Monroe County Board of Education,* 526 U.S. 629 (1999). See also George M. Rowley, "Liability for Student-to-Student Sexual Harassment under Title IX in Light of *Davis v. Monroe County Board of Education,*" *Brigham Young University Education and Law Journal* 1999 (winter 1999): 137–56.

47. Reports by advocacy groups such as the American Association of University Women have claimed that sexual harassment of girls is rampant in America's schools. But their definitions have been overly broad, and their social science methods suspect. See "Hostile Hallways: The AAUW Survey on Sexual Harassment in America's Schools," *The AAUW Educational Foundation Survey* (Washington, D.C.: American Association of University Women, June 1993), 6. Eugene Volokh criticized the AAUW's "Hostile Hallways" report by noting that it "defined harassment to cover anyone who has even once, in the four-year hormonal pressure cooker of high school, been the target of unwanted 'sexual comments, jokes, gestures, or looks.'" Eugene Volokh, "The Dangerous Drift of 'Harassment,'" in Simon, ed., *From Data to Public Policy,* 47.

48. Independent Women's Forum, amicus curiae brief in *Davis v. Monroe County Board of Education,* 6–7.

49. Ibid.

50. That was the reasoning of Judge Gerald B. Tjoflat, writing for the majority, in the Eleventh Circuit's decision against the *Davis* claim. *Davis v. Monroe County Board of Education,* 74 F.3d 1186 (11th Cir. 1996), reviewed en banc, 120 F.3d 1390 (11th Cir. 1997). See also Sasha Ransom, "How Far Is Too Far? Balancing Sexual Harassment Policies and Reasonableness in the Primary and Secondary Classrooms," *Southwestern University Law Review* 27 (1997): 265–97.

51. Cynthia Grant Bowman, "Street Harassment and the Informal Ghettoization of Women," *Harvard Law Review* 106 (January 1993): 518, 520.

52. Bowman also said: "In sum, the continuation and near-general tolerance of street harassment has serious consequences both for women and for society at large. It inflicts the most direct costs upon women, in the form of fear, emotional distress, feelings of disempowerment, and significant limitations upon their liberty, mobility, and hopes for equality. It also increases distrust between men and women and reinforces rigid gender roles, hierarchy,

and the confinement of women to the private sphere. Street harassment thus performs a function as a social institution that is antithetical to the acceptance of women into American public life on terms equal to men." Ibid., 542.

53. With feminist provocateur Andrea Dworkin, Catharine MacKinnon helped draft a municipal ordinance that would have made pornographers liable for violating women's equality, for example. In part because of the efforts of free speech advocates, the ordinance was declared unconstitutional. *Ronald E. Richards v. Indiana*, 461 N.E.2d 744 (April 1984). See Frances Olsen, "The Outsider," *American Lawyer*, December 6, 1999. Feminist law professor Susan Estrich said: "I would have no objection to rules which prohibited men and women from sexual relations in the workplace, at least with those who worked directly for them. . . . I do not see this as going too far." Estrich, "Sex at Work," 860. For opposition to the ordinance, see Hank Grezlak, "An Interview with ACLU Head Nadine Strossen," *Pennsylvania Law Weekly*, March 27, 1995. See MacKinnon's rationale for and history of the ordinance in MacKinnon, "Pornography as Defamation and Discrimination." For a review of the Indianapolis ordinance and the right to free speech, see Marilyn J. Maag, "The Indianapolis Pornography Ordinance: Does the Right to Free Speech Outweigh Pornography's Harm to Women?" *University of Cincinnati Law Review* 54 (1985): 249–69.

54. One of the most recent examples of that phenomenon was the case of Miller Brewing Co. employee Jerold Mackenzie, who was fired after discussing a racy episode of the television show *Seinfeld* with a female employee. Mackenzie later won a lawsuit against Miller and was awarded $26.6 million from a jury comprising ten women and two men. *Mackenzie v. Miller Brewing Co.*, 608 N.W.2d 331 (2000). See also John Greenya, "Canned," *Washington Post*, October 5, 1997.

55. Young, "Sexual Harassment in the '90s"; Young, "Sexual Harassment"; and Ellen Frankel Paul, "Sexual Harassment as Sex Discrimination: A Defective Paradigm," *Yale Law and Policy Review* 8 (1990): 335, 350.

56. See the EEOC guidelines above. That argument is ably made as well by Young, "Sexual Harassment in the '90s."

57. The researchers also found that power differentials were not as important as feminists have claimed and that while women based their judgments of what was harassment on the "perceived intent" of the man, men based theirs on "welcomeness." Richard L. Wiener and Linda E. Hurt, "Social Sexual Conduct at Work: How Do Workers Know When It Is Harassment and When It Is Not?" *California Western Law Review* 34 (fall 1997): 61, 96.

58. Kozinski, "The False Protection of a Gilded Cage."

Chapter 7: Restructuring the Workplace: Mandatory Benefits and Optional Results

1. *Americans with Disabilities Act of 1990*, Public Law 101-336, July 26, 1990.

2. Betty Friedan, *Life So Far* (New York: Simon & Schuster, 2000), 369.

3. Ibid., 370.

4. Rebecca Korzec, "Working on the 'Mommy-Track': Motherhood and Women Lawyers," *Hastings Women's Law Journal* 8 (winter 1997): 117–40.

5. Sylvia Ann Hewlett, "Have a Child, and Experience the Wage Gap," *New York Times,* May 16, 2000.

6. Karen Kornbluh, "The Mommy Tax," *Washington Post,* January 5, 2001.

7. Suzanne Nossel and Elizabeth Westfall, *Presumed Equal: What America's Top Women Lawyers Really Think about Their Firms* (Franklin Lakes, N.J.: Career Press, 1998), xvii.

8. Ibid., xviii–xxii.

9. Ibid., xxiv.

10. Korzec, "Working on the 'Mommy-Track,'" 117.

11. Ibid., 140.

12. Congressional Budget Office, *Measurement of Employment Benefits in the National Accounts* (Washington, D.C.: Government Printing Office, September 1998), 5.

13. *Americans with Disabilities Act of 1990,* Public Law 101-336, July 26, 1990; and *Family and Medical Leave Act of 1993,* Public Law 103-3, February 5, 1993.

14. Jane Waldfogel, "Family Leave Coverage in the 1990s," *Monthly Labor Review* 122, no. 10 (October 1, 1999): 13.

15. Joe Wilson, PermaTreat owner, personal communication with the authors, May 19, 2000.

16. George Daniels, president, Daniels Manufacturing, personal communication with the authors, May 22, 2000.

17. Dixie Dugan, "Is the Department of Labor Regulating the Public through the Backdoor?" testimony before the U.S. House of Representatives, Committee on Government Reform, Subcommittee on National Economic Growth, Natural Resources, and Regulatory Affairs, February 15, 2000, http://www.workingforthefuture.org/dixie_dugan_testimony.html, accessed May 23, 2000.

18. William J. Clinton, "Remarks by the President on Parental Leave," White House, Office of the Press Secretary, November 30, 1999. See also Associated Press, "Parental Proposal a Slow Starter," November 30, 1999; and Anne Gearan, "Subsidies Proposed for Parents on Leave," *Washington Post,* December 1, 1999.

19. Kimberley K. Hostetler, "Unemployment Compensation and the Family and Medical Leave Act," testimony before the U.S. House of Representatives, Human Resources Subcommittee of the House Ways and Means Committee, March 9, 2000, http://www.workingforthefuture.org/hostetler_testimony.html, accessed May 23, 2000.

20. Ibid.

21. Ricardo J. Caballero and Mohamad L. Hammour, "Jobless Growth: Appropriability, Factor Substitution, and Unemployment," NBER Working Paper 6221, National Bureau of Economic Research, October 1997.

22. Thomas J. Bliley, Jr., *Survey of Federal Agencies on Costs of Federal Regulations,* staff report prepared for the Committee on Commerce, U.S. House of Representatives (Washington, D.C.: Government Printing Office, 1997). For an up-to-date analysis of what the government knows about the benefits and costs of regulation, see Robert W. Hahn, *Reviving Regulatory Reform: A Global Perspective* (Washington, D.C.: AEI Press, 2000).

23. Bill Summary and Status for the 105th Congress, http://www.thomas.loc.gov, accessed August 2, 1999. See, for example, H.R. 1374, H.R. 1200, H.R. 4178, H.R. 1113, H.R. 4844, H.R. 4102, S. 886, S. 183, S. 280, S. 756, S. 1610, S. 19, and S. 2593.

24. Ibid. See, for example, H.R. 4178, H.R. 2842, H.R. 1113, and S. 183.

25. Australia, for example, mandates fifty-two weeks of parental leave for men or women who have worked for the same employer for twelve consecutive months. Mothers and fathers in France are legally entitled to three years of leave for the purpose of raising a child. But French employers are not required to pay for such leave, although unions and employers have established a variety of agreements. Greek parents receive three months each of nontransferable, unpaid leave. In the Netherlands each parent is allowed six months of reduced work hours. The Swedish government pays 90 percent of the salary of the parent who stays home with the child for the first year and mandates a reduced work day until the child is eight years old as well (information obtained from interviews with countries' respective embassies).

26. Rick Melchionno, "The Changing Temporary Work Force: Managerial, Professional, and Technical Workers in the Personnel Supply Services Industry," *Occupational Outlook Quarterly* 43 (spring 1999): 24–32, http://www.stats.bls.gov:80/opub/ooq/1999/Spring/art03.pdf, accessed June 5, 2000. See also U.S. Department of Labor, Bureau of Labor Statistics, *Employment and Earnings* 48, no. 1 (January 2001): 228–29, table 50, "Employees on Nonfarm Payrolls by Major Industry and Selected Component Groups."

27. International Labor Organization, "More Than 120 Nations Provide Paid Maternity Leave: Gap in Employment Treatment for Men and Women Still Exists," Geneva, Switzerland, February 16, 1998.

28. Kirsten Downey Grimsley, "Study: U.S. Mothers Face Stingy Maternity Benefits," *Washington Post,* February 16, 1998; and Del Jones, "Drive for Paid Family Leave Raises Cost Issues," *USA Today,* March 3, 1998.

29. Except in the highest income bracket, parents are eligible for some federal tax relief through the child care credit. Moreover, many low-income parents may be eligible to send their children to local government-sponsored child care centers.

30. Eli Lilly and Company, "Managing Your Work and Personal Life: A Resource Guide"; and Eli Lilly and Company, "Corporate Policies—Balancing Work and Personal Life," http://www.lilly.com/about/overview/policies/life.html, accessed February 26, 2001.

31. Bill Summary and Status for the 105th Congress, http://www. thomas.loc.gov, accessed August 2, 1999. See, for example, H.R. 3686, H.R. 4844, H.R. 4102, H.R. 2719, H.R. 3768, S. 1697, S. 1470, S. 19, and S. 2489.

32. Marcia K. Meyers and Janet C. Gornick, "Early Childhood Education and Care: Cross-National Variation in Service Organization and Financing," paper presented at A Consultative Meeting on International Developments in Early Childhood Education and Care: An Activity of the Columbia Institute for Child and Family Policy, New York, N.Y., May 11–12, 2000; revised July 31, 2000. See table 2.

33. Barbara R. Bergmann, *Saving Our Children from Poverty: What the United States Can Learn from France* (New York, N.Y.: Russell Sage Foundation, 1997).

34. U.S. Department of Labor, Bureau of Labor Statistics, Office of Productivity and Technology, "Comparative Civilian Labor Force Statistics, Ten Countries: 1959–1999," April 17, 2000, 20, table 4, "Civilian Labor Force Participation Rates by Sex, 1960–1999," http://www.stats.bls.gov/special.requests/ForeignLabor/flslforc.pdf, accessed May 17, 2000.

35. Ibid., 34, table 8, "Civilian Unemployment Rates by Sex, 1960–1999."

36. Ibid., 33–34.

37. Ibid.

38. U.S. Department of Labor, Bureau of Labor Statistics, Office of Productivity and Technology, "Comparative Real Gross Domestic Product per Capita and per Employed Person, Fourteen Countries: 1960–1998," March 30, 2000, 9, table 2, "Real GDP per Capita, Converted to U.S. Dollars Using EKS PPPs (United States = 100)," http://www.stats.bls.gov:80/special. requests/ForeignLabor/ flsgdp.pdf, accessed May 17, 2000.

39. Ibid., 12, table 5, "Real GDP per Capita, Average Annual Percent Change."

40. George Daniels, president, Daniels Manufacturing, personal communication with the authors, June 19, 2000.

Chapter 8: Playing Hardball: Title IX and Women's Athletics

1. *Newsweek*'s cover story on the World Cup win featured the headline "Girls Rule!" (*Newsweek*, July 19, 1999), while *USA Today* opted for a slightly more subdued "Women's Sports Take Giant Leap" (Jill Lieber, *USA Today*, July 12, 1999). See the summary of media coverage by William Saletan, "Cups, Bras, and Athletic Supporters," *Slate* online magazine, July 14, 1999, http://www.slate.com.

2. Amy Shipley, "This Team's Biggest Fans Are Little," *Washington Post,* July 1, 1999.

3. Garry Wills, "Women as the New Blacks," *Tahoe Daily Tribune,* July 23–25, 1999; Ruth Conniff, "The Real Women's Sports Revolution," http://www.IntellectualCapital.com, accessed August 5, 1999. See also Patricia Schroeder, "Listen to the Sound of the Glass Ceiling Shattering," *Los Angeles Times,* July 14, 1999; "A Cultural Win for Women's Sports," *Atlanta Journal and Constitution,* July 14, 1999; and Glenn Dickey, "World Cup Harvest Was Sown in the 70s," *San Francisco Chronicle,* July 14, 1999. *Time* referred to the team as "the daughters of Title IX." Robert Sullivan, "Goodbye to Heroin Chic. Now It's Sexy to Be Strong," *Time,* July 19, 1999, 62.

4. Joyce Gelb and Marian Lief Palley, *Women and Public Policies: Reassessing Gender Politics* (Charlottesville: University Press of Virginia, 1996), chap. 5.

5. See U.S. Code, vol. 20, sec. 1681 (b).

6. In July 1974 a House-Senate conference committee added language from the Javits Amendment to Title IX effectively to ensure that "reasonable provisions" for women's participation in college athletics be included in Title IX. See Gelb and Palley, *Women and Public Policies,* 104. At that time, the committee also rejected Senator John Tower's amendment to exempt revenue-producing college sports, such as football, from the Title IX equation.

7. *Congressional Record* 117 (1971): 30403, 30406–7, 30409.

8. Quoted in David Aronberg, "Crumbling Foundations: Why Recent Judicial and Legislative Challenges to Title IX May Signal Its Demise," *Florida Law Review* 47 (December 1995): 748–49. See also *Congressional Record* 117 (1971): 30403, 30406–7, 30409.

9. That point is made by Gelb and Palley, *Women and Public Policies,* 103–4, as well as by Walter B. Connolly, Jr., and Jeffrey D. Adelman, "A University's Defense to a Title IX Gender Equity in Athletics Lawsuit: Congress Never Intended Gender Equity Based on Student Body Ratios," *University of Detroit Mercy Law Review* 71 (summer 1994): 852. In 1979 the U.S. Department of Health, Education, and Welfare split, and enforcement of Title IX was given to the U.S. Department of Education and its Office for Civil Rights.

10. Gelb and Palley, *Women and Public Policies,* 100–101.

11. Department of Health, Education, and Welfare, Office for Civil Rights, "Title IX of the Educational Amendments of 1972; A Policy Interpretation: Title IX and Intercollegiate Athletics," *Federal Register* 44, no. 239 (December 11, 1979). Policy historians Gelb and Palley noted that "when new athletic guidelines were issued in December 1979, it was clear that the women's movement had been successful in holding the line on the intent of Title IX." Gelb and Palley, *Women and Public Policies,* 95.

12. Ibid., 116–17.

13. *Federal Register* 44, no. 71 (1979): 413–18.

14. Connolly and Adelman, "A University's Defense to a Title IX Gender Equity in Athletics Lawsuit," 863. For more on the general feminist goal of statis-

tical parity, see Deborah Rhode, *Speaking of Sex: The Denial of Gender Inequality* (Cambridge: Harvard University Press, 1997), and Virginia Valian, *Why So Slow? The Advancement of Women* (Cambridge: MIT Press, 1998).

15. Valerie M. Bonnette and Lamar Daniel, Office of Civil Rights, Department of Education, *Title IX Athletics Investigator's Manual* (Washington, D.C.: Government Printing Office, 1990).

16. David Tell, "The Myth of Title IX," *Weekly Standard,* July 26, 1999, 25.

17. *Grove City College v. Bell,* 465 U.S. 555 (1984); and Gelb and Palley, *Women and Public Policies,* 120.

18. *Civil Rights Restoration Act of 1987,* Public Law 100-259.

19. In 1992, for example, the Women's Sports Foundation (with the help of the National Women's Law Center) published a booklet that explained how female athletes could file a Title IX complaint with the Office for Civil Rights or a lawsuit. Also contributing to the escalation of litigation was the Supreme Court's opinion in *Franklin v. Gwinnett County Public Schools* in 1992, which said that plantiffs filing Title IX lawsuits were eligible for punitive damages. Kimberly Schuld, "A Commonsense Ruling on Sex Harassment May Change Rules for Lawyers Harassing Schools for Huge Fees," *Insight,* July 27, 1998, 29.

20. "Title IX Impact on Women's Participation in Intercollegiate Athletics and Gender Equity," hearing before the Subcommittee on Commerce, Consumer Protection, and Competitiveness of the Committee on Energy and Commerce, House of Representatives, 103d Cong., 1st sess., February 17, 1993, 13 (hereafter cited as Title IX Hearings, 1993).

21. Terry Don Phillips and Paul Makris, "Colleges Can Achieve Equity in College Sports: A Response," *College Football Association Sidelines* 6, no. 9 (May 1993): 8–10, 14.

22. Aronberg, "Crumbling Foundations," 783. The SAT data are from the 1993 Student Descriptive Questionnaire.

23. National Federation of State High School Associations, *NFHS Participation Survey 1999–2000* (Kansas City, Mo.: National Federation of State High School Associations, 2000), http://www.nfhs.org/part_survey-99-00.htm, accessed March 6, 2001.

24. National Federation of State High School Associations, *National Federation 1992–93 Interscholastic Activities Survey* (Kansas City, Mo.: National Federation of State High School Associations, 1993).

25. Little League Baseball Headquarters, Media Relations Department, "Baseball Only" and "Softball Only" statistics for the United States, 1999, facsimile, June 29, 2000. In 1999 the baseball program consisted of an estimated 1 to 2 percent girls (no numbers are available), while the softball program was 99.75 percent girls, according to Lance Van Auken of Little League Baseball Headquarters. Lance Van Auken, personal communication with the authors, September 13, 2000.

26. Cathy Young, "Where the Boys Are," *Salon.com,* July 10, 1999; and Jack McCallum, "Out of Joint," *Sports Illustrated,* February 13, 1995), 44.

27. McCallum, "Out of Joint."

28. Information on the *Brown* case was drawn from *Cohen v. Brown University,* 101 F.3d 155 (1996), Aronberg, "Crumbling Foundations," 772–78, and R. Lindsay Marshall, "*Cohen v. Brown University:* The First Circuit Breaks New Ground Regarding Title IX's Application to Intercollegiate Athletics," *Georgia Law Review* 28 (1994): 837–61.

29. Marshall, "*Cohen v. Brown University,*" 848, 842–43. In the *Colgate* case, for example, where plaintiffs filed as individuals, the Second Circuit vacated the lower court's ruling and declared it moot since the plaintiffs would graduate before the court order to reinstate the ice hockey team was set to take effect. Later, litigants launched another Title IX suit, then as a class action. In 1997 Colgate agreed to a settlement of the suit, and women's ice hockey was elevated to varsity status. See *Haffer v. Temple University,* 678 F. Supp. 517 (E.D. Penn. 1988), 688 F.2d 14 (3d Cir. 1982); and *Cook v. Colgate University,* 992 F.2d 17 (2d Cir. 1993).

30. Marshall, "*Cohen v. Brown University,*" 850–51.

31. Ibid. The relevant part of the ruling stated: "If a university prefers to take another route, it can also bring itself into compliance with the first benchmark of the accommodation test by subtraction and downgrading, that is, by reducing opportunities for the overrepresented gender while keeping opportunities stable for the underrepresented gender." Quoted in Aronberg, "Crumbling Foundations," 775.

32. To the first claim, the court opined that since Brown had demonstrated early enthusiasm for women's athletics, including considerable expansion of women's teams in the 1970s, but had not kept up the same pace of expansion through the 1980s, when budgetary constraints prevented it, the university failed the expanding opportunities test. The court effectively punished Brown for being on the leading edge of female athletics development. Had the university waited until the 1980s to initiate the women's athletic program expansion, it likely would have met the expanding opportunities test, though many female athletes attending Brown in the 1970s would then have had far fewer opportunities to participate in sports.

33. David Roach (athletic director, Brown University), "No Competition: A Desperately Wrong Idea of Fairness in College Athletics," *Washington Post,* October 5, 1995.

34. Vartan Gregorian, testimony before the Subcommittee on Postsecondary Education, Training, and Life-Long Learning, U.S. House of Representatives, May 9, 1995.

35. *Roberts v. Colorado State University,* 998 F.2d 824 (10th Cir. 1993); and *Favia v. Indiana University of Pennsylvania,* 812 F. Supp. 578 (W.D. Penn. 1992) and 7 F.3d 332 (3d Cir. 1993).

36. Michael W. Lynch, "Title IX's Pyrrhic Victory," *Reason* 12 (April 2001), 29.

37. Welch Suggs, "Miami U. Drops 3 Men's Sports," *Chronicle of Higher Education*, April 30, 1999.

38. Associated Press, "Miami Drops Diving, Swim Programs," February 28, 2000.

39. Leo Kocher, "There Ought to Be a Law," in *The Impact of the Current Interpretation of Title IX, 1992–1997*, April 1997 NCAA Gender-Equity Study Results (Overland Park, Kans.: National Collegiate Athletic Association, 1997). Kocher is associate professor of physical education and athletics and head wrestling coach at the University of Chicago.

40. Ibid.

41. Aronberg, "Crumbling Foundations," 765–66.

42. Ibid., 778. The *Kelley* case was heard in the District Court for the Central District of Illinois and affirmed on appeal to the U.S. Court of Appeals for the Seventh Circuit. The Supreme Court denied a writ of certiorari (as it had also done in the *Brown* case). *Kelley v. Board of Trustees of the University of Illinois*, 513 U.S. 1128 (1995).

43. The Office for Civil Rights' *Investigator's Manual* outlines the major areas of investigation: athletic financial assistance; accommodation of interests and abilities; equipment and supplies; scheduling of games and practice time; travel and per diem allowance; tutors; coaches; locker rooms and practice and competitive facilities; medical and training facilities and services; housing and dining facilities and services; publicity; support services; and recruitment of student athletes. Bonnette and Daniel, *Title IX Athletics Investigator's Manual.*

44. The hearings examined specifically the office's enforcement of school desegregation plans. See "Failure and Fraud in Civil Rights Enforcement by the Department of Education," hearing before the Committee on Government Operations, 100th Cong., 1st sess., September 29, 1987.

45. The failure to release documents is especially appalling, given the standards for disclosure universities must meet. The passage of the Equity in Athletics Disclosure Act in 1994, an amendment to the 1994 Elementary and Secondary Education Act cosponsored by Senators Carol Mosley-Braun and Edward Kennedy, required colleges and universities to gather statistics on gender equity in their athletic programs. The Department of Education requires that the university's report "be made *within a few days after a request is made*" and sent to the Department of Education. See Diane Heckman, "Scoreboard: A Concise Chronological Twenty-Five Year History of Title IX Involving Interscholastic and Intercollegiate Athletics," *Seton Hall Journal of Sport Law* 7 (1997): 391–422, footnote 118 (emphasis added).

46. Copies of letters from the general counsel, Johns Hopkins University, to Dr. Robert A. Smallwood, regional civil rights director, U.S. Department of Education, February 14, 1995; and to Norma Cantu, assistant secretary, Office for Civil Rights, Department of Education, December 8, 1994, in the authors' possession.

47. Gerard St. Ours, Office of the Vice President and General Counsel, Johns Hopkins University, personal communication with the authors, May 31, 2000.

48. That confusion was not abated by the office's release in 1996 of the "Clarification of Intercollegiate Athletics Policy Guideline." While Department of Education Secretary Norma Cantu claimed that "OCR does not require quotas," her agency's "clarification" incorporated none of the many suggestions for reform made by outside groups. The office also neglected to clarify what "substantially proportionate" meant in the context of Title IX enforcement in college athletics and offered only a few examples of acceptable ratios, always less than 5 percent. The clarification amounted to a continuation of the status quo, and the status quo was quotas. Department of Education, Office for Civil Rights, "Clarification of Intercollegiate Athletics Policy Guidance: The Three-Part Test," May 16, 1996. See also Vartan Gregorian's letter to Norma Cantu, October 20, 1995, http://www.brown.edu/Administration/News_Bureau/Special_ Reports, accessed December 8, 1998. See also Aronberg, "Crumbling Foundations," 763–64.

49. National Coalition for Women and Girls in Education, "Report Card on Gender Equity," Washington, D.C., June 23, 1997, http://www.edc.org/WomensEquity/resource/title9/report/index.htm, accessed July 24, 2000. See also National Coalition for Women and Girls in Education, "Education Coalition's Title IX Report Card Gives Nation a 'C' Grade in Efforts to Fully Implement Landmark Law," press release, Washington, D.C., June 23, 1997.

50. Feminist Majority Foundation, *Empowering Women in Sports, Empowering Women Series* 4 (1995): 1.

51. *Task Force on Intercollegiate Athletics,* special edition (Northridge: California State University, January 9, 1998): 8.

52. Ibid., 8.

53. Ibid., 9.

54. Jeff Barry, "Title IX at CSUN," *All Things Considered,* transcript, June 19, 1997.

55. Marshall, "*Cohen v. Brown University,*" 857, footnote 150.

56. Debra E. Blum, "University of Texas Settles Sex-Bias Suit," *Chronicle of Higher Education,* July 28, 1993.

57. Brian Metzler and Carol Rowe, "Schools Still Struggling with Title IX Compliance," *Anchorage Daily News,* June 22, 1997.

58. *Boulahanis, Vanduyne et al. v. Board of Regents of Illinois State University,* 198 F.3d 633 (7th Cir. 1999).

59. On the NOW lawsuits, see Scott M. Reid, "School Hit with Title IX Complaints," *Orange County Register,* December 11, 1998. On *Neal v. CSUB,* see Jeremy Rabkin, "Gender Benders," *American Spectator,* April 1999. See also *Neal v. California State University, Bakersfield,* 198 F.3d 763 (9th Cir. 1999).

60. Denise K. Magner, "Judge Blocks Cal State–Bakersfield's Plan to Cap Size of Wrestling Team," *Chronicle of Higher Education,* March 12, 1999.

61. Welch Suggs, "Two Appeals Courts Uphold Right of Universities to Reduce the Number of Male Athletes," *Chronicle of Higher Education,* January 7, 2000.

62. The twenty-five schools listed in the lawsuit include five colleges and twenty universities: Bethune-Cookman College, Boston College, the College of William and Mary, Coppin State College, Wofford College, Boston University, Bowling Green State University, Brigham Young University, Colorado State University, Duke University, Hampton University, Liberty University, Northeastern University, South Carolina State University, the University of Colorado at Boulder, the University of Maine at Orono, the University of New Hampshire, the University of North Texas, the University of Oregon, the University of Texas at El Paso, the University of Toledo, the University of Tulsa, Utah State University, Vanderbilt University, and Wake Forest University.

63. National Women's Law Center, "Citing a $5M Scholarship Gap, National Women's Law Center Files Title IX Complaints against 25 Colleges," press release, Washington, D.C., June 2, 1997.

64. Kevin M. Gray, "Bias in Scholarship Charged at 25 Colleges," *New York Times,* June 3, 1997; and Amy Shipley, "Title IX Complaints Filed against 25 Universities," *Washington Post,* June 3, 1997.

65. "Dear Colleague" letter issued by the Office for Civil Rights, with enclosure of Mary O'Shea's letter of clarification, July 23, 1998. In an interview O'Shea insisted that the 1 percent rule was "a guideline and not a quota." See Jim Naughton, "Clarification of Title IX May Leave Many Colleges in Violation over Aid to Athletes," *Chronicle of Higher Education,* July 24, 1998.

66. Bonnie Erbe and Josette Shiner, "Game Plan from the Big Bench," *Washington Times,* May 3, 1997.

67. Title IX Hearings, 1993, 20–23, 26. Lopiano also advocated other punitive measures such as a rule that "would prohibit the allocation of an automatic national championship berth to any institution that has not achieved gender equity or to any conference without a conference-level presidential review requirement for the control of athletics expenditures." See her testimony, 22. For the golden-goose remark, see Donna Lopiano, "Will Gender Equity Kill the Golden Goose of College Football?" http:// womenssportsfoundation.org/templates/res_center/rclib/results_topics2 .html?article=64&record=36, accessed July 20, 2000.

68. Ibid., 911.

69. *All Things Considered,* transcript, April 22, 1997.

70. Metzler and Rowe, "Schools Still Struggling with Title IX Compliance." June 22, 1997.

71. Connolly and Adelman, "A University's Defense to a Title IX Gender Equity in Athletics Lawsuit," 771.

72. Title IX Hearings, 1993, 26.

73. Kimberly Schuld, personal communication with the authors, March 6, 2000.
74. Title IX Hearings, 1993, 10, 17.
75. Constitution Subcommittee Markup of *The Civil Rights Act of 1997,* H.R. 1909, July 9, 1997.
76. Title IX Hearings, 1993, 2.
77. William J. Clinton, "Women's Equality Day, 1997—By the President of the United States of America, A Proclamation," White House, Office of the Press Secretary, August 19, 1997.
78. Title IX Hearings, 1993, 7.

Chapter 9: Preference Programs for Women

1. Mary Becker, "Patriarchy and Inequality: Towards a Substantive Feminism," *University of Chicago Legal Forum* 21 (1999): 21–88.
2. Equal Employment Opportunity Commission, Office of Federal Operations, Federal Sector Programs, *Annual Report on the Employment of Minorities, Women, and People with Disabilities in the Federal Government for the Fiscal Year Ending 1998* (Washington, D.C.: Government Printing Office, 1999).
3. Equal Employment Opportunity Commission, Office of Federal Operations, Federal Sector Programs, *Annual Report on the Employment of Minorities, Women, and People with Disabilities in the Federal Government for the Fiscal Year Ending 1999* (Washington, D.C.: Government Printing Office, 2000), A18–A34, table I-8, "Federal Agency Trend Summary for Agencies with 500 or More Employees for 1990–1999."
4. Those and other tables can be found in Department of Health and Human Services, *Affirmative Employment Program and FY 1998 Update for the Department of Health and Human Services* (Washington, D.C.: Government Printing Office, September 1998).
5. For the purposes of the tables, statistical balance is no less than two standard deviations below the expected value. If employment opportunities were normally distributed, there would be less than a 5 percent chance that employment would fall below two standard deviations less than the mean.
6. Department of Health and Human Services, *Affirmative Employment Program and FY 1998 Update for the Department of Health and Human Services,* supporting data, standard deviation report, "Work Force Inventory Profile System (WIPS) Permanent Career/Career Conditional Employees Standard Deviation Report, Males," 54.
7. Donna E. Shalala, secretary of Health and Human Services, letter to Paul M. Igasaki, Equal Employment Opportunity Commission, September 14, 1998.
8. Department of Health and Human Services, *Affirmative Employment Program and FY 1998 Update for the Department of Health and Human Services,* Objectives and Action Items, 7.
9. Department of Housing and Urban Development, *Departmentwide Fiscal Year 1998 Affirmative Employment Program Update Report,* Program

Element 2—Work Force, "Combined Hiring and Internal Movement Numerical Objectives by Major Occupations," DII-26.

10. Department of Interior, *Fiscal Year 1999 Affirmative Employment Program Report,* Program Element 3—Ensure Accountability at the Secretarial and Bureau Levels for Improving Diversity, Objective A, Strategy 3, http://www.doi.gov/diversity/aep_report/part0.htm, accessed July 14, 1999.

11. Small Business Administration, "SBA Announces Plans to Increase Contracting Opportunities for Women Business Owners," News Release No. 98-52, June 19, 1998, http://www.sba.gov/news/current/98-52.html, accessed December 22, 1999.

12. Small Business Administration, "Federal Agency Advocates for Women," http://www.sba.gov/GC/wobadvocates.html, accessed December 22, 1999.

13. Pat Hodge, Department of Transportation, personal communication with the authors, March 23, 2000.

14. Small Business Administration, "Memorandum of Understanding between the U.S. Department of Defense and the U.S. Small Business Administration," 1999, http://www.sba.gov/GC/dod-mou.pdf, accessed December 22, 1999.

15. For the EEOC's 1999 survey (at this writing the most recent completed survey), the EEOC received 38,675 forms from employers. Brenda Kyne, EEOC Surveys Division, personal communication with the authors, February 23, 2001.

16. Equal Employment Opportunity Commission, *Standard Form 100, Rev. 3-97, Employer Information Report EEO-1 Instruction Booklet,* OMB No. 3046-0007, 4–5.

17. Ibid., 2.

18. Karen Jones-Budd, personal communication with the authors, March 30, 2000.

19. Anonymous personal communication with the authors, March 24, 2000.

20. Department of Education, National Center for Education Statistics, *Integrated Postsecondary Education Data System Fall Staff Survey 1999,* OMB No. 1850-0582, http://www.nces.ed.gov/ipeds/form1999/S.pdf, accessed March 30, 2000.

21. Ibid., 5–13.

22. Ibid., 3.

23. For a detailed review of the literature, see Elizabeth G. Creamer, *Assessing Faculty Publication Productivity: Issues of Equity,* Ashe-Eric Higher Education Reports 26, no. 2 (Washington, D.C.: George Washington University, Graduate School of Education and Human Development, 1998). See also Yu Xie and Kimberlee A. Shauman, "Sex Differences in Research Productivity: New Evidence about an Old Puzzle," *American Sociological Review* 63 (1998): 847–70; Yu Xie and Kimberlee Shauman, "Gender Differences in Research Productivity," *Scientist* 13, no. 9 (September 27, 1999): 10; and Linda J. Sax, Alexander W. Astin, William S. Korn, and

Shannon K. Gilmartin, *The American College Teacher: National Norms for the 1998–1999 HERI Faculty Survey* (Higher Education Research Institute, University of California, Los Angeles, September 1999).

24. Department of Labor class-action complaint against Stanford University, November 1998. See "Stanford Gets Probe Name List, Women Say Promise of Anonymity Violated," *San Francisco Chronicle,* January 25, 2000; and Bill Workman, "Women's Claim against Stanford Headed to Trial," *San Francisco Chronicle,* March 14, 2000.

25. Massachusetts Institute of Technology, *The MIT Faculty Newsletter, Special Edition: A Study on the Status of Women Faculty in Science at MIT* 11, no. 4 (March 1999).

26. University of Illinois at Urbana-Champaign, Chancellor's Committee on the Status of Women, *The Status of Women Faculty at the University of Illinois at Urbana-Champaign 1999,* http://www.admin.uiuc.edu/oc/csw/report, accessed February 23, 2001.

27. Cable News Network, "Ivy Bias; They Called It Murder," transcript, January 31, 2000.

28. See Diana Furchtgott-Roth, "MIT Report Flunks Statistics 101," *Investor's Business Daily,* May 4, 1999.

29. *The MIT Faculty Newsletter,* March 1999, 8, table 2, "Number of Women vs. Men—Undergraduate to Faculty in the School of Science, MIT 1994."

30. Carolyn Stout Morgan, "College Students' Perceptions of Barriers to Women in Science and Engineering," *Youth and Society* 24, no. 2 (December 1992): 228–36; Kristy K. Johnson et al., *Focus Groups: A Method of Evaluation to Increase Retention of Female Engineering Students* (College Park: University of Maryland, 1995); and Richard M. Felder et al., *Gender Differences in Student Performance and Attitudes: A Longitudinal Study of Engineering Student Performance and Retention* (Raleigh: North Carolina State University, 1994).

31. University of Illinois at Urbana-Champaign, *The Status of Women Faculty,* 28–30, figures 11–13.

32. Massachusetts Institute of Technology, *The MIT Faculty Newsletter, Special Edition,* 12.

Chapter 10: Recognizing Success

1. See, for example, Stephan Thernstrom and Abigail Thernstrom, "The Consequences of Colorblindness," *Wall Street Journal,* April 7, 1998; Ward Connerly, *Creating Equal: My Fight against Race Preferences* (San Francisco, Calif.: Encounter Books, 2000); and William G. Bowen and Derek Bok, *The Shape of the River: Long-Term Consequences of Considering Race in College and University Admissions* (Princeton: Princeton University Press, 1998).

2. Thomas Snyder and Charlene Hoffman, *Digest of Educational Statistics, 2000* (Washington, D.C.: National Center for Education Statistics, 2001), 289, table 248, "Earned Degrees Conferred by Degree-Granting Institutions, by Level of Degree and Sex of Student: 1869–70 to 2009–10"; Robert N.

Anderson, "United States Life Tables, 1998," *National Vital Statistics Reports* 48, no. 18 (Hyattsville, Md.: National Center for Health Statistics, 2001); and Bureau of the Census, Population Estimates Program, Population Division, "Resident Population Estimates of the United States by Age and Sex: April 1, 1990 to July 1, 1999, with Short-Term Projection to November 1, 2000," January 2, 2001, http://www.census.gov/population/estimates/nation/intfile2-1.txt, accessed February 21, 2001.

3. Richard A. Epstein, *Forbidden Grounds: The Case against Employment Discrimination Laws* (Cambridge: Harvard University Press, 1992). See also Richard A. Epstein, "Liberty, Patriarchy, and Feminism," *University of Chicago Legal Forum* 21 (1999): 89–114.

4. William J. Clinton, Executive Order 13152, "Further Amendment to Executive Order 11478, Equal Employment Opportunity in Federal Government," White House, Office of the Press Secretary, May 2, 2000.

Index

About the Authors

Diana Furchtgott-Roth was a resident fellow at the American Enterprise Institute from 1993 to 2001. She is coauthor with Christine Stolba of *Women's Figures: An Illustrated Guide to the Economic Progress of Women in America* (1999). Her articles on labor and tax policy have been published in the *Washington Post,* the *Wall Street Journal, Investor's Business Daily,* the *Los Angeles Times,* and other publications. Before joining AEI in 1993, Ms. Furchtgott-Roth was the deputy executive secretary of the Domestic Policy Council and later associate director in the Office of Policy Planning at the White House under President Bush. She served on the staff of President Reagan's Council of Economic Advisers from 1986 to 1987. Ms. Furchtgott-Roth received an M.Phil. in economics from Oxford University. She has appeared on numerous TV and radio shows, including the *NewsHour with Jim Lehrer* and programs on FOX News, C-SPAN, and National Public Radio.

Christine Stolba is a senior fellow with the Independent Women's Forum, where she writes about a range of issues, including women and the economy, feminism, and women's studies. She is also an adjunct scholar at the American Enterprise Institute and is coauthor, with Diana Furchtgott-Roth, of *Women's Figures: An Illustrated Guide to the Economic Progress of Women in America* (1999). Ms. Stolba has written numerous opinion pieces for the *Wall Street Journal,* the *Manchester Union-Leader,* the *Houston Chronicle,* the *Salt Lake Tribune,* and the *Orlando Sentinel* and has contributed essays to

Commentary, the *New England Journal of Medicine,* the *Women's Quarterly, Women in World History, iVillage.com,* and *National Review On Line.* Ms. Stolba holds a Ph.D. in history from Emory University, where her studies focused on American intellectual history and women's history. Ms. Stolba has been a contributor on many radio and television shows, including *C-SPAN Washington Journal* and programs on MSNBC and FOX News.

Nelson W. Polsby
Heller Professor of Political Science
University of California, Berkeley

George L. Priest
John M. Olin Professor of Law and
  Economics
Yale Law School

Thomas Sowell
Rose and Milton Friedman
  Senior Fellow in Public Policy
Hoover Institution
Stanford University

Murray L. Weidenbaum
Mallinckrodt Distinguished
  University Professor
Washington University

Richard J. Zeckhauser
Frank Plumpton Ramsey Professor
  of Political Economy
Kennedy School of Government
Harvard University

Research Staff

Leon Aron
Resident Scholar

David Asher
Associate Director, Asian Studies

Claude E. Barfield
Resident Scholar; Director, Science
  and Technology Policy Studies

Walter Berns
Resident Scholar

Douglas J. Besharov
Joseph J. and Violet Jacobs
  Scholar in Social Welfare Studies

Robert H. Bork
Senior Fellow

Karlyn H. Bowman
Resident Fellow

Montgomery Brown
Director of Publications

John E. Calfee
Resident Scholar

Charles W. Calomiris
Visiting Scholar

Lynne V. Cheney
Senior Fellow

Dinesh D'Souza
John M. Olin Research Fellow

Nicholas Eberstadt
Henry Wendt Scholar in Political
  Economy

Mark Falcoff
Resident Scholar

J. Michael Finger
Resident Fellow

Gerald R. Ford
Distinguished Fellow

Murray F. Foss
Visiting Scholar

Hillel Fradkin
W. H. Brady, Jr., Fellow

Harold Furchtgott-Roth
Visiting Fellow

Jeffrey Gedmin
Resident Scholar; Executive
  Director, New Atlantic Initiative

Newt Gingrich
Senior Fellow

James K. Glassman
Resident Fellow

Robert A. Goldwin
Resident Scholar

Michael S. Greve
John G. Searle Scholar

Robert W. Hahn
Resident Scholar; Director,
  AEI-Brookings Joint Center
  for Regulatory Studies

Kevin A. Hassett
Resident Scholar

Thomas W. Hazlett
Resident Scholar

Robert B. Helms
Resident Scholar; Director, Health
  Policy Studies

James D. Johnston
Resident Fellow

Jeane J. Kirkpatrick
Senior Fellow; Director, Foreign and
  Defense Policy Studies

Marvin H. Kosters
Resident Scholar; Director,
  Economic Policy Studies

Irving Kristol
Senior Fellow

Michael A. Ledeen
Freedom Scholar

James R. Lilley
Resident Fellow

Randall Lutter
Resident Scholar

John H. Makin
Resident Scholar; Director,
  Fiscal Policy Studies

Allan H. Meltzer
Visiting Scholar

Joshua Muravchik
Resident Scholar

Charles Murray
Bradley Fellow

Michael Novak
George Frederick Jewett Scholar
  in Religion, Philosophy, and Public
  Policy; Director, Social and Political
  Studies

Norman J. Ornstein
Resident Scholar

Richard N. Perle
Resident Fellow

Sarath Rajapatirana
Visiting Scholar

Sally Satel
W. H. Brady, Jr., Fellow

William Schneider
Resident Fellow

J. Gregory Sidak
F. K. Weyerhaeuser Fellow in Law
  and Economics

Christina Hoff Sommers
Resident Scholar

Daniel E. Troy
Associate Scholar

Arthur Waldron
Visiting Scholar; Director, Asian
  Studies

Graham Walker
Visiting Scholar

Peter J. Wallison
Resident Fellow

Ben J. Wattenberg
Senior Fellow

David Wurmser
Research Fellow

Karl Zinsmeister
J. B. Fuqua Fellow; Editor,
  The American Enterprise